A Refugee's Journey

A Memoir

by Walter Hess

Blue Thread Books, an imprint of *Jewish Currents* magazine

For information, write to: JEWISH CURRENTS, PO Box 111, Accord, NY 12404.

ISBN 978-0-9978978-6-9

A Refugee's Journey

Dedicated to my grandchildren:

Max

Zoe

Allie

Jenny

Stephie

And what I shall never in the world return to
And look at, I am to love forever.
Only a stranger will return to my place. But I will set down
All these things once more, as Moses did,

After he smashed the first tablets.

—Yehuda Amichai

Prologue

In August of 1939 I was eight years old, and I and my family were on the North German Lloyd's 30,000-ton steamship *Caribia*. We had left Germany and were now on our way to the country of Ecuador. Three weeks later, our ship let down its anchor in the harbor of Guayaquil. The day was steaming, and I remember the odor of cocoa on the dock. The date was September 1st, when the German army began its invasion of Poland and World War II began.

In the spring of 1940, my family and I arrived in New York City from Ecuador on the *Santa Rosa*, a sleek Grace liner with sparkling green and white smokestacks. The day was glorious, the million windows of downtown Manhattan gleaming and sparkling a greeting as the great ship moved slowly up the Hudson to its mooring. I leaned over railings and saw faces and waving handkerchiefs down on the dock, the faces jumping up and down, excited, anticipating happy reunions.

In the spring of 1953, I was on a ship again, an Army transport, the dull-gray *General Buckner*, along with a thousand other GI's. The day was gray, but a band played marches as the ship pulled out of its Staten Island dock. The Sousa tunes faded away as the Buckner nosed out into the harbor. The million windows of distant Manhattan were now gray and without sparkle. I saw them disappear as we rounded Fort Wadsworth, and as gray clouds dropped like a curtain over the island's skyscrapers.

As our ship moved out into the Atlantic, I began to feel fear. Not a powerful fear, just the beginning of a small knot in my stomach. Somebody said, "Those lights, that's Cape Cod." The *Buckner* tended north to make its way along the great circle route, tended back to swallowed anxieties and angers long denied, tended back to Bremerhaven and Germany.

As I leaned over the ship's railing, what I had neglected or denied for so very long began to assert itself. The knot grew larger. It took me a while, staring over the railing into the foam, to realize that it was not simply a memory of fear that stimulated the knot, but the real thing: a reassertion of all those fears generated by all those many absences, threats, and abandonments, which had threaded themselves through all those early years. They were fears so powerful that a substitution had had to be found, a way to translate what had been imprinted onto the nerves of a child so that their living threat might be diminished. I had found that substitute by telling myself, and everyone about me, that it had all been a wonderful adventure. But now I was on a ship again, returning to Germany, the place where all those fears began.

Chapter One

New York's Central Park is close to where we live. Soon after I retired, I began walking in Central Park as part of my daily exercises. And in walking, I discovered a marvelous pond, at about West 102nd Street. Walking the park, circling the pond, soon became my only exercise. This pond, properly called the "Pool," is surprisingly hardly ever mentioned in any description of the park. On any map, to the northwest of the Reservoir, there might be a blue dot without any explanatory note. Finding the dot, finding the pond, made it mine.

In every season, in every weather, walking was a great joy. The pond produced a grand revelation of color from the trees' reflection in its water, a shock of color for every visitor, every time. Maples, oaks, hickory, cypress, willow (especially willow), black cherry; the afternoon sun slanting on leaves created a new and remarkable palette, every hour, every day, every season.

Although it was my pond, I shared: with the young college students with computers and white papers in front of them, writing their theses; with mothers and nannies jiggling carriages so their charges might sleep, or bringing them closer to the shore to see the ducks; with elders, reading their books, looking up occasionally to check the reflections of trees in the water, then smiling and returning to their books. After a while, walking my rounds, I became aware of tourists, and the good New Yorker arose in me. If I saw several people muddling about a park map, I would ask where they might want to go. Then there would be a short lesson in New York geography: Yes, Broadway was west and Fifth Avenue was east. The Palace Hotel and Cleopatra's Needle were south. Haarlem Meer was a short walk north.

Then there was She, beautiful, her back to the varied shore, and He, standing back, taking her picture. I thought I might help out by asking the couple if I could take a picture of them together. Smiles of gratitude, and complicated teaching about what to push and what to look through on a camera or phone, and we became three happy people. Frequently when I thought to help there were answers in foreign languages, European, South American, Asian.

This time it was German. This time it was a warm May day. He was bending over the wooden bridge with an enormous camera in front of his chest, photographing the waterfall as it shot through the black stony grotto. He stood up, turned, looked a bit confused, and called out, "*Wiefiel Uhr,*" before shaking his head and rubbing his face with his hands. As I neared him, I said *Halb drei.*" He looked relieved, and said with a happy smile, "You speak German?" "*Ya. Und wo sind Sie heer?*" Still smiling, he turned to English: "I'm waiting for my wife. She told me about this marvelous place. And I come from Marburg — the university." He looked immensely happy and pointed to a bench: "Can we sit down?" I nodded, and we sat. He seemed to be in his mid-fifties, with a wide, handsome, tanned, wrinkled face and a full head of gray hair.

"We are on vacation," he said. "This is our first time in the U.S. Usually we go to places like Thailand, China, Australia. But this time my wife insisted on the U.S. She wanted to go shopping in New York. And the dollar and mark exchange is so very favorable right now."

I was a bit anxious, but Marburg interested me greatly. "Marburg. Isn't Marburg near Wetter?"

"Hah." He was astonished. "How do you know about Wetter?"

"My grandfather came from Wetter."

"Your grandfather . . ."

"Yes. My Opa, he came from Wetter. He died in Trescin in 1942."

"He was killed . . . murdered."

"He died, I think, of bladder problems. It's common in my family. My Oma was murdered in Auschwitz, maybe 1944." My words came out so easily. I wasn't angry, nor did I want to hit a German with history; he seemed to have a kind and guilty sense about him. I smiled, looked at him. "Yes, Opa came from Wetter, and as a young man to Ruppichthroth, married . . ."

"What?" He was almost yelling. "I was born in Rupp!"

With a grand happy smile on my face: "And so was I. Actually, in a Siegburg hospital. But I lived and grew up in Rupp, went to school there. That two-room village school."

He took some deep breaths, put his hand on my shoulder, and very tenderly asked, "When were you born?"

"1931."

He waited a bit, rubbed a finger to his upper lip. "I was born in 1945, after the war. During the war, my father, he was a mechanic in the *HuWil Werke* in Rupp."

"The Willach factory."

"Yah."

We both took some deep breaths. "This is so remarkable," he said, "the two of us, this tiny Rhineland village. So strange. We left, my family, I was two. In Stuttgart my father found work with the U.S. Army. Also strange."

I smiled. "There was a distant cousin of my father's, Leo Baer, he was from Nûmbrecht . . ."

"I know the place."

"He was an officer, and he arranged to be the first U.S soldier in

3

Rupp. On a visit he told us about the *HuWil Werke*. There were lots of dead bodies lying about everywhere."

Silence for a while. He lowered his head. "Yes, my father told me also. They were mostly French prisoners." More silence. His arm shot out and pointed: "Wonderful colors, this is so beautiful." And then a change: "You didn't see any of this?"

"No, but I saw enough. *Kristallnacht*. My father taken to Dachau…"

He bit his lip. "Your father?"

"He was okay. After six weeks he made it out. Out to Holland."

He reached into a jacket pocket and pulled out a card, which he handed to me. I read: Karl Hecker: Professor of Physics, Marburg University.

I waited for my smile to return, but it took a while. "My parents went back several times, in the sixties, seventies. It angered me."

"Yes."

I shrugged my shoulders. I tried not to look at him. "I was afraid that they still thought that Rupp was their home"

"No. No. But you knew that your home, our home, the place of our birth, our cradle," he said, "was crippled — destroyed, for you, for others. Germany."

I was almost in tears, so I quickly said that I had also gone back. "The first time as a GI in the fifties."

"You were angry."

"If I was angry it was because where I remembered green gardens, I now saw mud."

"My father told me . . . the troops stationed in Rupp cut down all the trees they could find, for fuel. Turned everything into mud. Streets, green gardens, even the pastures that surrounded the village, where they put up their tents. All mud."

We stopped talking again, and looked at the colorful reflections in the water.

In a low voice he said, "I know about *Kristallnacht*." It was a while before he continued: "You must have been . . . what?"

"Eight."

Again low, and slowly, a voice full of astonishment: "How did you get out?"

Chapter Two

In 1936, shortly after my fifth birthday, I was given a new pair of shoes. They were ankle-high, hobnailed, black. Instead of eyelets, they had little metal hooks around which leather laces were wound. The shoes were shiny, not from polish but from a black greasy covering that I was told would make them waterproof. They were just like my father's work-day shoes — farming shoes, for the meadow and the cow stall. I walked out of our house, out through the flower garden, which looked like a bright apron in front of our house, out onto the cobbled street, and with sharp downward kicks, my metal-hobbled soles struck white, yellow and red sparks from the cobble stones. I could make lightning.

I walked the streets of our village, striking the cobblestones, confirming my power. I walked to exhibit the shoes, to show off, but every once in a while I would hack at the cobblestones, checking the power. With each step I lifted my shoes high in the air. I thought that there was a string that connected the tips of my shoes all the way up to where God lived, where someone, maybe God himself, pulled on the strings like a puppeteer, helping me to get my feet high up in the air so that everyone in the village might get to see the wonder.

Mrs. Schumacher, our neighbor, saw me and said, "Very nice new shoes." Mrs. Schumacher was a widow, tall, always in black with a white, rice pudding kind of face. Her son had a car. Every Easter she hid colored eggs out in the meadow behind her house. And even though we were Jewish, my brother and I were invited to hunt, along with other village children, among them my friends Willibald, Horst, and Daniel. We searched for eggs, running from one possible hiding place to next, all of us laughing and screaming on cold April mornings among the pale and frosty green hummocks of the Schumacher's meadow. I looked forward to it with great excitement: If there was talk of Passover in the air, I knew that the hunt for eggs was close. I wanted to hunt for those eggs even more than to hunt for the *afikomen,* the hidden Passover matzoh, and the gifts that went with finding it.

I walked through streets lined with chestnut trees. One of them was my tree. Under its enormous canopy I could stand dry and secure while the blue rain fell, and from its shiny brown nuts I could make a pipe with the insertion of just a skinny twig. Sitting outside, leaning back on the last house step, pipe in hand, legs crossed, I could imagine being like my tall father, driving a herd of cattle to market.

I walked past our synagogue, which was made out of large, square, cut fieldstone. I say our synagogue but it was really my synagogue where my grandfather, my Opa led the service, and in whose hand my hand rested when we walked Friday night and Saturday morning to his service. We'd walk and he'd ask me questions.

"How did God create the world?"

"I don't know."

"You don't know?"

"Well, He said . . . "

"That's right, He said. And how did He say?"

"I don't know."

"Of course you don't know. When He spoke, when He said 'Let there be . . .' it sounded just like a blast from the *shofar.* With that sound of the *shofar,* He made the world."

"Nice."

"That's how he did it. And when He speaks again, sounds it again, the world is going to be destroyed."

"That's not very nice."

"But that won't be for a very long time." He picked me up, held me and carried me. "You don't have to worry your head. Not for a very long time."

Gustav Gartner, the white-haired butcher, stood in his bloody apron in front of his store. He, too, lifted me, hugged me, and made me come into the store. From behind the counter he handed me slices of salami. "I saw your shoes all the way down by the synagogue. Very nice. Here, they deserve another slice."

Then I heard the tune of the blacksmith's hammer. The blacksmith was next to the butcher shop. His iron timpani called me. The hammer rang more beautifully on the anvil than the bells from either the Catholic or Protestant churches. One strong and powerful ring, then many fast, light ringing repetitions, gentle touches in a slightly higher tone that faded to silence; then again a hammer blow and the great ringing. Were I sent on an errand and was overdue at home, someone was sure to come and get me from in front of the blacksmith's.

His shop was a vast black hollow of a barn, open to the street. It allowed entrance to the farmers and their plow horses, enormous Belgians and fiercely snorting Percherons. At the very rear was the high black furnace with its small round opening glowing red. The blacksmith was at the furnace, pumping the bellows, and with each heave, thin blue wreaths of flame shot out of the furnace mouth, and with each blast of air, the coals bubbled a fiercer red. The smith reached into the furnace mouth with his iron tongs and drew out a glowing orange horseshoe. He placed it on the anvil and began beating. Red and white sparks flew from the beaten horseshoe, the same sparks that I made with my hobnailed shoes. The tongs lifted the glowing iron and plunged it in the nearby trough of water with a great hiss and boiling; smoke and bubbles rose from the water. The hiss, smoke, and bubbles were repeated several times, and then the smith lifted the enormous forefoot of the great Belgian, rested it in his leather-aproned lap, and fitted the hot iron onto its gray hoof; then a hiss from the iron doused in water, smoke and an odor like that of burning hair. I knew the smell. After my mother cut my hair she would gather all of it up and throw it into our coal stove. "Why do you do that, Mamma?" "So no one can make magic with your hair."

The hammer pounded, and the iron was nailed into the horse's hoof. The smith straightened up, came over to me and ran his rough hand through my hair. "He's going to be my apprentice." The farmer, brown-faced, holding his horse's halter, said, "A Jew working in a smithy? I want to see that one before I die."

The cobbled street ran upward, past my Aunt Lydia's house, a large, half-timbered house with a pear tree orchard in back. Aunt Lydia's mustachioed husband Fred had been pruning a tree when he fell from the ladder and, reaching out a hand to ease his fall, was cut by a shard of glass that was just lying there on the ground. Two weeks later he was dead from tetanus, whatever that meant. I was sorry that he died because often, on a Saturday afternoon visit, he would let me have a taste of the Kümmel he was sipping. He would be reading a book, with the glass in front of him on a hassock. I would stand and wait until he looked up and nodded. The liquor was thick as oil and sweet; it scratched my throat, raising white sparks as it went down, raising sweet fumes that smelled like the seeds on rye bread, and the fumes went up my nose and out of my eyes.

Mrs. Shumacher's son lent his car to drive the casket to the little hillside cemetery. He drove very slowly while all the rest of us followed slowly behind the car to the hillside cemetery where my great-grandfather Oma's father, Jacob, had been buried just a little while before. My great-grandfather had a white goatee, and never paid any attention to me, but he was famous. Our town had a picture postcard — Mamma said it was for tourists — that showed a long stretch of our main street, the mountains in the distance the gas station on the right side, and right in the middle of the picture, right in the middle of the street, was a little man with a goatee.

Every time I looked at the picture — Mamma had it stuck in the mirror of her bedroom — she would say, "That's your great-grandfather. That picture is sent all over Germany, and he's all over the world." He was the first person that I ever knew who died.

I was on my way to Regensburgers, but decided to stop first at Schorn's store. This was the local market, the big grocery store in town. I clambered up the long stone stairs and breathed in the well-mixed odors of flour and soap and chocolate. I stood in front of the counter for what seemed a very long time before Mrs. Schorn came looming over me: "Well, Wolfgang, what are you here for."

"Nothing." My face burned with embarrassment and I ran out.

"Wait. Wait. Come back here." The voice was commanding and I came back, afraid. "Close your eyes and hold out your hand." My palm tickled. "Open your eyes." A handful of nonpareils were in my palm. "What did you call them when you were a baby? Little pearls with sugar? Go. Regards home." She didn't say anything about my shoes.

Regensburger's bakery was across the street. It was afternoon and the store had its cold-baking smell. If you came in the morning it had the hot-baking smell, because all the baking was done early in the morning, even before dawn came up.

Harry sat in one corner reading a newspaper. Harry was strange: He had white hair like my *Opa*, but he wasn't old. He put the paper down. "Here comes Mr. Wiseguy." I hated him calling me that. Once, at some holiday party, I had seen him looking very peculiarly at Gertie Nathan. Gertie used lipstick and smoked cigarettes right out in the open, out on the street where everybody could see. I had piped out loudly, "He's looking at Gertie." From then on, to him, I was Mr. Wiseguy. Nevertheless, that day I walked up and down in front of his counter lifting my legs high, showing my shoes.

"Who are you today, Mr. Wiseguy, one of Hitler's soldiers?"

"No, that's not nice to say."

I knew from what I had picked up at home from overheard adult conversations, conversations they thought were guarded, that Hitler was not nice. I think I heard the anger in their throats. The mention of his name made me feel afraid.

"Well, what do you want?"

"Nothing." I kept on high-stepping in front of him.

"We don't sell 'nothing' here. We sell bread and rolls."

"Cake too."

"And cake. I got enough people buying nothing these days; I don't need you as a customer. Take your shoes and get out of here." At least he had noticed the shoes. I made my way to the door.

"Where are you going?"

"You said I should go."

"Yes, but where are you going?"

"To Willy's."

"Here." He pulled out a sugar-coated jelly donut from under the counter. "You shouldn't starve on the way."

I thought that was very funny. Willy was only one street over and two streets up. I would never starve going there.

In the whole town, except for my younger brother Karl, Willy was the only Jewish boy near my age, almost two years older and my best friend. I played with Willy all the time. We were in each other's houses, together in the synagogue, together at all the holiday celebrations. From time to time, I might play with my Christian friends, but was I then disloyal to Willy, who had no one else? My memory is that I played with Christian friends out in the open air, but I don't remember ever being inside one of their houses. Poor Willy.

Willy and I were both going into first grade in the fall, Willy for the second time. Reading was difficult for him; he was awkward and somewhat slow. "You read newspapers when you were still little," I was told. I read when I was sick, and that was often. There were mumps and measles and colds and tonsilitis. The throat pained and things were hard to swallow. There was tenderness and fever. The ears hurt, the jaw hurt, and when the doctor came to look at my tongue and feel my neck, I always knew what he was going to say: "The tongue is coated and the glands are swollen. Give him aspirin."

"Those germs just love you," said my mother when she anointed my throat with eucalyptus ointment and bound my neck with a red woolen scarf that scratched even more than the enlarged tonsils. And my *Oma* called me her "delicate child." This happened sometimes two or three times a year, maybe more often. Reading books eased the worst of the initial hurt and made the convalescences easy. My favorites were *Robinson Crusoe*, *Carl May* and *Shatterhand*, and the books of travel by Sven Hedin. I can still hear the howl of hyenas in the night on distant Persian mountain deserts . . .

My friend Willy's father was a cattle dealer just like mine, but while they followed the same trade, there was a difference between the two households. We had indoor plumbing, they had an outhouse. (Our plumbing didn't always work, so we, too, sometimes used the outhouse.) My father played the flute, Willy's father distilled a terrible-smelling liquor from a big round copper bowl, with a long pointed neck, in their kitchen.

They had a meadow in back of their house and a cow stall attached to their house. They also had a small pond on which ducks floated, along with their goose. I was afraid of the goose, which was almost as tall as I and probably heavier, and which one day fiercely waddled at me with a grim hissing of its yellow beak and an angry waving of its tall neck. After that, visiting alone, I would stand some distance from their house and call out, "Willy!" He'd come and tell me that the goose had been penned; he'd then take my hand and lead me into their compound.

This day they saw my shoes: Willy, his mother, and his somewhat older sister, Lera. They were all properly impressed. I waited, thinking that some chocolate was due, but praise was the only food forthcoming. We played with hoops on the street outside their house. We were auto racers on the Neuburg Ring. Finished with hoops, Willy called me over to their outhouse. He looked through a knot-hole in the wooden structure, stepped back and invited me to look. There sat Lera. My face burned. I was awed, awed also by the fact that Lera wiped herself only in front while I knew that I wiped myself only in back. How could that be? For the rest of the afternoon we played Parcheesi.

It was almost dusk when my father picked me up. Willy's house stood on the rim of the bowl that was my village. Standing in front of Willy's house, we watched as several stars appeared. Below, the familiar houses and streets began to darken. My father took my hand, and we walked toward home. In daylight I had always made this walk by myself, but now it was getting dark. We passed houses that, in the light, on white-washed walls crossed by black timbers, I saw thin black lines, fine cracks that looked like snakes, complicated letters, strange birds, and wild forest animals. My father held my hand, and as we walked in the darkening light, windows that had been reflecting silver now, one after another, turned orange.

Chapter Three

If I approached our house from the street, I first walked up three broad brick steps, and then I passed through Oma's flower garden. There were brick towers at the corners of the garden that were connected by a surrounding black spiked fence. There were two wooden benches in the garden and tall lilac bushes at the fences. The front of our house looked like a face. My mother said it had the face of a man who needed to be tickled.

Upstairs, the two side windows were staring eyes and the third, the middle one was a nose; the front door was a mouth. The dark moldings over the two side windows were eyebrows. The two downstairs windows were a problem, but I said to myself that they were cheeks, the cheeks of a skinny man wearing a dark suit and tie.

The front door of our house had a large oval glass in a dark wooden frame. The glass had incised curlicues and frosted wreaths of interlocking leaves. I could stand in front of our door for long periods of time tracing the course of this white streaming strangeness. "Dreamer," said Fat Liesl, the girl who sometimes worked for us. "My dreamer," said my Oma.

In back of the house there was mud and a barn for the cows, a manure pile from the top of which the rooster crowed, and off to one side a small chicken house. But the chickens never laid their eggs in the house as they were supposed to do, so my grandmother, my Oma, had always to look for the eggs in the grass of the meadow that bordered the barnyard. The barn was timbered; great areas of white plaster between black beams that looked like they wanted to make block letters but couldn't. The barn was two-storied. Hay was stored in the rafters above the cow stalls, and I would climb the ladder to lie in the odor-filled hay and read my book.

The meadow in back of our house rose to a small hill and then stretched ever backward to meet with a pine wood in which Oma and I searched for mushrooms. There were small and contorted apple trees that dotted the meadow and at the border of the wood there were several tall pear trees. This meadow was a kind of holding place where my father and Opa kept a cow or two or three that had recently been bought before they were sold again or added to the herd.

Sometimes they kept a few sheep there and once, I remember, two brown-coated colts.

Up the hill and off to one side of the meadow was my mother's garden, and beyond that my father's potato field, where I helped him plant potatoes in the upturned earth, making sure that the piece I dropped into the furrow had its eyes turned down into the dirt.

Most of our cows were not kept in this meadow, but in fields outside of the village, past the Catholic church and past the black-surfaced pond they called the *Sperber*, the hawk, where a man was supposed to have drowned. When my mother and I passed this pond going to retrieve the cattle from the distant field, she would make hooting noises to keep the ghosts away.

One day at supper my father told me that I would have to get to bed early that night. Why? Because in the morning he would be driving cows to market, to the market in *Waldbröl*, and he thought that I should go with him. I looked to my mother and she nodded. Four-thirty in the morning; we'd have to get up in the dark. I ran to bed.

My father shook me, woke me, and held a finger to his lips. I was to be quiet, as my brother Karl slept in the same room. My father held up clothes for me, then went downstairs to the kitchen while I washed, then dressed on the darkened landing to the stairs. I was struggling to get into my shoes when I sensed, by his sweet sweat, my father's being back. He squatted down to my level and quietly smiled at my labors.

We went to the kitchen, where there was black coffee and large slabs of farmer bread slathered with fresh butter. Then we went into the barn, and I saw white steam streaming from the skin of the cows. Out on the meadow, coils of fog wove and dipped like dancers. We released the half-dozen cows from their stanchions and herded them down the street, where their padding raised echoes over the dew-wet cobbles, then onto the narrow, macadamized highway, the ordinary black surface of which seemed streaked with silver and pewter on this early, wet morning.

It was still dark as we entered the highway, but there was a patch of milky whiteness out beyond the hills on the right. Soon the patch turned as red as the flames from the blacksmiths' furnace, then orange. In full light, the sky seemed very high and light blue. It was eight miles to *Waldbröl*, a five-hour walk.

The macadam road ran through a green valley. A green wood bordered the road on both sides, and through openings I could see meadows, and beyond the meadows the sloping hills, with banks and braids of gray fog sliding down their green tops into the valley bottom. On the left, dodging in and out of the woods, ran a small brook.

We walked through the green, the cows plodding in front of us, and I watched the rhythmic rise and fall of their bony behinds. My father darted down into the woods where the stream ran and disappeared. I stopped, afraid. He came back smiling, with a long, thin willow switch in his hand. He snapped it in the air. It whistled. He handed it to me, "You can guide the cows with this. Make sure they don't go off the road, down into the brook. They like the water."

"After we sell these, when are we going to get more cows?"

"Of course, soon. That's the business. We sell cows. We get money, and with the money we get more cows. That's how it works."

It was important that we get more cows. My grandfather did the evening milking, and I usually made it my business to be there with him. He would sit on his stool and strip milk from the cows. I would hunker down beside him. "In the barn, right with the swallows," he'd say, and "Watch it. Don't get caught." He meant the swishing of the cows' tails. He'd get angry when the swinging tails caught and stung his face, then he'd push the cow hard and yell and curse at it. I waited, sitting on my haunches until he said, "Ready?" Then I opened my mouth and Opa, with a turn of his wrist, directed, from the teat he was holding, a stream of warm, sweet milk right into my mouth.

We needed more cows.

Cars and trucks clattered by. Sometimes they waved. Sometimes they honked. Sometimes the loud noise startled the herd and they veered off, down toward the brook. I looked at my father, he nodded, and I ran down after the cows. I touched their sides lightly with my willow. I waved my arms and yelled like my grandfather. The cows stopped, slowly turned their great necks, looked back at me with their shiny black eyes, and then, as if their joints were badly connected, strained or heaved their bodies forward in separate successive sections until they reached the flat landing of the road and clattered down the asphalt, their bony back-sides riding up and down like the cars on a roller coaster. My father said, "Good. Well done." I looked down at my shoes, embarrassed by the praise.

Waldbröl on market day was large, busy, and full of color, not gray-busy like Bonn or Cologne, where I had been several times. Waldbröl had the feel of a village very much like ours, only many times larger, and in its center was the cobbled market square. To get to the square, our cows passed flower stands and farm stands, attended by farmer's wives in their aprons.

The houses ranging the square were as much as four stories high. The shops carried awnings of red and brown, gold and blue. Little tables and spidery metal chairs clustered in front of the cafés, and in the center of the market stood curved metal cattle stanchions like so many motionless and sullen teenagers at school, hands in their pockets. Round the area of stanchions were large carts and wagons holding bleating sheep and calves. Farmers were throwing hay and straw into the wagons. My father found empty stanchions and fed the heads of our cattle into them. Now the German farmers gathered round my father. Some wore knee-length boots, others long gray coats.

"Well, Oscar, how goes it? And who is this sparrow? Learning the business? Gonna get his nice shoes all covered with cow flop?"

"Your pappa is a good guy. Not one of those cutthroats. Not one of those putting our acres into his strong box." My face turned red, embarrassed. He meant, I knew, that there were other Jews who were doing this, and whatever it was, it wasn't nice.

"You tired? Later, after we do some business we'll have a Coca Cola over there. Yes?" He nodded toward the spidery tables. He dug a strong hand into my shoulder and released. "Your oldest, Oscar?"

The German farmers went round to all the cattle, felt their wattles, dug their hands into the shoulders of the cows, passed their hands under the udders and felt for knots, slapped them on their rumps. "No. Not there," my father called out. "She kicks."

Their bargaining was something I had only seen once before, when a Christian farmer came to our house and bought a cow. Opa and the farmer stood across from each other, in front of the barn. They slapped, hard, into each other's palms and each time they did, they called out the price that they were willing to pay and to get. They kept on slapping until they came to an agreement. Later I asked Opa how come the farmer talked in Hebrew when he was a

Christian. Opa said, "We've been in this town for a very long time."

"How long?"

"Well, before my great-grandfather, and before his great-grandfather and before his great-grandfather."

"Is that long?"

"Long enough for us to learn German and long enough for them to learn a little bit of Hebrew."

Now, at the market, a farmer and my father stood close together and looked straight into each other's eyes. They then started to slap their hands together, hard — from the shoulders down, their palms crashed into each other. With each slap, each man would, in turn yell out a number. Their calling out was in Hebrew or German-Yiddish, both of them: "Kof nun," *slap!* "Mem lamed," *slap!* With each slap, a number was called. My father started out high, the farmer low; my father came down, the farmer up. They met somewhere in the middle, where both knew they'd meet, and the deal was done, a cow was sold. They both shook their hot hands from the wrist and smiled. The two then walked over to the spidery tables and celebrated the sale with a *schnaps*. My father came back and then, with another farmer, the slapping began all over again.

By noon, all the cows were sold and I was looking forward to my Coca Cola. The farmer who had offered it was gone; he had forgotten, but my father had not. "Come on, you deserve a drink." We both sat on the spidery chairs in front of the spidery tables, at ease, sipping our drinks, my legs crossed just like my father's, and we watched all those others who still had animals to sell. All through the market square, one could hear the slapping of palms and the Hebrew numbers called out.

Chapter Four

In summer, when the days grew longer and the weather turned warm, our big-city relatives, from Frankfurt or Cologne or Hanover or Amsterdam, would come to visit us in our green hills. Opa said, "It's nice when they come, and it's nice when they leave."

The most surprising thing was that nearly everybody who came wanted to walk — from our small town to even smaller towns a few kilometers away. They wanted to walk over the hills and they wanted to walk through the woods. They wanted to walk over the main streets and over the narrowest, wagon-rutted path.

I always liked it when our cousins from Hanover came. The first to arrive, usually, was my other Oma, Oma Krämer, our mother's mother, who came all the way from the big city, Frankfurt.

The number of suitcases she brought with her announced the length of her stay: one suitcase per week. Usually my father would bring up four from the railroad station. Oma Krämer had large gray eyes, gray hair, and a face with soft wrinkles that bounced when she suddenly turned her head. I felt her soft hands when she stroked my face.

There were gifts when she came, wind-up toys, little red and yellow cars for Karl and me. And books. For three years it was the same large-size *Grimm's Fairy Tales*, with hard covers, dark green with the title stamped in large gold letters. The illustrations were in color and beautiful. Mamma said, after the third time, "Just say thank you and give her a hug and a kiss and don't you dare say anything else."

Sometimes, if the door to her room was ajar, I might see her wrap her legs in bandages from her knees down to her ankles. When she would leave, back to Frankfurt, the room still had an odor that was a mixture of linament, face powder, and lilac perfume.

Oma had been a widow since age 37. "You were named for your Opa," she would say, and sigh and gently rub my hair. Louis was my middle name.

Middle names were useless. Ugly middle names were even more than useless. My mother would pronounce it, "Looee." Looee was foreign, useless, not German. All my classmates had names like Horst or Wilhelm or Heinz or Klaus or August. Actually, it really didn't matter what my middle name was, it was only my middle name and useless, everyone called me by my first name, anyway, which was Wolfgang, a name I liked. Looee had little to do with the green mountains, my father's dirty work boots, cows, chickens, or the steaming dung heap. And when Herbert Gärtner would sometimes grab me and heave me up on his shoulders, he'd ask, "And how do you like that, Ludwig?" I wouldn't answer but I liked the idea of having my middle name changed from Looee to Ludwig.

Oma Krämer, everyone said, complained a lot. Pappa had a hard time fixing the mattress just right, and the closet was too small for her. When the plumbing went out, which was often, the only resort was the outhouse beyond the downstairs kitchen. Very indignantly, Oma would say, "I'm simply not used to that any more." Mamma said that Oma had too great a sense of family pride. Her maiden name was Hess; my mother's and father's families were very distantly related. But Oma Krämer's Hesses, so she said, went back to a long line of rabbis, all the way back to the Middle Ages, as if Pappa's Hesses didn't. And Oma often repeated, "Some of them were famous and even wrote books." But her most immediate source of pride was that her husband who was dead, her Looee, had been in the United States. At the end of the last century, Louis and a half-brother had traveled to America. The brother stayed, but when an economic slump had made life in America just too hard, Louis had returned to Germany. While still in America, however, and while he had some money, he put some of that money into a new company called U.S. Steel.

Back in Germany, he opened a store that sold fabrics. The store did very well and he forgot all about American stocks. After some years, after World War I and after grandfather Louis died, the half-brother wrote Oma asking what she wanted to do with those stocks because now she was rich. I once heard Mamma say that Oma always acted rich even when she had no money; after all she came from a long line of rabbis who wrote books.

Oma liked to walk. And when she walked, she wore shoes with heels, a long, dark-print dress, and over her arm hung her black leather bag. The town streets were paved with cobblestones, and two steps out of the town you encountered dirt roads. When Oma came back from one of her walks, we would hear her say loudly, "Oh, my legs, my legs!" Fat Lisl, who worked for us, would roll her eyes and say in a harsh but low voice, "Where do you think you are? We don't have fancy boulevards in this shit town."

The first thing to do in the morning was to walk. After lunch and a nap, too, everybody walked. Uncle Theo, Mamma's brother, first thing after he arrived, would whittle himself a walking stick. He would look for some knobby branch on the side of the road somewhere and attack the wood with his pocket knife until it had zig-zag designs from top to bottom. When he finished his stick, he was prepared to walk. Aunt Irma, Mamma's sister, would walk day and night but only if she had a hat that covered her face. She hated the sun but loved to walk in the woods because she loved the pine smell so much, and there was not so much sun in the woods.

Tante Ella would come, Pappa's cousin, the daughter of Tante Mina. Ella had been coming to Ruppichteroth since she was a small child. She always brought her daughter with her, Eva, who was one or two years older than I. Ella walked, but it was to visit all her old friends. Then there were my cousins from Hannover, Karl and Gerhardt. They came with their father and mother, my Uncle Albert and Tante Anna. Karl and Gerhardt were also several years older than I. They would go walking over the dirt roads and over the fields with their mother Anna, and sing loud songs while tramping through the woods.

Whenever they came, I would look at my Opa real hard. Once I had heard my mother say, "It takes something out of him." I looked to see what might be taken out of him but could see nothing. It took me a while to understand what my mother meant. Tante Anna was Catholic. Uncle Albert had married out of his religion and, Mamma said, it affected Opa. Maybe it was words that were taken out of him, because he seemed silent whenever Albert and Anna came.

Uncle Albert was a doctor, a veterinarian. He and Pappa would sometimes walk out onto the pasture behind the house. They would talk, and Albert would look at cows, and I would tag along behind them. Once, they walked out to the pasture and Albert had his doctor satchel with him. They came to this one red cow, and Albert poked it all over, then he rolled up one sleeve of his shirt and shoved his whole arm up the rear end of the cow. I decided then that I would never become a veterinarian. Aunt Anna was also a doctor, a doctor of history. But why history needed a doctor no one was ever able to tell me. They only laughed when I asked.

People also laughed at Aunt Anna. They did this behind her back. Aunt Anna was big and pink, and round and fat and she ate a great deal of everything. I was a fussy eater, I liked anything chocolate; vanilla pudding with raspberry syrup; potato shalet, which was a big fat potato pancake that was baked in an iron pot in lots of fat; hutzelsclos, which was something like a plum pudding, stuffed spleen, and apple fritters; and I would eat anything Opa cooked for me. But Aunt Anna ate everything: meat and vegetables, bread and rolls, in huge portions. Fat Lisl would say, "She's going to eat your Omas' whole store and drive your Opa to the poor house." At breakfast people would secretly watch her. There was a huge farmers' bread that was as round as I was. Anna would hold the bread to her breast and cut off a whole round slice. Once I heard my mother say to my father, "Did you see how she slathered that whole slice with all the butter in the tin? And then the strawberry jam? No wonder." My father gave Mamma a mean look.

One day all of us kids were out on the lawn behind the house. Eva was there, my brother Karl, and my cousins, Gerhardt and Karl. We were being entertained by Ilse Gärtner, our babysitter, who sat us on the grass while she read to us. What she read was the Chanukah story of Hannah and her ten sons who refused to bow to Antiochus Epiphanes, the Hellenistic dictator of Israel. King Antiochus was determined to place himself above the God of the Jews, and it was demanded of the ten sons that they bow to his statue. One after the other they refused to obey the command, and each son, in turn, was skinned alive before his mother. The Greek commander, each time, begged the mother to tell her sons to obey the command, but each time she refused.

When it came to about the fifth or sixth son, I began to bawl. Every muscle and bone in my body heaved, and I felt my own skin being flayed. I felt pity, but even more: anger. Is this what happened to Jews? Eva looked sad, and my brother Karl, too, began to cough a bit as tears appeared on the edges of his eyes.

But I was inconsolable. Gerhard pointed at me and began to laugh. His brother, too, joined him in pointing and laughing. Ilse stopped reading and stroked my hair. Gerhardt and Karl ran away toward the cow barn.

Tante Mina came. We waited for her at the train station, Oma and Opa and I. It wasn't really a station, but simply where the train stopped on the way further down the valley to Waldbröl. Opa yelled at me when I leaned down to put my ear on the silver railroad track. That was what the Osage chief dressed in Eagle feathers did when he wanted know how far away the iron horse was. There was a low, hooting scream like the owl at night, only longer. There was gray smoke. The train was coming.

Tante Mina wore a broad brimmed hat and a dress that waved in the wind. It was shiny and sparkled like fish scales. She stood at the little platform of the last car of the train with her hands on the railing and she smiled down on us. Opa clapped his hands together, then held one out to help her down. Her smile grew bigger, but she waved Opa's hand away and quickly hopped down the steps to Oma, where the two embraced.

Tante Mina was our savior. There were so many stories about her. First, that she had married Mr. Mayer from Cologne, who was rich but she made him richer. Mr. Mayer had a steel importing business and Tante Mina also got him into the steel exporting business. They had a car with a chauffeur, but lots of time Mina drove the car herself. She was the first woman in Cologne to have a driver's license, and she was the first woman to drive a car over one of the Swiss mountain passes to Italy — and she wore pants.

What was even more strange than the pants was the fact that she liked to go about with Oma gather eggs in the yard. If Tante Mina found a warm one that had just been laid, she would pick it up, hold it up to the sky, wipe the egg with a handkerchief she had with her and then, taking a pin which she also had with her, put her mouth to the hole she had made and suck out the eggs' insides. She said she liked that a lot. She also liked to walk.

Chapter Five

My Opa cooked. No other grownup man I knew cooked. Ever. Not even my father.

Sometimes, when I'd get to the Gärtners, Willy's mother, Meta, who was always ironing clothes, would ask me: "And what did your Opa make for you today?" She said it while looking down at her ironing, then looked up expecting an answer. But her question always contained such a peculiar mixture of disdain and admiration, criticism and regard, that I would be left confused. The fact that Opa cooked was something that seemed to set him apart from the rest of the male population of our village, that and the fact that he read and, in the words of one of the townspeople, "Your Opa, he knows a lot."

It wasn't that Oma didn't cook — she did most of the cooking — but the fact that he cooked at all seemed to make him remarkable in the eyes of the village. And he cooked for me. Even before my father was taken to Dachau, Opa cooked, just for me.

"What shall we have today?"

I sat at the kitchen table in front of the plate he had set, and just looked at him, knowing what would come next.

"Stones and straw. That's what I'm making today. Stones and straw."

What I liked best were his fried potatoes and the little carrots that came, mostly, out of a can from Oma's store, but from her garden when the season was right, and he made them sweeter than the carrots cooked by anyone else.

Maybe others might, possibly, get close to the taste of Opa's carrots, but no one could get near his potatoes. I watched him as he stood at the coal stove, hunched over, digging the butter out of a small tun, cutting the boiled potatoes into the sizzling pan, turning the potatoes in the pan.

Opa had a bald head, very deep-set eyes, a gray mustache, and a cleft in his chin. He shaved with a straight razor.

Sometime in the middle of summer, Mamma told me I would accompany Oma and Aunt Irma back to Frankfurt for a little vacation on top of summer vacation. Frankfurt was lovely, it felt generous. It had color, unlike our little town, which I saw as black and white and gray. I remember sun over wide boulevards in Frankfurt, where people didn't walk but "strolled." Tall houses colored cream or a shiny gray edged the boulevards, with large windows that lit up orange when the sun was reflected in them.

We walked the boulevards, Aunt Irma and I. On the days that we walked, we would stop in at a café that had small tables with cream-colored marble tops and spidery chairs.

"What would you like," asked Aunt Irma, and my answer was always the same: "a glass of seltzer with raspberry syrup in it and . . ." I would hardly dare finish the sentence, since that one request, I felt, was all that I was entitled to have. But Aunt Irma would finish the sentence for me by telling the waiter, with a nod, "and some vanilla ice cream." First came the syrupy soda, which I drank in time to Aunt Irma sipping her coffee. Then came the ice cream, piled high in a silvery metal cup that sweated beads of water.

I took my time with the ice cream. It was not on any menu, ever, in Ruppichteroth. There were never ever any menus in Ruppichteroth. There were hardly any restaurants in Ruppichteroth, just a bar with tables and everybody called out what they wanted because everybody knew everything that was served.

While I dawdled with my ice cream, Aunt Irma looked out of the cafe's glass window at the passing crowds. At times I would go shopping with Oma or Irma, frequently to Falk, the butcher. I would stand quietly in front of the counter hoping, and then, every time, the broad Mrs. Falk, in her white chef's hat and white apron would lean over the counter and ask, "Are you a good boy?" I would nod, and then she'd reach over the counter and hand me a large slice of salami, or head cheese, or corn beef that was almost as delicious as the ice cream. Maybe it was just the generosity of the gift, given without any reckoning of whether I deserved it, that made it so delicious. I knew that Mrs. Falk's question was just a repetition, something that grown-ups always had to do, but had I shaken my head rather than nodded, I still would have gotten the gift.

Very many years later, in Washington Heights, on the corner of Broadway and 174th Street, stood the butcher store of Bloch and Falk. The first time I entered the premises, probably with one of my parents, I saw broad Mrs. Falk in her white apron but minus the chef's hat, tending to customers. When she turned to my parents, I spoke up: "I remember you from Frankfurt."

"You, you are Irma's nephew?"

I nodded. She turned away, then turned toward me again holding up a large piece of balony. "And are you a good boy?"

I nodded and was handed the delicious meat. For many years, that act would be repeated each time I entered the store. Very much later, when I came there with my young daughter, Mrs. Bloch would repeat our old scenario with her. People always said that Bloch and Falk had the very best cold cuts anywhere in Manhattan, but to me, just entering the store was as as great joy as having new shoes.

After about three weeks in Frankfurt, I came home with my Aunt Irma. As I entered our house, a smiling Oma greeted me and took my hand. She led me upstairs to our apartment, into our kitchen-living room. The room was full of people, including Herbert Gartner and several of my father's cousins. They all looked at me with smiles, then turned their heads toward the couch where my mother lay smiling, too, with a little bald baby at her breast.

"Come, see little Peter."

I looked, then began to cry and screamed, very loud: "Get that little thing out of here! Get it out. I don't want it. We don't need it. Why do you have it?"

The multitude laughed at my indignation. The raw indignity of being laughed at angered me even more than Peter at my mother's breast. I ran out of the room, down the stairs and out of the house. I ran wildly, crying, down the road and out of our village, up another road, hardly knowing where I was running to. I wound up in an adjoining village at the door of fat Lisel who took me in, wiped my face, and hugged me. Some hours later, or so it seemed, my Oma stood before me, Pappa behind her. Oma hugged me and between the two, Oma and Pappa, holding their hands we walked back home. "You are a very fast runner," said Pappa. His sympathy was no consolation for being laughed at and for feeling displaced. It was no consolation for feeling betrayed by being sent to Frankfurt and not really told why I was being sent.

Fat Liesl had upper arms from which lots of flesh hung down and jiggled when she moved. She had red spots on her face and arms. She sweated a lot and breathed very hard, and she always told me stories. She told one to me when I was standing looking at the front door and she wanted to clean it but I wouldn't move. She said that she was cleaning the front hall first and that when she came back to that front door, I had better move.

Her story was this: When Oma was a little girl, maybe five years old, her younger brother Karl did something bad. He was about three years old, and old Opa Nathan, to punish him, put him down into their potato cellar.

We had a potato cellar. Five stone steps led down to it. It had a very low ceiling and was very dark except for light allowed in by the door and by a narrow ground-level window at its far end. The potato cellar was large, dark and musty. It smelled of mice and turned-up earth. Right by the door of our potato cellar, there were two tall wooden barrels. One contained sauerkraut, the other pickles, and whenever I saw the door to the potato cellar open, I stole down the steps. I had to get up on my toes to reach into the barrel, to lift up the heavy piece of slate that was pressing down on the pickling and then quickly grab a few handfuls of the delicious sauerkraut.

Oma's brother, her Karl, cried for a very long time after he had been shut in the dark cellar. After a while he stopped crying, and maybe the family forgot about him, or maybe not. When they remembered that they had a little boy down in the cellar, somebody went to get him, but he was already dead, lying right in front on the other side of the cellar door. The door had long scratches in it that Karl had made with his nails.

"Anyway, that's why everybody says your Oma always looks so serious," Fat Lisl said. "Maybe she thinks that somebody might still put her in the potato cellar and keep her there. She's always looked serious ever since she was a little girl and that was the reason." She looked at me hard and raised her eyebrows. "Get away from the door. I have to clean it now." I got away.

Oma didn't look very serious when she worked in her vegetable garden in the large plot right across the street from the house. The garden had a mesh-wire fence, but it was mostly hidden by the thick green branches of Oma's gooseberry bushes, which ran all around the garden's border. I would pull the golden yellow berries from those bushes, pop them in my mouth crunch down on their tough skin, and the sweet pulp would burst in my mouth and run down my throat.

There were warnings associated with eating gooseberries: First, that we shouldn't eat them, but Oma knew that my brother Karl and I would, which meant, second, that if we did eat the berries, we must not under any circumstances drink cold water right afterwards because once, some hundreds of years ago, the Princess of Julich und Berg, who was then the owner of the land on which we lived, drank cold water right after eating gooseberries and then died, right then and there.

The water warning was also extended, for us, to apricots, peaches, plums, and cherries. If we argued that the princess' death had only come after gooseberries, the answer was always, "Better safe than sorry" and "Fresh fruit is fresh fruit."

"Anyway," I once said, "why is it so terrible to drink water after gooseberries but you never say anything about currants?" I received a quick slap in the face from my mother when I asked that question.

When the weather was right, Oma was in that garden almost every day. I would see her down in the black dirt, moving forward on her knees and pulling weeds among the radishes, lettuce, strawberry beds, and pea plants. Then she'd stand up, make a face, place a hand on her side and say, "Oh, my back!"

In the middle of the garden was a large section, low to the ground, that was covered by panes of glass. "My hot house," Oma said. In this part of the garden she seemed to work the hardest, because under the glass, which could be raised like wings, was the thing she loved best: her asparagus. Every time she finished working there, even if I saw nothing that had really changed, she would stand and look down for a minute with an expression on her face that was the same as when she looked down at my brother Peter as a baby in his crib .

Every spring, Oma raised long rows of dirt under the glass. Trenches were dug on each side of each row, which had been prepared for the asparagus roots. A wheelbarrow brought dung from the mountainous heap outside the cow-barn. Oma would take one handle and I the other. She shoveled the dung carefully into the trenches she had prepared, and as she shoveled she would repeat, "It takes a lot of dung to make good asparagus."

Oma spent a lot of time tending the beds. "Asparagus should be eaten as soon as they're picked" was another motto. And on the day the asparagus was picked, Opa would be in the kitchen making the mayonnaise, hunched over at the table, stirring yellow egg yolks in a wooden bowl while adding oil to the mixture, drop by drop, from a crystal cruet.

When we would finish in the garden, Oma would take me back into the house and into her store. I waited while she went in back of the counter, bent down, and then emerged with a bar of chocolate. "That's for helping so nicely. Share it with Karl, all right?" Why I should have to share it with my brother Karl, when I had done all the work for Oma, was beyond me.

The front right room of the house was Oma's grocery store, though these days it was rare to see a customer at the door. There was a counter with a silvery scale, and near the ceiling behind the counter hung strips of stockfish, dried cod-fish. On the other side of the counter, creating a narrow aisle, were bins for vegetables, beans, peas, asparagus, potatoes, rhubarb, and gooseberries. At the other end, opposite the door, were shelves filled with jars and cans.

Sometimes, on Fridays, Oma took a bus to Bonn to buy articles for sale in her store. My father went with her.

One time when we were tending the asparagus, I asked her, "Why do you have a store, when Opa has a business?" She replied, "Sometimes things don't always happen the way you might like. Sometimes."

One time I saw Fat Lisl in the potato cellar, stuffing Opa's sauerkraut into her mouth with both hands. She saw that I saw her. Another day I saw Lisl cleaning Oma's silver in the special dining room in which nobody ever ate, and I sat down next to her and asked her why Oma had to have a store when Opa had a business. She said, "It's not a great business and it's not a great store. Go ask your Oma."

"I did."

"And what did she say?"

I told her what Oma had said and then Lisl said, "You're a real wise guy. You want to know everything."

I said that I knew that I was a wise guy. Harry Regensburger called me that.

She said, "Well, since you know that, I guess I can tell you the story. Your Opa used to be rich."

"Really? How rich?"

"I don't know, but everybody says he was rich. You want me to tell you the story?"

"Yes."

"Well, right after the Great War, he had a very large herd of cows. He had more cows than anybody."

"Wasn't he a soldier in the war?"

"Yes. But he was wounded almost right away, at the beginning, so they sent him home. Didn't you ever see the scar on his chest?"

"No. Did you?"

"You really are a wise guy." At that point she was going to stop telling the story, but I begged and pleaded because I wanted very much to hear this story, which had started out so very like a fairy-tale of somebody who was rich and then poor and then because of some wonderful thing that happened became rich again. I pulled at her apron and whined and wouldn't let her go back to work until she raised her eyebrows at me, and then I stopped, and she said all right, but no more wise guy.

"You know," she said with some surprise, "your Opa and your father are the only farmers in this town who don't wipe their noses on their forearms." She stopped, seemed to think, and then went on. "Anyway, this was 1914, maybe '15, and your Opa came home something of a hero. That he was a Jewish hero some people didn't much like, but anyway, his business did well. So he bought land for the cattle and the more cattle he had the more land he needed. He was rich. In the war, farmers did well. Not the ones who had to go to war and be soldiers, but the ones who stayed home, they got rich."

"But Opa was a soldier. He got wounded."

"Anyway, one day in the early '20s, after the war, your Opa sold all his cattle, and he had a lot. The next day, right the very next day the inflation started. You know about the inflation."

"Pappa says that just to buy a loaf of bread you had to take a wheelbarrow full of money to the bakery — if they had any bread."

"That's right. So from one day to the next he was poor. All his cash became worthless. It was as if he never had any cows or any land, and the land he still had, he sold most of it just to keep going. Those were very hard times for just about everybody. People starved. People on the land, farmers, they starved because they didn't have money for seed. Can you imagine? We would have starved if my mother hadn't taken in this little girl with tuberculosis from Cologne. Her parents thought the air in the country would do her good, and they paid us good money in silver to keep her. I guess they heard about Dr. Hertzfeld's Sanitarium. And then when your uncle died . . . Karl . . ."

"My uncle?"

She had stopped talking and was wiping her eyes.

"The little boy Karl?"

"Your uncle was named after the little boy."

I don't think I had ever heard of an Uncle Karl, but I didn't know, I was confused; there were so many Karls that died. My younger brother was named Karl; now an uncle had that name, but if he was ever mentioned, it was out of earshot. I knew that I had an Uncle Albert, who was Pappa's brother, and two cousins — one of them named Karl.

"He was so good, so good," Fat Liesl said. "Such a shame . . . awful shame . . ."

"My uncle?"

"He was in my class. He was so smart! So funny. Everybody loved him." I waited while she cried. "His appendix ruptured. Didn't you know? In Beul. In the hospital. They couldn't do anything. And he was so young."

"How old?"

"Twenty-four. So smart! He already had a business."

"What . . ."

"A grocery store up near your aunt Lydia. It was doing so well. He was going to make the family fortune all over again."

"So . . ."

"So your Oma, after he died, took the goods in your uncle's store and brought them down here. I helped carry them. And she started a store, too."

"But my uncle . . ."

"He died. I guess that's another reason she looks so sad . . ."

"It makes me sad, too."

She raised her eyebrows at me and mumbled, "Parents shouldn't have to see their children die."

I ran away. I climbed up to where we stored the hay, up above the cows in the barn. I lay in the hay with a book.

One day, nobody knew when, but it must have been some holiday evening when we were all at synagogue, Opa discovered that all the glass panes, every one that covered the asparagus beds, had been smashed in, broken. After that Oma stopped working in her garden. The shovels and shears she had used turned rusty, and the garden turned to seed. It was the beginning of my looking at people, stopping to look. No more skipping, arms flying, shirt flying, free. I was a kid. I wasn't free.

Chapter Six

Going to Schorn's store, doing errands, I had to pass the Hertzfeld villa. Hertzfeld was a Jewish doctor who in the 1920's had established a hotel and "rest home" in the hills outside our town. I had often heard my parents call it a spa without a spa, and that this *Kurort* was responsible, in no small measure, for the economic revival of our area after the disasters of the First World War.

A low masonry wall abutted the street for about a block. Behind the wall was a lawn that seemed forever green, and then between tall trees there rose a very large house, the villa. The Hertzfelds were gone, however, and the villa was now owned by Herr Löwenich, a man whom I had never seen, but who was, from the way people talked, as frightening as any gnome or dark King of Fogs. Löwenich was the town's leading Nazi. On his stone wall there now hung a glass case in which were displayed several pages of Nazi newspapers. I remember, the huge Teutonic letters: *Der Sturmer*, The Fury, and *Der Volkischer Beobachter*, the People's Observer. Each time I passed the case I looked; it seemed as if I were compelled to look. What forced me to stand in front of the glass case were the cartoons, caricatures in black and white of what the text said were Jews. They looked like no Jews I had ever seen before: heavy men in long black coats and wide-brimmed black hats. They had great hooked, pocked noses, beards and sidelocks. They carried suitcases; sandwich crumbs dropped from their mouths; sausages hung out of their side pockets. Their wives, trailing behind, were heavy, black-coated, great-bosomed, with jowly, ugly infants.

They were like no Jews that I had ever seen before. These were, the papers repeated, the scum of the earth. The words most used to describe them were terms describing sickness: scab, infection, germs, bacteria, contagion, plague. These were supposed to be Jews like me, but I was nothing like them. I knew that. Still, I had to repeatedly look at my father and mother, my grandparents, at all the others — they certainly looked like nothing I saw in these papers. Yet if these were Jews, and these were their descriptions, what was I? Every time I passed that glass case it was as if someone forced me to look at these ugly people. I was them; I was not them.

Every morning, in school, we lined up in the yard and in loud voices sang patriotic songs. I somehow always managed to be the last in line, and edged a bit away from the others when these songs were sung. One day, our teacher stepped close to me and, in a very low voice, told me that I really did not have to sing these songs if I did not want to. I felt grateful, almost comforted, but I did not tell him that. What I really wanted was to be able to sing these songs along with everyone else in school. What I wanted was not to feel that peculiar heaviness, that burden that felt physical, that was extra flesh, like a hump on my back — feelings that made me feel different and had me mouthing the words to the songs rather than singing out in full voice with the others who had no burden like mine.

The terrible caricatures, as well as the teacher's kind words, piled on weight. I knew that I was "the other." The weight never lightened. It remains to this day.

When we had our class picture taken I found myself at the end of one of the lines. The class stood on a hillside, the big fourth grade kids stood high on the hill, my grade on the bottom. I sat apart from the others, or maybe they sat apart from me. Joseph

Frisch, sitting next to me, looked angry, his arms folded. Was he angry that he was sitting next to the Jew? Until about then I still had a few German school friends, and we played together, but it seemed more and more as if it was just Willy and me.

One day, in the middle of a lesson, a girl near the front of the class rose and said, pointing to Willy, "He let one go. He stinks." She did not say, "The Jew stinks," but of course that's what I heard. There was a hateful sound to her voice, a sound that ground into me. Everyone around Willy moved away. The teacher told Willy to leave the room and wait outside. Along with everyone else I watched him as he slowly walked out the door, and as I watched I thought, horrendously disloyally, of the cartoons in the glass case, that they applied to him.

The teacher asked me to take Willy home and then return to class. I was bewildered. I was joined to the Jew, yet made to feel different from that Jew.

It was about then that my German school friends stopped playing with me. It was about then, too, that I was no longer invited to our neighbors' Easter egg hunt.

Very many years later, as a film editor in New York, I received an assignment to edit a documentary on some aspects of the Holocaust. One sequence in the film dealt with the rounding up of Jews in the various cities and towns in Germany and Poland preparatory to their being sent to concentration camps. Since the Germans were assiduous in documenting practically all phases of what they called "Jewish resettlement," there was a great deal of material available both in film and stills, and so a great many reels of 16-mm. film were handed to me. There were Jews assembled on city streets, Jews herded onto freight trains, cars, and trucks, Jews marching in columns along bombed-out city streets, Jews marching in their black coats against the cold. Fathers held onto bundles and suitcases, mothers held on to their children. I had to look at many reels to make my selections from these miles of black grainy footage. At one point, the film's producer called me into his office and complained that I was slow in completing this sequence. We had been friends, and his complaint was gentle, but I was costing him money. I promised to speed it up and went back to my cutting room to look at more film.

I could not tell my friend the reason for my slowness. For days and nights I had been poring over the film almost frame by frame, examining each for a face that might be familiar: Oma or Opa, Aunt Lydia, Harry Regensburger, or any of our towns' Jews who had been unable to make it out of Germany in time. Most of all, I think, I was looking for Willy.

At one point I did come across a long column of marchers in a close middle distance: the emptying out of the Warsaw Ghetto. There was one young boy at the edge of the column who could have been about my age at the time, in knee socks and a short coat and brimmed cap. With one hand, he held on to a woman who might have been his mother, but whose face I could not clearly see, and with the other he held a small suitcase. I looked for a long time at that face. There were cases of German Jews being shipped to the Warsaw Ghetto. It could have been Willy, but I don't really know.

At about that time of my alienation at school, my family bought a new radio, a large Grundig. My brother Karl and I watched my father place it on a low settee beneath the kitchen window. Our old radio had sat on a living room shelf right above the RCA Victrola, so it seemed strange to me that this new radio should sit so peculiarly in the kitchen. We watched him set it up, bending over to straighten wires and find connections while our mother stood over him, smiling and nodding. He attached hooks above the window, one on each side. The sound from the radio was beautiful.

"Tell them," said our mother, "if they touch the radio they're going to get it."

Father, on his knees, still occupied and fiddling with wires, mumbled, "You're going to get it, both of you," then looked up, puzzled, at Mamma: "What did they do?"

We all started laughing, and our mamma held both of us and said, "Nothing, nothing." Then Karl called out, "Not yet."

Mostly on weekends, but often enough during the week, when it got dark, my father would stretch a bedsheet across the window, attaching the sheet to the curtain hooks. This time, before stretching the sheet, he attached one end of a rolled-up wire to the back of the radio and then, opening the window just a bit, let wire trail from the kitchen down to the ground below.

My father, mother, grandfather, and sometimes one of the Gärtners were soon huddling around this radio. There was a bit of music that I would later recognize as "The Internationale," and then a voice saying strange words such as "Bilbao, Valencia, Negrin, Catalonia, Madrid." When the adults heard these words, their faces, when they rose from their stooped positions, were stony. Then my mother sighed, "It's all right. You'll see. You'll see." My father took down the sheet and slowly hauled the wire up from the ground.

My Opa was soon objecting to having to listen to this particular station, with its music, "Why do we always have to listen to *them?*" And my mother would reply, with some heat: "All the others lie."

There was now a law: Jewish bulls could not mate with Aryan cows. The law took my Opa's and my father's business from them. None of the Jewish families in town were allowed to do their usual work: No more butcher and a slice of salami; no more baker and a jelly doughnut. Instead, the men were forced to work in one of the local stone quarries. Each day, my handsome father came home covered in gray dust, in his hair, his eyebrows, his hands, his face. His clothes were gray, and my father now complained of aches and pains — and of all the many things my mother had, that day, neglected to do. Never before had I heard my father complain.

Our mother wanted to leave Germany to go to Palestine, or America, or anywhere. My father did not. "Are there cows in Manhattan?" he would say. "What am I going to do in America?"

Tante Irma, Mamma's sister, was in New York City; Uncle Theo, her brother, in England. My parents began having terrible arguments, and then I would run out of the house. Once, my mother took a book and shoved it under my father's nose. "Here, damn it! Read it yourself!" The book bunked him and father's nose bled all over it. The book was *Mein Kampf*.

I ran out of the house.

Some days before, forced laborers had been working on the street in front of our house, fixing cobblestones and street drainage, pick-and-shovel work. These were some of the early enemies of the Nazis, whom Hitler had rounded up and jailed or put into concentration camps: Social Democrats, union people, communists, people like that. My mother, seeing them work so hard, brought them water, coffee, and bread and butter, for which these men were very grateful. She chatted with them, and they told her to leave Germany, to get out as soon as she could, because Hitler had it in for the Jews. It was they who had given her a copy of Hitler's book.

Our father wouldn't read it. "This kind of thing happens all the time all over Europe," he said. "Hitler's a cheap politician. It'll blow over. Do you think that the people who really count will let him go on with this? Never!"

My grandmother and I were in a pine wood searching for mushrooms when we saw German Army vehicles parked on the roads beyond. The army was on maneuvers.

We ambled slowly through the soft pine needles, hunting on the forest floor. When we separated, our loud hallooing told each other where we were.

I reached the edge of the forest. There were green bushes and then a wide meadow. Through the bushes, I saw a soldier sitting at what looked like a peculiar desk, a desk with little wheels. It seemed to be made of wire and little slats of shiny wood, and on a board in front of him were lots of little buttons and levers. There was a horn jutting from his chest, into which he was talking while his hands danced, turning levers, pushing buttons. He was blond, in a brown uniform, and he talked and laughed and ran his machine with an ease that I envied. Here was this wonderful figure, and there was my father, all covered with gray dust, and I a bug, an insect, a scab . . .

It was very hot when Oma and I came out of the woods. We crossed the railroad tracks, the highway, then our green meadow, which stretched from the highway all the way down to the edge of the Bröl, the brook for which the whole area where we lived, the Brölthal, the Bröl valley, was named.

I was sometimes a bit embarrassed that this little brook, in which I could dangle my feet on a hot day when everybody else was gathering hay, had given its name to so wide an expanse of land. I knew from my books that ours was a big world, and that the Nile and the Mississippi, the Amazon and the Orinocco were very large rivers, yet except for the Amazon, they hadn't been used to name the countries they flowed through — not even the Rhine, which was a great deal closer. Still, the Bröl was a nice brook, and when I looked at the pool where the water eddied, black with silver strings, I thought, *Where did this water begin?*

Oma said there were springs up in the hills. She pointed. Up there, she said, the water bubbled up out of the ground and all of the springs bubbled together to make the Bröl.

At the edge of the meadow, the water ran in this lovely steel blue color, except where it flowed over stones and frothed white. On the forest side, where branches arched over the water, it was this dappled color, dark brown where the shadows lay and silver-blue where the sun shone through the branches. I sometimes stood at the water's edge for long periods watching a leaf flow on the current. The leaf would come around the bend and slowly flow on the current through shadow and sunlight. Would it flow swiftly past me and disappear around another bend, or would it get caught in the swirling around one of the rocks and sink in the swirling, or be pushed flat against one of the rocks and kept stuck there by the pressure of the water?

I had watched many leaves float down the brook. Now the water was low, and Oma and I could hop from stone to stone until we reached the other side.

We walked into a green pine woods. The floor of the forest squeaked and crunched as we trod on the dark pine needles. "They're going to cut the tall grass for hay in a few days," Oma said.

She knew where she was going and soon we came to the place where the forest floor was covered with thin, crooked, yellow-brown morrels. The forest floor was dappled like the shadow part of the brook, sun and shadow. The morels seemed to grow in shadow. When one patch of them was almost exhausted, Oma moved on, searching for the next patch, and left me to pick the last few by myself. Her loud halloo told me where she was, and I hurried after her.

Oma held her apron out in front of her, we threw the mushrooms into the bellying apron. It was soon filled and we started home, retracing the way we had come.

We reached the highway, turned right, and there in front of the Nathan house was a huge wooden crate. It was a barn of a crate, as big as our living room. Its wood was blond, and the box was open at one end, and empty. Oma said, "The lift."

The Nathan house was the largest Jewish house in the whole town, really one of the largest houses in the whole town. It was the house in which Oma grew up, and where her brother Julius lived with his son Wolfgang, Wolfgang's wife Ruth, and their new baby.

The house had a large garden in back that ran almost down to the brook. It had a summer house in which I drank cold cider, and it had willow trees that gave shade. I would sit under the shade of the willow trees and squish ants with my thumb.

Oma turned from the crate to the house said, "I have to go in."

"Can I stay here? I want to look at the box."

I was very surprised when she said yes. Oma went into the house, and I ran toward the crate and walked carefully into its dark interior. The crate smelled of sawdust and shellac. It was massive. Its height disappeared in darkness, but its sides were a smooth blond wood, which I touched very carefully, feeling the way I felt in synagogue.

Suddenly there was a boom, then another boom, and I ran out of the box. Outside there were two men laughing, carrying a chest of drawers. "Can't have vermin in the crate; got to drive them out," said one of them, and they carried the chest into the crate.

Oma came out of the house and took my hand and we resumed our way home. "Wolfgang is going to Palestine. Did you know that?"

I knew that. Wolfgang was her nephew; he had the same name as mine.

"The Lift is going to carry everything to Eretz."

"And Aunt Ruth and the baby in there?"

"No, that's silly, just their household things."

I knew that. I was making a joke. Aunt Ruth and the baby were not going to Palestine, just Wolfgang. Wolfgang was something of a joke, too, in our town; not me, him. When their baby, Rolfe, was born, he was not "all right." His skin was brown and he had lots of black hair. He had large peculiar eyes, and his face was all flat. He cried all the time. Some people said that his crying was louder than the whistle of the train whose tracks ran on the other side of the highway. I could sometimes stop his crying with a stupid game. When he visited, or I was at his house and he lay in his little crib, I made believe that I was catching flies. "See Rolfe, see?" — and I would quickly whisk my hand through the air and then close my fingers into a fist. I would show him the fist then open my hand, see. All gone. It's all gone." I would do that over and over again, and all the while he would be quiet, fascinated, I guess, by the movement of my hands. The minute I stopped, his wailing would begin again.

If I were at her house, Aunt Ruth would say that I could not leave, I would have to stay all the time and entertain her boy. Then she would get me a piece of cake or a pink marzipan pig.

Aunt Ruth was tall with black hair and very smooth white skin. She would say, "When Wolfgang is gone you'll come and stay with me. All right? Then I won't have lost a Wolfgang, I'll just have another Wolfgang. All right?

The reason that Aunt Ruth's Wolfgang was something of a joke in the town was that when the baby was crying so hard, Wolfgang would put it in the little cream-colored carriage and wheel the baby right out on the highway, which ran in front of his house and where all the people could see him. He would wheeled the carriage up and down the road until the baby was quiet, and then he would wheel it some more until the baby was asleep. The people all said, "What kind of a thing is that for a man to do, wheeling a carriage? That's nothing for a man. Ruth doesn't have anything else to do? Hmm and hmm." There was a lot of hmming going on.

But because the baby was not "all right," the Germans would not let the baby out of the country, so Wolfgang was going to leave by himself, leave Aunt Ruth and the baby, and then see what he could do to get them out of Germany from outside the country.

By the time we left the country, two years later, Aunt Ruth and the baby would still be in Ruppichteroth. Many years later we heard that both Ruth and their baby had transported to a concentration camp in Riga, Latvia, where both were killed.

Ernst Gärtner, Otto's son, left for America. Next, my favorite Gärtner, Herbert, left for America, for New York. He was my favorite because whenever he saw me, I would get to ride on his shoulders. Herbert had sisters, Kate and Irene, who many years before had left our town for America.

The United States existed for us as a word called "America." The word was always, always, "America." It was a name that had an almost holy feeling to it, a feeling that was soft like the deep red carpet in the synagogue, from where looked up onto the soft and shimmering red velvet curtain, decorated on its borders with gold braid, and where, behind the curtain, there were the burnished oak doors behind which were the scrolls of the Torahs with their silver crowns and silver bells. America was as real, as were the stories of Indians and the wilderness. America was *Schlaraffenland*, Utopia, the land of milk and honey, the big rock candy mountain, a place of luxury, hard work, and delicious idleness. How could a land exist where buildings were built on hard rock and could reach the sky so that their tops scraped the clouds?

Herbert called me "Big Ears" because he said I would always "snuffle," put my nose in where adults were gathered and try to listen to what they were saying. So: Kate and Irene had left for America even before I was born, and they were both rich, in Newark, New Jersey. Kurt Gärtner, Otto's son, had also left for America. I did not like Kurt very much because unlike any of the other Gärtners, he never bothered much with me. He was small and had a narrow face. Then Werner Gärtner, Herbert's brother, had left.

There were parties for all of them just before they left, parties to which I was not invited. Then the Isaak girls left, blond Selma and blond Elsie. I was at the party for them, and quite a few Christians were there. Else's mother and grandmother were both midwives, and I had heard that the two of them delivered babies in our town and in the towns round about. The grandmother, Sarah, walked stooped, had white hair and a slate-gray face, and always wore black; I avoided her because I thought she was a witch. When Sarah walked along the streets of the town and a Christian man walked by, he would take off his hat to her; if a little girl walked by, she would curtsy.

One late afternoon, I watched at the kitchen table as Oma lit a candle and carried it over to a nook in the wall, where there were small shelves with small frames holding small framed photographs of great-aunts and uncles and Opa in an army uniform.

Opa was near that nook, praying his usual afternoon and evening prayers. He watched Oma with some surprise, all the while praying and at the same time making questioning motions to her with his arms. While he gestured and prayed, Oma looked for more candles, found them, and put them on the table. She turned to the stove where she rattled some pots.

When Opa finished praying, he turned, wide-eyed, to Oma. "Who in God's name is that candle for? For what? For what are you lighting candles now?"

Oma never said much. So often, when I saw her speak, it was as if she were just discovering words. They came out smoothly but slowly, so that when she said something, it really seemed more important than when most other people said something — as if she were answering some very deep and important question.

"For Karl," she said. "I thought I should."

"It's not his *yortsayt* yet. It's not until October."

"Why not light them when we feel like it?"

"If we did it when we felt like it, we might never do it."

"Or we might light them one a minute until the kitchen looked like an acre of candle lights, like in the Cologne Cathedral!"

"An acre of lights would be too expensive for us."

Oma went to a cupboard and took some saucers and put them on the table. She took the candles and put them, after melting some wax at their bottoms, on the saucers.

"What, in God's name, are these for, now? These four — but what four?

"Five."

"No. We won't mourn them. No. There's nothing to mourn. They're going to leave, that's all. You are killing them before their time, aren't you? Aren't you?"

"I'm not killing them. Except I know that there'll be a time when we won't be seeing them any more. Once they're out the door they're gone. And I feel sad."

"You are a nun, you with your candles." Opa snuffed out five candles. "One candle is enough. One is enough."

Chapter Seven

There was talk of war. The nights grew longer and the days were chillier. There was talk of Sudetenland and Czechoslovakia, of cutting it up. How could one cut up a country? Did one use a knife? Of course not. Spain was being cut up with bombs and guns. Hitler wanted to cut up Czechoslovakia, and the Germans who lived there were going to live as Germans. All Germans everywhere were one people. But we, Opa and Oma, my parents, the other Jewish families, we were Germans, too, weren't we? How could they say that Czechs were Germans and that other Germans, Germans like us, were not Germans?

Along with talk of war, of cutting up a country, there was talk of names. And the names felt like arrows pointed at us. In the warm evenings after supper, when the talk turned to names, it was as if the names did things, created actions, just names alone. One name was good, another bad, others just so-so. Some names were courageous, others cowardly. Whatever the names did, I understood, would have an effect on our lives. When the adults spoke of the names, their voices were intense. Whenever the talk turned to names, it would frighten me. There was Runciman and Ciano, Bonnet and Mussolini, Roosevelt, Hitler, Benes, Chamberlain. I was frightened. All the men seemed to pull hard on their cigarettes. And though I was frightened, I wanted to hear all that my cigarette smoking, chin stroking adults had to say. When I was shooed off to bed, I walked away very slowly.

I spent most of my days in the hay loft, reading. When not reading, I examined the gray spider webs being spun in the darker corners of the loft. There was something terribly exact about the woven lines and circles of their webs in which the small flies struggled. Whenever Opa came to milk the several cows we had left, I would climb down from my loft and wait, as I so often did, and hunker down beside him and wait for the spray of milk into my mouth. But he was distracted so often these days that he hardly ever noticed me beside him. This day, however, he did, but not in the way I wanted.

"Just wait here," he said. "Oma needs some milk."

When he returned he had a pail with him. "Let's go collect some pears." He held out his hand, I took it, and we walked through our hilly meadow. It was noon and the sun shone. Holding hands, we came to the meadow's edge where stood our ancient pear tree. The tree was huge. Strips of bark were shed from its sides. A cow stood in its shadow, eating pears that had fallen. Opa drove the cow away by hitting it in the rump with the pail.

"Got to leave some pears for us humans, she's got all this grass." He smiled. There were a great many pears on the ground and I jumped to collect them into the pail. Opa found a stick and hit the branches so that more pears tumbled down. We soon filled the pail. Opa looked about on the ground, found one, picked it up and rubbed it hard, and gave it to me.

"Eat. These are the best pears in Ruppichteroth." I ate. The pear was sweet and tart; white and yellow sparks were in it. We walked down the small rise on which the pear tree stood. There was a hum in the air. Opa stopped. "Look up there." I saw a sliver of silver far overhead. "Look up there. A plane." I had seen planes in the air before, but they were always black and had double wings. This one was brand new to me. The plane was silver and had only one set of wings and even more, as I looked at it, it was surrounded by a black halo. The plane flew on surrounded by this black circle. Opa put down the pail and pointed.

"That's Chamberlain on his way to Bad Godesberg. He's on his way to Hitler. Too bad for all the Czechs. Too bad for the rest of the world." We resumed walking. Opa looked down at me, smiled, and squeezed my hand. I held onto his hand until we reached our door. I looked back up toward the meadow. I couldn't see the tree or cow. They were gone.

One day at school, in the yard during recess, someone called out, "Look down there. Smoke." We all ran to a low wall that edged the playground. From there we could look down on the roofs of the town, on the yards and the streets, on the washing that hung out in the yards. Down below, I could see that it was our synagogue from which the black smoke rose.

Children moved back from the wall and looked at me. They moved away from me, as if I were Willy and had committed something foul. I stood very still. Our teacher came to me and took my hand. "I'm going to walk you home." We found my brother, Karl, who by then was also attending school. He was in first grade, I in second. Our teacher took each of us by the hand, Karl on one side and I on the other, and walked us home.

We walked down the cobbled streets, past Schorn's store, past Aunt Lydia's house, past the blacksmith's. There seemed to be more people than usual out on the street; there seemed to be women in aprons who had just stepped out of their houses, some with towels still in their hands, as if, in their rush outdoors, they had been overtaken by surprise, and were chatting as if in front of their own houses, but they were further out in the open, on the street. As we passed, they stopped their talk and silently looked at us.

I was excited by what seemed to be a totally extraordinary event. I did not at all mind the attention our walk was getting. A crowd stood in front of the synagogue: townspeople, men and women milling, several gray-uniformed policemen, Brownshirts with red swastika armbands. White smoke billowed from the front door of the synagogue.

My grandfather, my Opa, appeared in the smoke. He stood in the doorway with a Torah on his shoulder, as if he had just lifted it from the Ark. I was afraid, I pulled at our teacher's hand, I wanted to run to Opa. The teacher squeezed my hand hard, looked down at me, and shook his head. He threaded us along the back of the crowd. He held our hands tight and looked straight ahead. But I wanted Opa.

We arrived in front of our house. Our grandmother stood on the front steps. Our teacher nodded at her, maybe bowed, then turned and left. Grandmother came down and embraced us. She was crying. We were crying.

Opa came in the door, smelling of smoke and carrying a Torah. "I have to go back, get the others." He laid the Torah on the kitchen table and hurried out again. A few minutes later he came back with another scroll. As he started to rush out again, Oma said, quietly, "The *shul* is burning." Opa looked at her, said nothing, and hurried out again.

Several of the older men, Gustav and Otto Gärtner, Harry Regensburgers' father, old Mr. Isaaks, Oma's brother Julius, all came to the kitchen with armsful of old leather-covered books and Torahs. The Torahs lay on the kitchen table, and all the old men sat around on chairs, with their hands in front of their mouths.

The policeman, Laddach, appeared in the kitchen door, with several young SA men behind him. Laddach was about to say something when one of the young men jumped in front of him and yelled, "You old men, pick up those things and get outside." They all waited, then Officer Laddach nodded. Opa first and then the others picked up the Torahs and books and filed out the door. Outside, in front of our house, the Brown Shirts made the men stand in a line and then yelled at them to start marching. As they went off with Opa at the head of the line, one of them yelled, "Left foot, right foot," over and over again, soon all the other Brown Shirts began yelling, "Left foot, right foot."

Somebody ran up to Opa and forced an axe into his left hand. I saw them move out and round a corner. I tried to follow them, but Mamma pulled me back and pushed me into the house. Someone, later, told us that the old men were made to march through all the streets of the village with the SA men yelling, "Left foot, right foot" while laughing and enjoying themselves. The old men and Opa were then made to stand in front of the synagogue, where a bonfire had been started, and with guns pointing at them, they were made to throw the books and Torahs into the fire.

My grandparents lived on the ground floor. There was a center hall and their living quarters were off to the right. At the end of the hall was a door that led out to the barn, now empty of cows. Next to the stairs, in a small alcove, was the cream separator, a shining stainless steel tube, the top quarter pinched in before, like a large woman's hips, it flared out. I was in my grandmother's kitchen. There was a loud knocking on the front door. She and I both went to see. Officer Laddach, in a gray uniform, stood at the door.

He pulled off his cap, "I'm sorry, Oma. I'm looking for Oscar."

My father, in his shirt and open collar, came down the stairs, my mother behind him. My father stood in the middle of the room turning in a circle, looking at his mother, at my mother.

"What do you want, Laddach?" said my mother.

Laddach shuffled his feet, "I'm sorry, Melli, but I have to take Oscar."

"Why Oscar?"

"They're taking everybody. The Regensburgers, the Gärtners, everybody."

"Where is he going?"

Laddach pressed his lips together.

"Laddach, you two were in the band together, in the soccer club."

"First to Cologne, Messehalle, I think, then I don't know."

My mother ran upstairs. I moved from the stairs over to the cream separator. I leaned on it, I put my arms around its waist, embracing, holding on tight. Laddach and my father looked at each other. Neither said anything. My father turned in circles. He didn't see me. Nobody saw me.

My mother and grandmother ran at my father with clothes, warm clothes. My father just stood there, helpless, while they dressed him: my mother with coat and tie, my grandmother with a scarf, my mother with a sweater, then a heavy overcoat, then a hat.

Laddach said, "All right." My father moved toward the door, and my grandmother screamed, "Wait, I have to make some sandwiches. He has to take some sandwiches."

They all stood there saying nothing until my grandmother came with sandwiches. She embraced my father. Then my mother embraced him. My father went to the door, Laddach took him by the arm, and they went out.

Somewhat later, Laddach appeared at our door again.

"Melli, you have to come, you and the kids." My mother's knees buckled; she fell to the floor.

Laddach and my grandmother helped her up. "They just want you at the synagogue. They just want some pictures."

Another man came, saying, "Hurry, they're waiting. They have to get back to Cologne."

A small crowd still stood about the building, among them, several of my classmates. We were told to stand right in front of the synagogue, my mother, my grandmother, my brother Karl, myself. My mother held our youngest brother Peter in her arms. Although the synagogue had stopped burning, smoke still rose from the fallen roof. Now there was merely the smell of fire and ash, all around us.

Two men were taking pictures. My classmates, my playmates, Willibald and Horst, as well as some of the others, picked up small clods of dirt and threw them at us. Two SS men stood in back of the crowd, and as the flash bulbs popped off, they began to yell at us, "Just wait, soon you'll be burning, too. Just wait. Just wait." They were laughing and looking at each other, as if they were pulling off some great joke.

The following morning, Opa came out of hiding. He had spent that raw November night, first outside in the field and then, when he thought he heard some men, he ran down to a nearby brook where he spent most of the night immersed in the freezing water. What I remember about that particular morning was my Opa, outside the house somewhere, screaming, in great pain: "I'm pissing blood! I'm pissing blood!"

That night all the Jewish families in town gathered in the baker Regensburger's house. People slept in their day clothes on the floor in various rooms. We children were all in one upstairs room. We stayed up very late playing rummy and parchesi, and all night we heard our mothers, our grandmothers, our aunts, sobbing.

In the morning, we were home again. The only phone in the house was the one in the downstairs hall, attached to the wall. Making calls was a rare thing, but now we watched our mother make them frantically, call after call, trying to find out where our father had been taken. The following morning, she and several other women went off to Cologne to find out about their husbands and sons.

I was taken along. I was to hold on to mother's hand and not open my mouth. If she squeezed my hand, I could cry if I wanted to. We went to the offices of Jewish community organizations, but there were rows and lines of women already there when we came, many with children holding fast to their mothers' hands. We went to police stations and to the offices of the Gestapo, and always there were long lines, and nobody would tell us anything.

We returned home, and as we got off the train, Laddach was

waiting for us. He said, "Dachau. Dachau is where he is going."

There were no words, just screams. I had told Mamma that I needed Pappa back. With Pappa home, everything was right, everything was in its proper place. It had to do with the house: With Pappa home, every room in the house was in its proper place, the house stood foursquare on its foundation. With Pappa gone, the house was askew, it seemed to lean, maybe to tip over; things were out of balance. Mamma screamed and waved her arms up and down. I knew then that the strands that held my cradle together were being ripped apart. I was afraid. I didn't know what was going to happen.

Oma came, stroked my hair, and led me to her kitchen, where there were familiar smells. Karl and I sat on the bottom step of the stairs watching Mamma. All day she stood at the wall phone, calling, one call after the other. Opa fed us, and Oma watched over Peter.

Mamma was told to petition the Gestapo in Cologne. She learned that if someone had done service in the First World War, they might be released from the concentration camp. Pappa, at 16, during that war, had replaced a local postal worker and delivered mail for several years. She wrote up the petition and we returned to Cologne. The wait on a hard bench was very long. When we finally were led to an office, the black-uniformed officer looked up at mother from a sheet of paper and said that Oscar Hess, his name, had been erased. Mamma's face lit up with smiles; she bowed and said many thank you's, and made me say thank you. I hated her bowing.

At the railroad station we ran into Ilse Isaaks, and my mother told her what had happened, that his name had been erased. "Don't you know what that means?" said Ilse, "You'll never see him again."

I began to sob, but Mamma only said, "No." She kept repeating, "No," all the way back to Ruppichteroth.

About six weeks later, on a Friday night, Mamma took my brother and me down to the train station. It was dark except for a few streetlights. Our wait was short. Pappa stepped down from the train. The train pulled out behind him. His face was round and fat. He was bald. His wonderful black hair has been shaved off. He was a father I had never seen before. We stood across from him. His hands trembled. My brother and I looked up to him, but he didn't look at us, and everything he said was directed at our mother: "When do I leave? Are my papers in order?"

A week later, Pappa left for Holland. Much later I learned that the reason for his release from Dachau was that Aunt Mina in Holland had arranged it. She had contacts with Dutch government officials, and through them she had arranged for his visa, for his stay with her in Amsterdam. Only because of her efforts in Holland was our father released and allowed to leave the concentration camp and Germany.

All that week I was full of a fearful curiosity as to what had happened to my father, where he had been, what had happened to him to make him look so strange, what made him tremble so, to be so silent, to neglect us so.

On the morning of his leaving we all ate in my grandparents' kitchen. At one point, my grandfather left the room and then returned with an object wrapped in a large white linen napkin. I knew what it was, the *shofar*, the rams' horn, which was kept in the credenza, behind glass, on a glass pedestal, in the dark dining room in which no one ever ate. It was the *shofar* that had belonged to my grandfather's father and to his father before him and to the one before that. It had belonged to a whole series of fathers extending into what was for me a past, or rather, a distance, like Crusoe's island, or Shatterhand's America. It was a distance extending up into the night sky, where there was a constellation of stars, our teacher had told us, called the Ram.

I knew about rams. We kept them on the farm, for food. My

Opa would dig a little pit, struggle with the ram, his arm under its head until he was able to lift the ram's head high enough and then, with a quick stroke of a sharp knife, cut the ram's throat and let the dark red blood gush into the pit of dug-up earth until the pit was full and the ram stopped its struggling.

It was Abraham's ram that was up in the sky, the one he slaughtered instead of slaughtering his son, his only one. It was that distance that the *shofar* bridged, since it came from the horn of that ram. But I wanted to know what made Pappa look so strange and why he spoke so little, and why he looked out of the window all the time.

We walked over snow to the railroad that would take my Pappa to Holland. The snow crunched under my feet. There was a small crowd, maybe twenty people at the railroad station when we arrived, all Christians, all silent, the Protestant pastor among them. Except for the pastor, these were all old friends of Pappa's, friends from the town band, the soccer team. I thought it was strange that the pastor was there; the only contact with him that I knew of were the greetings that we exchanged whenever we passed each other on the street. Pappa embraced us, entered the train, and emerged on the rear platform of the last car. The train pulled out, and as it did, the Protestant pastor called out, "I wish I were going with you."

Over the next three months, Mamma traveled to almost every city in Germany in which a foreign consular office was located to try for a visa to somewhere, anywhere. When she came back from one of her trips she looked terrible. When there was black in the hollows of her eyes and her hair looked like wires and her slaps came fast for the least infraction, I knew there were no visas. Mamma's travels made Opa terribly angry. Once, I heard him yell at her that she was a whore. Mamma yelled back, "I want Oscar. We have to leave. It's hard, hard, hard."

When there was yelling I wanted to disappear, to run away, anywhere, but anywhere was black, anywhere was nowhere. I wanted to bury myself in the hay up in the barn, but the hay was old and rotting, it oozed a sticky wetness and smelled bad.

When Mamma was at home, nights, she would sit in a chair in the living room, silent, with her hands in her lap.

One day I brought a thick branch into the house. I wanted to whittle and decorate it like the shiny, knobby and shellacked walking stick that was Opa's. Opa screamed at me, "Get it out of the house." I took the branch and threw it out onto the midden. I had done something wrong, but I had no idea what it was.

Chapter Eight

We were going to Ecuador. The news came from Holland; visas and all the proper exit papers had been secured. Oma and Opa were not going with us. Opa was not going to go to a country of snakes and jungles, and anyway, he said, things eventually were going to be all right in Germany. Germany was a civilized country. He was a German. He had fought for his country. He was going to be all right. Opa took us to Cologne and from there it was on to Holland.

In Cologne we took a new train. Sometimes the train slowed or even stopped when it came near a station, and then I saw all those small garden plots on the edges of the tracks. There were rows of green plants, and women in aprons among the plants, on their knees, pulling weeds. There were wooden huts in the backs of the gardens where implements were stored, and beyond the huts were houses with ochre walls where bedding was being aired on window sills. I saw a young boy pull a wheelbarrow out of one of the huts. The gardens were separated by fencing, wood or metal wiring, and very often, along the fences, there were flowerbeds with red flowers and white. I wanted to pull a wheelbarrow.

Telephone or telegraph wires ran along the route of the train to Holland, from pole to pole. I watched them out of the window. The wires began even and level with a pole, but then bowed, sagged in a long soft curve, then rose up, lifting to meet the next pole. Rising and falling, rising and falling. I watched them against changing backgrounds, green woods, green fields. I watched them in the dark, too, light from compartment windows briefly striping them with flashes of orange, my face in the darkness reflected in the compartment window, and behind the window the rising and falling rhythm of the wires. We were going to meet Pappa; we were leaving Oma and Opa. The continuous repetitions, the rising and falling of the wires were soothing to me, even as they were keeping measure of my distance from Oma and Opa.

The train stopped at Emmerich, on the Dutch border. We heard a great deal of halooing outside the train. From the windows, we could see men in various uniforms, some that we recognized as the railroad people's olive, others dark blue, and they were all waving and shouting at each other. Suddenly, as if at a signal, passengers began to look at each other, then stood to pull their baggage from the overhead compartments. The doors to the car opened with a great clang, and a group of men in uniform entered and very loudly and cheerily called out, "Good afternoon ladies and gentlemen, Control, Control. We are from Control, any problems with languages? Please have your suitcases open when we come around." They were very cheery and smiled and said, "Anything to declare?" and "Thank you, thank you" a lot. They rummaged through our baggage, and when they were done placed a lead seal around the clasps of the suitcases.

While all that went on, one of the uniforms sat down next to my mother. He said that he was a border policeman; he had silver arrows on the tips of his lapels. He bent over the papers that she handed to him. We stared at him as he leafed through them. I was very afraid. After a while he looked up and shook his head. He turned and called out to men behind him, "You can stop with the baggage of these people." There was something wrong, something wrong with our papers, and the policeman with silver lapels said that we had to leave the train. Mamma began to cry, as we hung on to her skirts, "What can I do? My husband is waiting for us in Amsterdam."

"If you call him, maybe he can fix the problem quickly. He can talk to the Panama consulate and get it settled. There are trains all the time."

"But what if he can't? I have three children, and it's late, almost night."

He shrugged his shoulders and helped my mother take our baggage off the train. Our suitcases were stacked next to the track, and my brothers and I stood next to the suitcases. We looked at our mother, hurrying from one person to another asking where a phone might be, then disappearing behind a kiosk. Hissing and steaming, our train for Amsterdam pulled out and left the station.

Men pushed baggage trucks back and forth. Men and women with coats over their arms rushed for trains. Nobody looked at us. After a long while our mother reappeared; there was a man with a baggy pants and rumpled jacket and a tieless white shirt following behind her. "I can't find Pappa. This nice taxi driver thinks he knows a place where we might spend the night." It was already quite dark.

There was a Catholic cloister that had a hostel attached to it where, the taxi driver told us we might stay overnight. Mamma had the taxi driver stack our bags in front of the cloister door and, holding Peter in her arms, rang a bell on the side of the door. A nun in a dark habit and wimple opened the door wide. The light shone orange behind her, and I could see a wide staircase to the side. She had a pale round face and looked a great deal like Oma. Mamma tried to explain our situation: ". . . leaving Germany, husband in Amsterdam, something the matter with our papers, can't reach my husband, it will be all right tomorrow, just for one night." The nun patted Peter on the head. "Just for one night," Mamma repeated. I did not hear all their conversation, but I did hear, several times, the words "not possible." I heard "not possible" one last time, and then the door closed. There was no room. We stood there staring at the closed door. I felt as if someone had put their hand over my mouth, and it was hard to breathe. I felt the way I remembered when the teacher told me I need not join in singing the German anthems. There were things in this world that were just not for me. Our mother had the taxi take us to a hotel, but the hotel was full.

We stood on the sidewalk, under a streetlamp, in front of the hotel, when our taxi driver ran up to us. "One of my buddies told me of a Jewish family that might take you in."

They did. We were a week in Emmerich — a week of potato soup and cold meat; a week of playing rummy with my brother and an old man who lived in the house; a week of watching our mother make phone calls; there was nothing to be done. Our journey was not possible. Opa came, and looked at Mamma, who had both hands over her face; he shook his head and hugged her. He had come to take us back to our village.

We sat in our train compartment on slippery yellow wicker seats, my mother in a corner and Opa across from her. They sat by the window, and I didn't even care that I could not look out of the window. On the way out I would have fought for the window seat, but now I just watched my mother, slumped and silent in her corner, her arm around Peter, and my grandfather asking, "And this is what you got from all your running around?"

Mamma was stroking Peter and took a long while answering. The wait scared me. When she began to speak, she talked to the window, not to Opa. "Oscar was supposed to get the transit visa for Panama through the consulate in Amsterdam and send it to me."

"He didn't get it?"

"No. He didn't get it because somebody wanted too much money, and somebody else told him it wasn't necessary since we had the visa for Ecuador."

"So?"

"Our damn ship from Amsterdam doesn't go direct to Ecuador; it's too big to go through the canal or something. It lets us off in Panama, where we take another boat to Ecuador. We have to stay in Panama until we get the other boat."

"Mina would have helped."

"Tante Mina has helped and helped and helped. She got Oscar out of Dachau, she paid for all our tickets and gave us seven thousand dollars more. Oscar didn't think he could ask her one more time." She turned away from the window and looked at Opa, then yelled, "Do you know how it feels to stand in the dark with three kids and you don't know where to go? I didn't know where to go. I didn't know what to do! Damn it!" She cried and hit her head against the window several times.

Peter, Karl, and I began to cry. Opa stood up and took Mamma's head between his hands and kissed the top of her head.

It was night, but I didn't go to sleep. I counted all the stations on our backwards trip from Emmerich: Wesel, Oberhausen, Duisburg, Dusseldorf, Neuss, Cologne, Bonn. At Bonn we changed to the narrow gauge train that took us back to Ruppichteroth.

Three months later we were again on our way to Holland, and one week after that we were on an ocean liner, first class, on our way to Ecuador.

The reason we were traveling first class was that we were forced to. The German government had made it a condition of our emigration. Emigrants' tickets had to be paid for in hard currency, British pounds or American dollars, and so we were made to go first class, since that would bring the Nazis the largest amount of hard currency. Our family was very lucky to have had wealthy Aunt Mina, who was able to pay for first class, as well as providing for all the money we might need in our travels. I ache for those who had no such help. The Holocaust had its class aspect.

The voyage was a great geography lesson. The 35,000-ton *Carib-*

ia of the North German Lloyd was my teacher. The ship had nosed about ports on the North Sea scooping up passengers destined for Caribbean ports. Now it was docked in Ljmuiden, the port of Amsterdam, and when it was made clear to the white-uniformed officers that the gold had been paid and the cabins reserved, we boarded, and then it was out into the Channel and along the coast of France. Passengers leaned over the railing, pointing to the towns and cities that we were passing, naming them. These were seasoned travelers. I leaned over, too, or tried to, and I listened. Scheveningen, Ostende, Dunquerque, Calais, Boulogne, Dieppe, Le Havre, and "Were those lights Cherbourg?" Then out onto the ocean. "That's Madeira." Then Port of Spain. I loved all the new words, all the sounds of the new languages. At the Venezuelan port of La Guaira, brown-colored boys found ways to climb up the long black sides of the ship, then stood up on the railings, and passengers on the highest deck tossed silver coins into the brown harbor waters to see the boys jump and dive for them. There were sharks in these waters, we could see their fins cutting through the surf. Elders gave their children coins to toss.

Maracaibo, Baranquilla, Cartagena, Colon. The names were music.

Then there was luxury, first-class luxury. There was bouillon on the deck and mock turtle soup in the dining room, tea, toast, and butter cookies, and the string chamber group at four. Someone with a blanket wrapped me gently in the deck chair. We, who traveled behind cow flop, now had a shipload of obsequious servants. My mother reveled in it: the white table cloth, the heavy silver, the flowers, the smile from the captain's table. There were even scones, clotted cream, and strawberry jam.

Our father could not enjoy anything. He shied from everything and everybody. Anyone with black shoes, he thought, had to be in the SS. He was constantly looking for what was in back of him.

"Pappa," Mamma told us, "after Dachau, has become a real

coward. A *Washlappen*, a dishrag." My father? My father who had me walk with him, stride for stride, driving cows to market? A dishrag? Then what was I?

Yet there was much to divert a person from knots in the stomach. I had the run of the ship. There was the gymnasium that had all this fascinating machinery: a rowboat on dry land, a track on which I could run but which stood dead still and was called a treadmill; heavy iron weights which stood against one wall, over which men grunted when they pulled them up over their shoulders by a strong rope. And they kept up the pulling and grunting for no reason I could ever see. When I was alone in the gym, which was often, I rowed and ran and made the iron weights ring like bells when I pulled on the ropes and then quickly released them to smash on the ground.

It was all fun, but we, Karl and I, were severely reprimanded when we let 2-year-old Peter walk on top of the main deck railing. He accomplished three steps when there was a scream, a rush of adult arms, and a subsequent pounding of both our rear ends. Later, Pappa took us to the railing, "Look down there. Look." We were on the highest deck. Far down below, strands of white water separated the ship from the black that stretched to the horizon. Pappa lifted me up above the railing and ordered me to look. Suddenly he staggered back. He dropped me onto the deck. "I get dizzy," he mumbled, and sat down on a deck chair. Mamma later told us that Pappa had a lot of trouble, a lot, looking down from a great height.

Except for Karl and one boy, there was nobody near my age on the boat, on that long voyage. I was 8 and the boy was 10, maybe 11. He was blond, wore long pants and white short-sleeved shirts that were always creased as if they had just been ironed. He walked around as if nothing ever impressed him. This boat, this fantasy, this multi-colored fair, seemed to be something that was part of his ordinary life. That there were stewards who brought bouillon to the loungers on the top deck meant nothing to him. The gym meant nothing, the skeet shooting on the upper deck meant nothing — although I think it was his father who handled the gun most of the time, lovingly wiping down the shiny brown wooden stock with a chamois cloth, exchanging the gun he had just used with another, taking it from a wooden cabinet with a black handle as if it were an ordinary suitcase, a suitcase just for guns.

Was it a game? A tiny terrace bounded by a railing extended out over the side of the ship. It was just large enough for a man to stand on for shooting. The floor of the terrace was a braided metal weave of iron slats through which one could see the black ocean sweeping by below. A man could stand out there in safety, but a little boy would surely catch his shoes in the hollow openings. Might he not fall through, down to where the flying fishes jumped, down to where the porpoises raced the black iron sides of the ship? They were all of one kind of material, ship and porpoise, curved material bound and gathered by the thinnest slice of water. That was its skin, black and shiny above, its belly creamy and dun like a cowboy hat. I didn't think I would fall through the holes, but what if I did?

The ship would race on and I would be left behind in the empty ocean. I could imagine myself in the water. The high-walled ship would go past in a second, long before any cry of help could come from my mouth. I was caught in the wake, tossed and tumbled in the churning wash. Could I breathe? If I did, water would charge into my lungs, into my whole body and I would explode, my guts charging out of the rents in my body like the pulp of a gooseberry when cracked between my teeth. Once, I heard, when I was not supposed to be within hearing, my father told Mamma that when he was in Dachau the guards had taken a hose and pumped water down his throat. Pappa had said that he almost exploded. Maybe I would be caught by the ship's propeller and sliced and chopped into . . . what? I felt myself torn apart. A blade cut into my skull. Would someone see the blood?

I had been watching the men, the shooters, for a long while.

One of them would walk out onto the little terrace with his rifle. Off to one side of the terrace stood a strange machine, something like a man's arm, on a pedestal, like an arm and like a bow and arrow. It had ropes and wires that pulled in one direction and let go in another. Someone, not a sailor but one of the servants on the boat, someone like a waiter, would pull back the lower arm and put a large slate-colored disc where the hand would be. Then the man with the rifle standing on the terrace above the black sea would call out, but not in German, "Pull." The wonderful machine, just like an arm, flung itself out from the elbow, and the black disc sailed away from the boat as if someone were, backhanded, skimming a hat out over the lawn. Quickly the stock of the gun rose to rest in the hollow of the man's shoulder. Smoothly the man lowered his head over the gun, his head swivelled, the barrel moved just slightly. There was a crack, a puff of smoke, and the disc disintegrated into black crumbs that fell in an arc down into the ocean. My insides bubbled with the fact that people could be so clever.

"Good shot. Good Shot." All morning they called to each other, "Good shot. Good Shot." At each miss however, the men exchanged places and the other man would get his chance to shoot. He would get up from a canvas chair, put his drink on a table out of whose center a yellow umbrella sprouted.

I had been standing and watching for a long time, but to the men doing the shooting, I was invisible. Then the boy's father ambled over to me. "Is the shooting interesting to you?" I nodded, but was unable to say anything. He went back to his game. It was I who was watching him, not his son. I knew it was his son because he would sometimes bring him into the dining room where the children ate. This, too, eating apart from my parents, was something new for me. My parents ate in the dining room with the fresh-cut flowers on the tables and the gleaming glasses, and we ate away from them at the children's table. And the blond boy with the crisp white shirt sat there across from me, spooning hot soup into his mouth, each time scooping the liquid up by pushing the spoon away to the far end of the plate as my mother had been trying to teach us for many years. The boy sat there, and small bubbles of steam collected on the blond down of his upper lip. There was nothing I wanted so much as to have blond down on my upper lip and for little bubbles of steam to collect there.

Sometimes I would steal away from my parents to stand very near the ship's prow. It meant going down clanging metal stairs to second class, and then past the vast canvas-covered hatches, winches, and masts, up to the prow where anchor chains lay folded like undershirts in a bureau drawer. Then I would see the ship cutting through the hissing water, raising spray and white water, and, as if he were playing a game, I would see a blue-backed dolphin skipping and leaping just inches ahead of the prow, riding on the white waves it threw up. I knew that the dolphin knew that he was playing a game and that it was a great joy to him and it was a great joy for me to watch, but it was as nothing like seeing that blond boy, whom I wished to be more than anything else in the world.

There was a tap on my shoulder. I looked. It was Pappa. "We've been looking for you everywhere."

"Look. Look. Down there, the dolphin, he's leaping. Look down there."

Pappa shook his head, "I can't. Looking down from this height, I get dizzy. Come."

To get to Ecuador, we needed to go through the Panama Canal. The *Caribia* was not going that way. We were let off in the Panamanian city of Colon on the Atlantic side of the Canal. For a whole week, we waited in a hotel for the boat that would take us through the Canal and on to Ecuador. We slept in rooms with mosquito netting over our beds, and our mother started feeding us quinine pills to ward off malaria.

The boat to Equador was small and black, with one stack in the rear rather than with two tall, grand, racked stacks high and in its middle. There was only one class. Still, the dinner tables were set with white table cloths and shiny silver. What was most remarkable, however, was the Panama Canal itself: the locks with their immense and massive doors, which opened and closed to let the ship in and out, the black water that swirled in silver circles like the eddies on my Bröl stream and that filled empty space on the lock so that the ship might first be lifted, before the lock emptied and the ship was lowered. There was the marvel of the rectangular donkey engines that ran on rails besides the locks and pulled and guided the ship through the locks. Here were giants at work. I often had to be pulled from the ships' railing while making transit.

In the grand lake between the Atlantic and Pacific locks, I saw the American flag for the first time. It was flying at the rear of a sleek gray destroyer that tore through the water. I had the sense that there was something conscious about the vessel, that it had a sense of its own strength, and that, most of all, it knew to where it was speeding.

We disembarked in Guayaquil. A lighter, rocking over choppy water, took us to the dock. Two strange things: the wonderful odor of drying coffee, acres of coffee, all around the dock, men with rakes walking through the piles and turning the beans over to dry in the sun; and a shoeless boy in a ragged shirt and ragged pants walking past us dragging, by a rope tied to its neck, a long, dead, shiny brown snake.

We were standing there, my father wondering how to get to our hotel. He kept turning around and around saying, "Hotel? Hotel," while people from the lighter streamed past.

Mom wiped her face with a tissue. "It's hot. I hope it's cool where we're going." She waved her hand around. "I hope it's not as strange as all this."

"Hotel." When most of the crowd from the ship had gone past, the boy with the snake pointed across the street and said, "Taxi," and went on his way, dragging his enormous snake.

Machachi, near Quito, was to be our final destination, but we were forced to remain in Guayaquil for several weeks when Pappa came down with malaria. Our hotel was owned by a Jewish couple. The man wore a skullcap all the time, and the wife brought my father chicken soup. We spent our time standing around the bottom of Pappa's mosquito-netted bed. The couple came often to stand there, too, and to discuss the events in Europe.

We had landed in Ecuador on September 1, 1939, the day the Germans invaded Poland. There were long faces and worried groans from the adults. But there were stories, too, about our new country: its amazing poverty and crime. The most memorable one concerned a recently arrived Jewish couple. They lived in an apartment in a decent part of the city. Late one night, they were in bed and heard noises at the front door. Soon there were footsteps in the outer room. The two sat up, scared. With marvelous presence the wife cried out, loudly, "Thomas, *tome el revolver, ladrones aqui.*" With a crash the footsteps were gone and the front door slammed shut. The joke was that they owned no revolver at all, and that the man's name was Itzzig.

When not gathered around the bed, we were at the movies. The best one was a Tarzan film, maybe the first of the series. There was a swimming scene, Tarzan and Jane in the water — Maureen O'Sullivan diving in the water and smiling as she swam. Somehow, in one of her underwater motions, the top of her costume was parted from her body and I could see her breasts. I have been a lifelong fan of Maureen O'Sullivan.

As the crow flies, it is less than two hundred miles from the port Guayaquil to the capital Quito. In 1939, it took two days by train to cover the distance, a distance that seemingly crossed more climate zones than miles. It ranged from the hot, steaming port to the white city, nine thousand feet high, golden in the morning sun, basking in a perpetual equatorial spring. The Andes. The skyscraping mountain spurs forced the train to make long detours, switchbacks, where the rails ran along terribly narrow shelves scratched out of the mountain sides. We saw white peaks in the distance, while outside the window there were sheer drops of hundreds of feet into green jungles.

The train halted for water. Suddenly the cars were surrounded by dark people, men and women, wearing black hats and ochre-and-maroon ponchos. They held foods up to the windows, bananas, oranges, pineapples, and *cuyes* (guinea pigs), roasted to a shiny, crispy brown. "If you eat that you'll get a swat," said my father. "It's not kosher," said my mother.

"I want to see them closer," said my father, "maybe buy some oranges." He left our car, and through the train window we watched him saunter up and down the side of the train where the dark people were holding out their wares.

Suddenly, with a jerk, the train started to move. Pappa was not out in front of our railroad car any more, but in front of the one behind ours, and then the one after that. His head swiveled back and forth looking for our car, looking at the cars that were passing him by. Our mother was screaming, "Oh, God, oh God!" My brothers began to scream, "Pappa, Pappa, Pappa! Where is Pappa?"

The train was very long. Very slowly, it snaked around a curve and up a rise. I couldn't see my father any more. I started to run through the train, to the rear from where I might see my father once more before he disappeared in the distance. My mother and brothers followed me. We ran from car to car, the distance seemed interminable and difficult. To open each railroad car door seemed an overwhelmingly hard task, but we finally reach the last. What we saw was a little gandy dancers' cart — a railroad track workers' cart — attached just below where we were standing, and beyond it was our father, running, running trying to catch this car.

Our screaming increased as we saw the distance between the train and our father increase. But then the upgrade grew steeper.

The train chugged on, but slower. Father began to gain on it, and we urged him to run, run faster.

He made it to the attached cart and clambered up and across it. There was a long tongue that attached the cart to the train. Mother called out, "No, Oscar, no!" But he managed to sit on that tongue and slowly inch himself forward, his feet almost scraping the road-bed. I look around and saw a number of men standing with us at the open door at the end of the train. As father got closer and closer to the passenger car, these men, leaning over the last lip of the car, stretched their hands toward him, and finally, when Pappa was close enough, their hands linked and the men pulled him into the passenger car.

Marching back to our car, our father smiled as we children held fast to his coat. Once in our seats, he reached into his pockets and took out little oranges for us, but Mother grabbed them and yelled, "Don't eat them! Damn it!" Half laughing, she threw all the orang-es, one after the other, at my father. "Such stupidity, such stupidity."

We settled in Machachi, twenty miles from Quito, in the heart of the Andes. It was a provincial Spanish town of whitewashed buildings over three hundred years old. There was a town square and park surrounded by a low wall. Couples strolled through the square in the evening. Around and about the square was a mar-ket every Wednesday, and a band concert every Sunday afternoon. The houses were white, but in almost every other one there was a corner where the white was chipped away to show aging orange-yellow plaster beneath.

There were brown-skinned women in white blouses and black skirts who wore tall, rounded felt hats. Around their shoulders they wore black slings, and the bundles in front were their babies. There were brown-skinned men also wearing black hats and draped in ochre-and-maroon ponchos. The women took long, hard looks at us without changing a wrinkle in their faces. The men took quick glances and moved on. There were few cars on the street, but a good number of horses, horses with riders who were perhaps less brown than the walkers in the streets. The riders, too, wore black fedoras. They sometimes smiled at us, their horses' harnesses and trappings jingling as they went by.

Women sat, leaning against the houses on the square, and girls, I think their daughters, sat in their laps, on their wide skirts, with their back to them. The girls leaned back, they had long, straight,shiny black hair, and the mothers ran their hands through the hair, one strand at a time, it seemed. They would pick something off, look at it, then put it in their mouths.

"Lice," said my mother. "They don't eat it — they bite it to death. They don't have money for combs." Under her breath, she added, "Maybe they do eat it. Maybe they need to. God, I hate all the bastards that keep them poor."

I went to school, began to make friends, ate *chirimoyas*, fruit that tasted like egg custard and vanilla pudding with sparks of lemon in it. If I had *pesetas*, I bought them. I told my mother and father to please try it. Neither ever did. In that fact, I sensed their judgment about all of Ecuador, all of our surroundings. How could I like it when they didn't? I knew Mamma wanted to be away as soon as possible.

When I had a few more *pesetas*, I went to the vendors in the square who sold delicious, dark brown gobs of fried meat that tasted like the little friable pieces that were left over when my mother rendered the duck fat that she called *gribenes*. The vendors in the square sold them in paper shells for ten *centavos*. Caught buying them by my mother, I got a beating. "You don't know *who* made them, *how* they made them, *where* they made them, and it could be pork!"

It seemed as if I spoke Spanish almost the day we came off the ship. My mother said that I inhaled it. The teacher sat Chino in back of me, and if there was something I didn't understand, I would turn to him, *"Que es eso?"* Slowly, very slowly, he would explain.

I loved my teacher. He was tall with straight shiny black hair and a thin mustache. Instead of a dark suit and tie like my teacher in Germany wore every day, he often wore green pants and a shirt left open at the collar. Instead of *"Herr Lehrer"* we called him *"Professòr."* He got excited when he taught arithmetic.

"I always had problems with the sevens and nines tables when I was your age," he said, and quickly walked, almost jumped, from the middle of the room to the blackboard, where with loud bangs he chalked up the nines table. "The trick," he said as he wrote, "is to think of the nines table as the tens, and then you just subtract. Everybody knows the tens, so that's no problem. If it's times three, it's thirty minus three and that's twenty-seven; times four, it's forty minus four and that's thirty-six, and so on. Times nine it's ninety less nine and that's eighty-one. You see?" Then he took his guitar from the corner, sat cross-legged on his desk, and strummed and sang us a song.

For history, he told stories. "Ecuador was lucky. We had no gold or silver in the mountains like Colombia or Bolivia or Peru. So we are small. But we have gold in the water, don't we?" There were smiles and a hum of agreement from the class. "But don't you go looking for it." He shook a finger at us. "Lots of people died or were never found again when they did. There is this great lake at the bottom of Pichincha . . ."

He was looking right at me, talking to me. "The lake is black and deep and cold. And the deeper it gets, the colder it is. When the last Inca rulers fled the thieving Spaniards, fled Cuzco, they took all the treasure they could take, loaded gold and silver and beautiful treasures onto the llamas and onto their own backs, and they fled up here — the whole court, king, queen, all their attendants, to their second capital, Quito. Quito is Quetchua, not Spanish. But before they got to Quito, they were told Pizzaro's brother was already there. So when they got near Pichincha and to the lake, they took all the gold from their backs and threw it into the deepest part of the lake. It's true! Many years ago an explorer, an American, came here and brought up a tiny gold idol from the lake. So it's true. But nobody else ever did. Sometimes somebody tries and goes looking, but he is found floating on the black surface and then the condors come down and pick at the eyes, and they pick at the rest, and the condors have meat for their children.

"But there's also a nice story about the lake. In the days of the Incas, the lake was a holy place. The people here, then, like now, were farmers, and to insure that their crops would do well in the coming year they had a ceremony at the lake. There was a place, still is, where the cliff juts out, far into the lake, like the prow of a great boat. Every year, they would dress a girl, a young virgin, boys, don't snicker, in beautiful robes with gold and silver thread, and hand in hand with a boy, also dressed in robes like a great king, the two would jump down, a hundred meters down into the lake. There was music and people shouting and celebration. If the two sank and were never seen again, the harvest would be good. If they appeared again, there was a terrible sadness and the harvest would be very bad. It appears that the two may have been dressed in these heavy gold and silver clothing so that they would never come to the surface again. What do you think?"

The teacher talked about the Incas, how they had this marvelous civilization. It started when the Sun God, Inti, felt sorry for the people on Earth, and Inti decided to send his two children down to Earth to educate the humans so they could learn how to make things of their own. He sent down his son Manco Capac and his daughter Mamma Ocllo to Lake Titicaca, where they rose from the water like gods in the bodies of humans. They married and founded the Inca city of Cuzco.

Here *El Professòr* stopped and asked, "What does that sound like? Did you hear of something like that before?" Nobody raised their hands. He went on: "Well it didn't really start like that, nothing like that at all. All that is a legend, a story, a very nice story, but things don't happen like that. Be careful of nice stories. Nice stories are nice, but they don't help you to get the truth, and the truth is what you always want to have, what you always need to have if you don't always want to be poor and naked like a donkey that you always lead around by a rope around the neck. You have to be a mule that kicks and butts and bites and spits when they put too much weight on his back.

"Well, the Incas came down from the mountains," he continued, "in the twelfth century and made war on all the other tribes in the Andes and conquered them all. They started a culture that still amazes everybody in the world. Big professors can't figure out how they did their stone work and masonry. They are all amazed at the *quipu*, an ancient Incan recording tool, and the textiles and sculptures and the writing that nobody has figured out yet. From Quito to Valparaiso, they ruled, and you all are their descendants — all Indios and Mestizos are their children. You, too, Cèsar, if you want to be. That pig farmer Pizzaro and his brother had guns and horses, and that's why they won. That, and lies."

In school they called me Cèsar. One day, the teacher decided that Wolfgang did not properly fit in the mouths of the other children, so he stopped what he was doing and asked them, "What shall we call your new classmate?" Everybody shouted out something, mostly they shouted out what sounded to me like Herman. Herman was probably my least favorite name. I had an uncle with that name who was big and fat and smelly and never had presents when he came for a week in the summer.

The boy in back of me, Chino, who helped me with Spanish, then yelled out, "César," and then everybody else joined in: "César! César! César!" The teacher smiled. "And Gaul, that's Germany today, is divided into three parts," he said. "Stupid, disgusting and more stupid."

I was now César, but I didn't much feel like César, the conqueror, the ruler. The ruler, the conqueror is never afraid, but we were all afraid: My father and mother were afraid, never mind that Mamma railed against the Nazis and the Germans. We had run away, for no reason at all, from a place where I was the best in the class and where Oma brought me chocolate from the store, and now we were in a new country and I had to be quiet and listen to what my parents said and what they didn't say. There was too much I didn't know and felt stupid about to be a César, too much that I had to learn, too much for which I was in debt to others.

Wolfgang didn't suit anymore either. That name belonged, I knew, somewhere else. Neither name belonged. I knew everybody else's name, but nobody really knew my name, not my friends in school and not my parents. It felt as if I had no name. But I smiled and made believe I was a grateful guest.

The teacher told us about the marvels of the *quipu*. That when most of Europe couldn't read or write, when the Moors and Jews in Spain — he repeated it three times, Spain, Spain, Spain — were teaching the rest of Europe how to think, the Incas already knew how much corn was stored and many llamas the king had and how much the nobles of the country owed the king, things like that, because of the *quipu*, a knotted rope that contained mathematics that Europe wouldn't know for centuries.

They had great cities, too, Cuzco and the northern capital Quito, right near where we were. And *El Professòr* told us how they could make marvelous statues and decorations out of gold and silver. But then the Spanish pig farmer and his brother came, and they killed and burned and pulled down the great temples, and then I thought of my grandfather standing in the burning synagogue with the Torah in his hands. The teacher told how these two pig farmers turned all the people into slaves, and I thought of all those men who were working on the roads digging ditches and my father being forced to work in the stone quarries and coming home covered all over in grey dust. And the teacher said that someday there won't be any more slaves, and he climbed up on his desk with his guitar and sang a song in which all the children joined, but I didn't know any of the words.

Chapter Nine

Herbert Frisch and my father had become close friends in the concentration camp in Dachau. On those very rare occasions that my father spoke of Dachau, it always seemed as if Frisch was part of the conversation, and when he did mention Frisch, it was always in tones of great admiration. My father said that in Dachau they had helped each other out. When I asked how they had helped each other out, my father shook his head, then he said that they had shared things.

"What things?

"Aches and pains."

"No, really, what things?"

"We shared bread. He had a crust, when we were hungry, he gave me half. If I had a crust, when we were hungry, I gave him some. Not everybody in the KZ did that, especially the Viennese Jews. Most of them stuck together. Some of them had money and they could buy things in the canteen or they could buy off the kapos. They didn't get along very well with us German Jews, or maybe it was the other way around. We called them *Schlaviener*. I don't know what they called us. I should have asked Herbert sometime."

"But Herbert is Viennese."

"Let that be a lesson to you."

I didn't want to ask what he meant.

"And the reason that we are where we are is because of Herbert," he said. In the concentration camp, Frisch had told my father about Ecuador, a beautiful country that wanted trained Europeans. "What am I trained for?" said my father. "I'm a cattle dealer."

"No you're not, you have skills in farming. They need people with skills. See, I'm an economist with special skills in analyzing the international trade in pianos and other musical instruments. You see, they need people like us, agronomists and economists."

When my mother had exhausted all the other possibilities, my father, in Holland, tried for visas to Ecuador, and now we lived in Machachi, a few doors down from the Frisch family, who had a whole apartment to themselves, where Mrs. Frisch had a big kitchen where she would fry delicious chicken with even more delicious dumplings she called *"knödel."*

As we were leaving the Frisches, Mom said, 'The *knödel* really are delicious. Too bad everything else around us isn't."

We had only one room. It had a table and some chairs and was divided by a blanket that hung on wires that my father had strung. Mamma and Pappa slept on one side of the blanket; Karl and I on the other, in one bed, and Peter in a cot next to us. My mother cooked on a flat portable gas stove that had two burners. The stove rested on a large steamer trunk. One time, my mother was cooking scalloped potatoes on the stove. My father had gone to the Frisch's, and possibly my mother as well. I was to mind the children. Karl and I were playing a card game on the floor when Peter, now 3, toddled over to the steamer trunk and, wanting to see what was producing the nice smell on top of the stove, pulled at a handle of the steamer trunk. The stove toppled and the hot creamy potatoes covered Peter's chest and arms. Peter screamed. Within seconds, Karl ran outside with a pail scooped cold water from a horse trough and poured it over Peter. He ran in and out with water several times, while Peter screamed and I tried to get his shirt off.

For Peter, the result was nothing worse than several large red blisters on the backs of his hands. I, too, was blistered, by my mother, for not taking better care. Her unfairness burned.

All the while my father waited for the call that was to come, for a job as overseer of a large *hacienda* not far from Machachi. Mom wanted to be rid of Ecuador: "I can't breathe, we are so high." I saw her breathe, but very often she had to just find a chair and sit down.

The Frisch's had two daughter, Sophia, 11, with blond hair and braids, and Gerda, who was big, with blond hair and braids and whom I put with the adults.

Sophia and I hardly ever had any conversation. After all, I was only 8, but just about all the boys in my class wanted to meet her, and I was the person to make the introductions. Every day, several boys would surround me and beg me to find a way. My face would grow red, and I had some kind of intimation of Lera in the Gärtner outhouse. Then, substituting for an introduction, a group of boys would follow Sophia home, and I would follow them, trailing, in the rear, not knowing whether I was part of the group or not, or whether I was going along as a protector or a participant.

As Sophia walked home, seemingly oblivious, we would sneak after her, pasting ourselves against walls, peeking around corners, passing backward word of what she was doing now. "She's stopped and blowing her nose." "She's bending over and tying her shoes. I can see her panties, her panties." At the word "panties," the bunch threw secrecy to the winds and rushed out into the street for a better view. We clustered together in the middle of the cobblestones, when suddenly from behind us we heard, loud, *"Chicos, que pasa?"* Like pigeons on the street hearing a backfire, the group flew. No backward glance; they were gone, disappeared, all except myself, trailing in the rear, and now held fast by my collar.

I turned and there was Mr. Frisch, tall, skinny like a carrot, and red-headed — Mr. Frisch, my father's friend, who had helped my father, maybe saved him, and gotten us out of Germany by suggesting Ecuador. "Wolfgang, I'm surprised at you. What are you doing? Never mind. No more, you understand? No more. No more, and this stays between you and me. You understand?" I understood. And I slunk home, not Wolfgang or Cèsar, but Judas.

Days passed. I thought about the *hacienda*. What was it, really? I kept asking, "When are we going to the *hacienda*?" One evening, after I asked again, my mother grabbed my shoulders, pressed her fingers hard on my bones, shook me and shouted, "Just stop it! Stop it. We'll tell you when. All right? We'll tell you when."

Our one room seemed to be getting smaller and smaller every day, and I had run out of books to read. Mamma and Pappa were often snarling over stupid things and I started to go to bed earlier and earlier.

One night, there was some kind of noise and I woke up. I called out, "Mamma? Pappa?" Over and over again. No answer. I rose and looked behind the blanket that separated the room. Nobody there; nobody in their beds. Looking at their empty bed, I called out, "Mamma, Pappa," over and over again.

Peter was crying. Karl joined him. I looked toward the door. There had never been a lock in the door, only a hole where a lock should have been. Now there was a towel looped through the hole and tied around a slim stud that ran up toward the ceiling. I pushed at the door. The towel pretty much locked us in. Screaming out for my parents all the while, I found a serrated knife in a drawer and began to hack at the towel. Karl, through all his crying, begged me to stay. I would not listen and continued to cut. The knife did its job and I could push the door open.

I was in my nightshirt. My feet were bare, but I never felt the ground. I was now out on the sidewalk. There was darkness and there were no street lamps. It's possible that my parents had told us that they were going to a restaurant, it's more than probable that they had not. I was a sneaker, creeping, bending low along the walls of houses. The town square was a gray darkness. I held close to the low wall that surrounded the square. I bent low. No one should see me, yet I was calling out, "Mamma, Pappa, where are you?" Sauntering couples passed by, looked at me, and kept walking.

I don't know why I was drawn to this one particular restaurant. Maybe it was because there was guitar music that spilled out with the light when a door opened.

In the center of the restaurant sat my teacher and another man, both playing guitars and singing. I stood in the doorway and saw my parents at a table close to the two guitarists, and my father tapping out their rhythm on the table with a knife. The restaurant seemed full of people paying intense attention to the guitar players. I just stood there at the door.

Suddenly my mother called out, "What are you doing here? Peter, Karl, where are they?"

Suddenly I was scooped up by my teacher. There was an empty table near the center of the restaurant. The teacher put a chair on the table and placed me in the chair. I was at the center of the restaurant. The teacher and his friend sat in front of me and began to play songs that seemed to be just for me. *"Mamma yo quiero . . . De la Sierra Morena . . .Solo tres cosas de la vida . . ."*

They played for what seemed a very long time. My father carried me home on his shoulders.

I was walking home from school, which was somewhat outside the town, with my friend Chino, the Indian boy who had taken me in tow, sat behind me in class, taught me Spanish, and allowed me entry into his group of friends. We approached the great, many tiered, baroque Machachi church, built over an ancient Inca temple. A chill wind blew from the mountains.

In the forecourt of the church stood an old woman dressed all in black. The wind ruffled her clothes, and as we passed her she called out, "Judio, Judio." Chino broke the *chirimoya* he had been eating and handed me half. Looking back at the screaming woman, we two spit the black pits of the delicious fruit out onto the road.

I came home from school and there was a tall horse tied up at the bottom of the stairs to our room. A strange dark man sat in a chair between my mother and father, with Peter on his lap. Peter jumped down, and as he ran past me he said, "I got a ride." My mother yelled at Peter, "You can stand at the stairs and look. And you stay there." The dark man rose, when he took a step spurs on the heels of his boots jingled. He looked at my father and in a peculiarly accented German asked, "This is your oldest?" He rumpled my hair.

"Say hello to Señor DeLaBarca," said my father.

"Leon," said the dark brown man.

"He went to University in Bonn," said my mother, sounding greatly pleased.

"We spoke about the whole Rhine province," he said, looking at me. "Bonn, Cologne, Koblenz, the Rhine, the Moselle, Trier. All those wonderful wines." He looked at my mother. "Those were some of my happiest days." To me he said, "I got to Siegburg but I never got to . . . how do you say it . . . *Como se dice* . . ."

"Ruppichteroth, Ruppichteroth," said my father.

The man laughed, "I'll never get my tongue around that one. So. How would you like a ride on a horse?"

I looked at my mother. She smiled and nodded.

I sat in front of him on the saddle. "Wait!" yelled my mother. She had the bellows extended on her Agfa camera. "All right, now you can go." The horse padded off.

"Did you know that Marx went to the University in Bonn," said the dark brown man. I thought, *What Marx? My uncle who died of tetanus?* We rode around the town square while a late sun turned the white-washed walls to orange. Sitting on the tall horse, I felt as if I owned everything I looked at.

"Señor DeLaBarca invited us out to his *hacienda* on Sunday," said my father over supper at our tilting little table.

"Do we walk there, or is he bringing horses for us to ride, I hope," I said.

"No. He has a car."

"He has a swimming pool," said my mother.

I had, once very long ago, been in a swimming pool. I remembered liking it, but then they put up a sign, *"Juden Unerwüncht."* Jews not welcome. I never went again.

Leon's house was a wide rectangle that sat on the brow of a green hill. It was a very large house made of shiny brown and gray bricks, square bricks that had designs on them like something from the age of Athauhalpa. The house had large rectangular windows behind which flowed wide, white, crocheted curtains. We sat on white bent-wood chairs on a broad veranda from where we could see the land flow easily down the hill and then slope and stretch smoothly out for miles and miles of wide green fields. It reminded me of being on a high deck on the ocean when the water was all smooth and calm, with only the white thunderheads budding up from behind the far horizon disturbing the feeling of being happy, happy about nothing in particular. Here too, was a distance that seemed just as far as that ocean's horizon, green hills looming up that sometimes looked a grayish blue because there was a haze and because they were so far away. Behind the hills, snow-covered gray stony mountains reached halfway up the sky.

The swimming pool was built into the ground just below the veranda. For a foot or two, shiny green-and-white tiles rimmed the pool. My mother was already in the pool, happy. She waved to us on the veranda. "You have to come in. You have to." She meant us children; Pappa was not going to get into a bathing suit. He was deep in conversation with Leon.

Underpants were our bathing suits. Toe by toe by ankle, we stepped warily into the water at the low end of the pool. There was a slight feeling about my feet that was something similar to when I had to allow Karl to give my wrists a "burn" when I lost to him at some game or another. My mother was impatient, "Come on, come on," she called, "you've never felt anything like it." And as I slowly lowered myself, I felt this soft tug and this benign "burn" on every inch of my water-covered skin. *"Sprudelwasser,"* my mother called it — bubble-water.

I'd had *Sprudelwasser* for the first time in my life on the ship. "Soda," said the steward who handed it to me. Sparks had lit my mouth then, as they now flew all over my body. My eyes were wide, and Karl and Peter ran out of the pool. "It's eating me," cried Karl.

"Nonsense, nonsense," Mamma said, grabbing me under my arms and swirling me around the pool. "This is *Sprudelwasser*. All bubbles. A bubble spring feeds the pool. Isn't it wonderful? Come, I'll teach you the breast stroke."

When my lips began to turn blue, mother ordered me out of the pool. "This is wonderful," she said, "but America has swimming pools, too." She remained in the water, swimming laps. An Indian woman handed me a heavy clean towel. Karl and Peter were slurping orange juice at an umbrella-covered table. I went to look for my father.

I heard the men behind a heavy brown door, and I knocked. Leon ushered me into a room where the walls were all covered in a dark wood, and the wood was covered with lots of pictures and paintings in heavy, dark golden frames. "So? How did you like the water? Nice, eh?" I smiled and nodded. I looked toward my father who was standing, regarding the contents of a niche in the center of one wall. There, on a kind of small pillar, stood a candelabra with many arms.

My father turned. "Come look at this. What do you think it is?"

"Yes," said Leon, "what do you think it is?"

There was a peculiar smile on my father's face. "Is it?"

Leon said, "I think so. It belonged to my grandmother, and her grandmother, and her grandmother, and so on."

"Back to when?"

"Back to when somebody came not long after Pizzarro."

"Late fifteen hundreds?"

"Fifteen seventy-two. To New Granada. In the sixteenth century, some of his relatives got burned, so he moved here. To Quito first."

"What do you mean, burned?" I said.

Leon put his hand on my shoulder and pointed to the candelabra. "What do you think it is?" he repeated.

I looked hard for a moment, and then it seemed quite plain. "It's a menorah."

"Very good. I think so too. It belonged to my grandmother. And you see those candlesticks?" They rested on a shelf above the menorah. "Those also belonged to my grandmother, and she lit them every Friday night."

This puzzled me greatly. "My grandmother also lit candles every Friday night, but she was Jewish."

Leon started to laugh when my father said, "You are *conversos*."

"Goodness, no," Leon said. "My grandmother was a good Catholic, and so am I. Come, let me show you a key."

I didn't want to know anything about boring keys, so I went out again. The sky was now a blue-black, and I couldn't see the snow-covered mountains any more. My mother was drying herself off. Earlier, the low valley had been bright in the sun and the grass tinted a light green, a green that seemed so new and fresh that my brother called it "baby green." Now, in the absence of the sun, in the cover of that dark blue sky, the grass showed itself the way it really was, the most intense dark green I was ever to see.

It was early afternoon, but it seemed as if night were going to come very soon. As we stood there, yellow streaks suddenly divided the dark blue sky and touched the peaks of the faraway hills: lightning, without a sound of thunder. It began to rain, in the largest drops I had ever seen, pelting yet very soft, with a light blue color. My mother discarded the towel and dove back into the pool. Doing a lazy backstroke, she did slow laps while the soft rain kept coming down. Later, my father was angry with her for swimming while there was lightening, but she kept saying over and over again, "There is nothing like swimming when it's raining. Nothing. Nothing like swimming when the rain comes down." She smiled. "If only I could breathe better."

The call to the *hacienda* came. We arrived in two cars, with a man named Corrales driving ours. Near the *hacienda* we passed corrals, cows in some and horses in others. All about these many corrals the ground was stamped into bare brown dirt. There was a house in the distance — not a house, exactly, but something far larger that stretched and extended over the top of a green hill, with a crowd of moving, dark dots on the lawn in front. As we got nearer, the dots became people, and what had been dark resolved into color, sharp pieces of green and yellow, ochre and rust — ponchos, covering both the men and the women. They were all wearing bowler hats, the kind I had seen some people wearing in Machachi. As we neared the house, we heard music, like nothing I had heard before. I was used to my grandfather's singing in the synagogue, and Franz Lehar and Richard Tauber on the radio or gramophone, and the town band and the Radetzky March, and my father, in the living room, playing operatic hits and Sousa obbligatos on flute and piccolo. But this was something never heard before, high and piercing like many piccolos, and a thumping and thrumming behind the shafts of sound that not only stabbed but floated too, like scarves or flags free from their poles, drifting up and out in the blue sky around the white tops of the surrounding Andes.

We left the cars. Two men without hats were playing pan pipes. Next to them was a smiling man with a guitar, and next to him a boy, a teenager, smiling while thumping a big stick onto a drum. They all slowly retreated toward the house as we walked forward.

Then they stopped, and a smiling woman in a bowler hat came forward holding out a cup toward my mother, who was in the lead. Corrales said, "It's their greeting but I'm not sure you want to drink it. Make believe you're taking a sip. Then give it to your husband. It's a tradition."

Mamma was overjoyed by their greeting. She moved forward, smiling and nodding her head. She held out her arms, wide, as if to embrace the music, the people, the great house on the hill. She took the cup, threw back her head and emptied whatever was in it.

The music grew louder, and the people made muffled noises of approval. Then mother's legs gave way and she collapsed in front of the crowd, which moaned in surprise. We rushed toward her while Corrales called out, "It's all right! It sometimes happens. This is strong *chicha*. They chew the raw corn, spit it out and then let it ferment in a bucket." Father held Mamma's head in the crook of his arm. "Strong stuff, if you're not used to it," yelled Corrales. And I heard him add, in a lower voice, "And even if you are."

They carried mother to what was our apartment. She was out for several hours.

The house was enormous. Even standing at some distance from the house, it obliterated everything else, even the sky, it seemed, and the mountains. Three stories were built around an inner courtyard, and a second-story veranda ran all around its outer walls. A similar veranda faced the interior courtyard

Moving in consisted of dragging our three steamer trunks into the apartment. Then came the emptying of the trunks, but now there were new places to put our things: a kitchen-living room, a room for our parents, and a room for us three, as well as closets for clothes and cupboards for dishes.

A woman hovered at our door as we were emptying the steamer trunks. She wore an apron and had her hair in a European manner. She was dark but wasn't dressed like an Indian. As Mamma was taking out a white cup from the trunk, it fell and broke into two pieces. Mamma picked it up and looked puzzled at the way the cup had broken. As she attempted to fit the two pieces back together, the lady at the door came in and wanted to take them. She was apologetic, asking pardon over and over again, and as I translated for Mamma, it seemed that the woman knew how to repair the broken cup. She introduced herself as Olga, the wife of the foreman. They lived several doors down from us in an apartment that opened out onto the inner veranda just like ours.

"Espere un momento." Wait a minute. She rushed off with the pieces of cup and quickly came back holding it in front of her, tied together with black string. "Look," she told my mother, "the cup is white, see? If I boil it in milk the pieces will join back together."

The lady rushed off. We were about finished with the unpacking when she returned. "I thought I might help you, but it didn't work. Maybe you can do it. You come from Europe." She pushed the shards into Mamma's hands and rushed back to her own apartment.

Baerga was my friend — I don't know why, but he was. He seemed to be as old as my father, but where my father was tall and straight and his eyes looked forward, Baerga seemed bowed and scrunched as if he wanted to pull his body into himself. He walked with a stoop and he was very bow-legged. Most of the time he looked down, but when he looked up, he seemed to see everything. Baerga had a large head, but all the skin on his dark brown face, from his forehead to below his mouth, was scrolled and folded. There was a series of tatoos on his forehead: two thin black lines straight as railroad tracks, intersecting at various angles, like crazy railroad ties. And when he sweated, depending on how the light hit him, the drops on his face were either white or a yellow-gold. Baerga, it seemed, was in charge.

He wasn't the foreman of the ranch, but all the other men seemed to listen to him, and if he told them to do something, they did it. Baerga's main duty, it seemed, was to break the horses and mules on the ranch. I would hang on a rail of one of the corrals and watch as he went about his work. When he looked up and saw me, his eyes grew wide as if they were smiling. Breaking horses and mules in Ecuador was nothing like what you might see in a cowboy movie. It was much simpler.

There were wild horses that ran free on the *altiplano*, the grasslands up in the high mountains. Mules ran there as well. When horses were needed or were to be sold, large bunches were herded down from the mountains and held in the many corrals on the ranch. Bacrga would then break them: He would get one into a narrow chute where the horse would be practically immobile, and then he would tie coal sacks full of dirt on the horse's back. At first there were so many sacks that the horse would often buckle under the weight. Then he would lead the horse out of the chute by a halter. The horse could hardly move, but move it did. I had always thought that the expression on a horses face was always and ever the same, but I saw what they were thinking — the same thing, and looking the same way, as an Indian hauling a 150-pound bag of corn up a very long hill. There was no kicking or other wild gyrations, just the slow movement of a horse placing one hoof in front of the other. Baerga would lead the horse all about the ranch until he felt that the horse could go no further, by which time he would have it back in the chute. Each succeeding day, he would remove one more bag from the horse's back. By the time the last bag was removed, the horse was docile and amenable to control. Up to fifteen horses and mules were tamed this way in one week. The mules were more important than horses; they could go anywhere, their hooves could find the way on the narrowest trails, whether you went uphill or down. They were the working vans and pickup trucks of the high mountains.

In one of the herds brought down from the mountains was a huge brown mule. *"Muy hermoso, muy hermoso,"* said Baerga as he stroked its back while sitting on a rail above the chute. The mule was quiet as it was stroked, but when Baerga tried to tie the first bag on its back, it fought and shook violently, its shoulders and heels banging against the rails of the chute. The rails rattled and seemed close to breaking as the mule heaved, clawed, and shook. Yet Baerga, moving as the mule moved, got the first sack on its back and then quickly more, as many as he thought the mule could take.

There seemed to be many more sacks on this mule's back than on any horse I had watched Baerga tame. When it was time to walk the mule out of the chute, ranch workers were sitting up on corral rails, watching. The animal came out with Baerga leading it by a rope. It labored under its burden, but unlike horses the mule held its head high. Baerga was smiling as he led it round the corral. *"El Rey de los Andes,"* he kept repeating, *"El rey de los Andes."* There were shouts of *"Olé"* from the rails.

Some days later I sat watching the mule as the last sack was removed from its back. *"El Rey,"* the king, stood quite still in the chute, only its head moving up and down as if it were telling Baerga, "All right. Let's get me out." Someone removed the restraining rails from the chute and Baerga led *"El Rey"* as if on parade, all along the many corrals. The mule stepped as if it knew it was parading, and Baerga permitted it some slack on the rope.

Suddenly the mule ran. Baerga held on and dug in his heels, but the mule pulled and Baerga's heels made two little rills. The men working in front of the careening mule scattered. With the mule running at angles, Baerga was swept about in swift swerving arcs as he held onto the rope. Finally he was thrown against a heavy corral post, and I heard the crack. His hold loosened and *"El Rey"* was off, running up into the mountain meadows.

Several men ran to Baerga and lifted him. Their hands were a sling in which he sat. There was no sound from him, but one leg drifted back and forth as if there were no bone under the skin.

On the *hacienda*, Karl and I did not go to school. Mamma was our sometimes teacher. This day we were in the kitchen, it was after breakfast, and she was demonstrating to Karl and me a new way to write. In Germany we had been taught to write in an angular gothic script that was particular to German schools, but from now on, especially as we were someday going to the United States, we had to learn our letters in another kind of script, a smoother and more rounded one. It was important if we were to get ahead in American schools.

The learning was hard for me and even harder for Karl, and every once in a while the instruction was accompanied by a slap in the back of the head. It was a relief when Pappa called us out of the house: We were to come down into one of the corrals. We came, and there was Baerga, his leg healed, holding two small horses, not ponies exactly, or colts either, but a couple that seemed not to have grown up. They were saddled, *"Son un poco viejo, pero . . ."* (They are a bit old, but . . .)

Baerga handed the reins to Pappa, who looked down at us and smiled. "These are yours. Yours from now on. You can ride them. Want to ride them?" It was a joke, we had never ever ridden a horse. "No joke," he said. "Get upstairs, put on long pants, then you can try them out. Fast!"

We rushed upstairs and rushed back down — our own horses!

Baerga lifted me into the saddle and adjusted the stirrups for me. I squirmed about in the saddle and the leather squeaked.

Pappa and Baerga led us around the corral for a few turns, then we were given the reins. "All right," said Pappa, "they're yours. Go ride." Slowly, very slowly we paraded the horses through the maze of corrals. Baerga and Pappa watched from a distance. The horses were very obedient to the reins. Just the least tendency to the left or right and that's where they went. It was a bit uncomfortable though, the horses plodding through the hoof-pocked corrals while we bounced on the hard leather. Not quite Shatterhand or Old Winnetou.

My eyes roamed. Was anyone watching me? Baerga and Pappa, yes, but where was Mamma? I was a hero on the wild mustang. The awkward bounce in the saddle took something away from my equestrian nobility, and did Shatterhand ever feel an uncomfortable chafing on the inside of his thighs? Never mind. I pressed my feet hard into the stirrups. Yes, that allowed me to sit straight and upright, high on my courser, noble and bright-eyed. Baerga opened a gate for us and Pappa said, "Go ahead, ride around a bit." Baerga and Pappa turned and walked away. We were free.

A dirt road led up from the ranch to a paved highway that was the road to Quito. Karl and I didn't want to go that way. We wanted to ride around until Mamma came out and saw us on our horses. The horses, though, didn't see it that way. In the corrals they followed the slightest inclination of the reins, but now, no matter how hard we tugged left or right, they went their own way, and the way they went was up the dirt road to the highway. I was a bit afraid but not totally alarmed by these horses who went where they wanted.

The highway had nearly constant trains of sad-eyed mules that plodded along the sides of the road, and small herds of sheep guided along by old men with long staves. Cars were rare, and when they came, they slowed down almost to a stop to allow the sheep to flow forward around them. Once on the highway, the horses took the direction to Quito. Karl was now in the lead. His horse went into a trot. Karl seemed to like his pace and began to dig his heels into the horse's flank. After more thumps into the horse's side, it went into a canter. Karl liked that even more, and his legs began to fly into the horse's side. He was now in a full gallop. At Karl's every change of pace my horse followed suit. We were now flying. We cut through the herds of sheep like a ship's prow through the ocean. White flocks scattered, the mules were annoyed, their drivers too. Indians along the sides of the road stared after the white children on horses. We flew. We flew far and farther than any remembered landmarks. Karl, repeatedly, heaved back on his reins. His horse slowed and finally stopped, with mine following. Karl turned, then both legs flapping dug his heels into the horse's side. Our wild, joyous course was now run backwards. The herds of sheep were scattered again, and the mules and their drivers were again annoyed.

When we reached the road down to the ranch we turned again, back towards Quito. It was early twilight when we decided to stop flying and return down to the corrals. The horses, almost by themselves without guidance, sauntered towards one of the water troughs — where Pappa was waiting for us.

There was a look on his face I had never seen before. His eyes stared, and his lips were drawn so I could see his teeth. The second we were within his reach, he pulled us off our horses. With my foot stuck in a stirrup, I yelled.

"Shut up," he said. "Shut up. Damn it. Just shut up. Do you see what you've done?" And he started to whale my backside with his heavy hand as I had never been hit before. He threw me to one side and started in on Karl. "Do you see what you've done?" When he was finished with Karl, he pointed at our horses, whose reins were in the hands of Baerga. "Look! Look! You just don't treat horses that way."

All about us, though at some distance, stood an arc of what seemed to be the whole complement of Indian and Mestizo workers on the ranch. Pappa took my head in both his hands and with a jerk turned me to our horses. "Look, what do you see? What?"

The horses were covered with white foam. "They're sweating," Karl sobbed.

"Look at their mouths."

We looked. Red oozed from the side of the horses' mouths. Pappa removed a bit from one of them. "Look at this. Look at this." The bit was all red. Pappa ran his finger along the bit, then wiped the finger on Karl's cheek, then on mine. "How would you like it if this were in your mouth and I pulled so hard that I made it bleed?"

Pappa looked around and the workers looking on scattered. "It's probably my fault, you never had anything like this. Wipe them down." He handed large scraps of flannel to us and walked away.

Baerga removed the saddles and made motions how we were to wipe the horses down. He hovered over us and kept on mumbling, "I never saw anything like that before. Not ever. Nothing like that ever." I looked up and Baerga said, "I never ever before saw white kids paddled. Nobody ever did. I never saw it before."

Chapter Ten

I sat on the bottom railing of a corral, my feet stretching out into the mud. Men were running cattle through the corral, yelling and waving ponchos at them to make them run. The cows were squeezing through the narrow opening of the corral, forced through by the cows piled up in back of them, while the gate posts shuddered and squealed from the traffic. The men then herded them into the next corral box, but the calves running with them would stop after making the difficult squeeze through that first entrance. Dazed, bleating, maybe trying to locate its mother, each calf was grabbed by one of the men and thrown down into the mud. Once it had regained its feet, it would be herded into a connecting corral off to one side, where a other calves stood bleating for their disappearing mothers. I had no idea what was going to happen to any of them.

I could see my own mother leaning over the veranda railing in front of our apartment, speaking and gesturing to Baerga, who was looking up at her from the ground, speaking and gesturing in reply.

I was watching the bleating calves again and beginning to feel sorry for them when Baerga suddenly grabbed me under my arms and pulled me out from my perch. Our two horses, saddled, stood behind him, and Karl was already mounted on his. We were going to the wheat fields. Our father was already there.

From my saddle, I looked again toward our apartment, where

Mamma was still leaning over the railing. She blew us a kiss and disappeared back into our rooms.

I no longer liked to ride much. If I was on my horse for any length of time, the inside of my thighs would rub and chafe until they were red. Now, with Baerga in the lead, we were climbing up out of the valley bowl toward the previously forbidden highway on the bowl's rim. The horses' heads were bobbing up and down with the strain of climbing uphill. We cut across the road onto pale green grassland, following a trail that only Baerga knew. The sun was shining, but the air was still chilly. On some of the nearer craggy mountaintops, the sun made the ice and snow shine orange.

Now we were on a wide dirt road that led downward, then around a curve to the edge of a great hill. There was a drop of maybe ten feet; at the bottom, a small stream flowed over rocks.

The road turned away from the hill and down through a little pass. Views that had been hemmed in by a long, boring line of rocky hills opened up, and before us, somewhat below, stretched an immense vista of waving yellow. Baerga stopped and smiled at us. *"Vee. Oro,"* he said. Look. Gold.

From our left came the sound of a chugging motor and a swishing sound, like flicking whips. A harvester passed before us, a big wheel on its far side cutting the high stalks of standing wheat and laying them neatly in thick mats on the ground. Yards behind the harvester came three rows of hunched-over men who gathered pads of grain in their wide curving arms and then bound their armsful of wheat with twine pulled from bags attached to their waists. They dropped what they had bound and moved forward to repeat the action behind the moving harvester. What was dropped was then picked up by another man, who carried it back to a truck that was inching along behind the gatherers.

Baerga pointed across the field. Pappa. We raced toward him. Pappa was on his gray-blue stallion on a little ledge above the field, looking over it very much like a general observing maneuvers. He smiled. "What are you doing here?" Then he murmured, "What am I really doing here?"

Karl blurted out, in Spanish, "It's new to you; you're learning."

When Baerga laughed, Pappa laughed, too, then stopped abruptly. "I have to tell Señor Castillo that it would be useful to have a second truck. There's a lot of wasted time between when the full truck leaves and returns empty. It takes a while for it to return." After a while, he said, "Look, isn't it beautiful, something out of the Middle Ages? But they didn't have tractors then."

The harvester was making wide sweeps of the field, cutting through and across what seemed maybe a quarter of its length. After clearing a wide alley, it turned to make another pass, soon leaving just an island of wheat in the middle of the field.

Suddenly all the crouching gatherers stood up, pointed and yelled. In the middle of the island of wheat was a leaping deer. Pappa said, "A doe. She's big." The deer made for that further section of the field that had not yet been touched by the harvester, but already, there were a number of gatherers, in the open alley between the sections, waving their arms up and down and yelling at the bounding animal.

The doe turned, recoiling from the flailing arms. It turned in the opposite direction, but there, too, was what seemed like a wall of men who were all waving their arms and screaming. The doe ran at a right angle towards the road from where we had come, but there, too . . .

The deer stopped. We heard a faint bleat from across the field. The deer turned in circles, then leaped towards the farthest stretch of men who were still maybe a hundred yards away. She reached them, then turned in the opposite direction. So she ran, back and forth, as the men closed in on her like a human, three-sided moving corral on the ledge on which we stood.

One or two men from each side ran yelling and waving at the deer. If one stopped, another or several others took up the chase. The deer ran wherever she thought there might be an opening for her. She came close to our ledge and we heard the pounding of her hooves and her hard breathing. She took another direction, but the runners were very close. Again, she passed right under our ledge, her skin scraping the wall. She was cornered now, right beneath us.

She reared up, her front legs striking nothing but air. Someone ran at her and put his shoulder into her side but she didn't fall. Then another ran at her the same way and she went down, her legs still working. Someone grabbed the doe's head, then fell backward still holding her head. With his feet anchored in the dirt, he pulled that head with all his might, while another man stepped up with a machete and hacked at her throat. A gush of blood arched into the air, and the men who were now all around her threw themselves down at her throat and took the pouring blood into their mouths. Some rolled away from the fountain, their faces smeared all red, and others then took their place.

Pappa had us hand him our reins, "I will take the boys back to the *hacienda*. See if you can get them back to work."

Baerga nodded.

"Where's Peter?" My mother leaned out over the veranda railing. "Where is he?"

I could barely hear her. I was watching some of the men castrating calves in the near corral. Several held down a thrashing and bleating bull calf; a large knife flashed, and before any blood spurted a large black brush slathered tar over the cut. The tar smelled like asphalt. The cut part was thrown into a nearby pail, but before it was thrown into the pail someone held it up so I would see it. Over the yelping of the calf, he called called out, *"Cojones."*

Baerga stood over me. "Very good to eat, *cojones*. Makes you strong." He held up a clenched fist, *"Muy fuerza.* Your mamma is calling."

"You were supposed to watch him," Mamma scolded me.

"No, I wasn't."

"Yes, you were. Just wait until I come down."

"He was with Pappa."

"Where is Pappa?"

"Talking to the Señor."

"Where is Karl?"

"He's with Pappa, too."

"Just wait until I come down."

Before she could come down, I ran to find my father. I found him at the compound gate, looking at a piece of paper. Karl was holding on to Pappa's pants. The Señor's car was just pulling out past the gate.

"Pappa, where's Peter?"

"I have no idea. I saw him with Cansada, upstairs, a little while ago." Cansada was our name for the foreman's wife. Her real name was Olga. She was thin and bustled about all the time and always had a rag in her hand, and whenever my parents engaged her in conversation, at some time or other during their talking she would blurt out, *"Soy tanto muy cansada. Tengo mucho trabajo."* (I'm always very tired. I've got a lot of work.)

Mamma rushed at us. "Where's Peter?"

Pappa said that he had seen him with Cansada upstairs, a little while ago.

"No," she said. "He's nowhere upstairs. He was supposed to be with you."

"How could he be with me? I had Karl with me and I had an important discussion with Castillo. How could he be with me?"

Pappa looked at me but I just shook my head. Mamma grabbed my collar. "Didn't I say you should watch him?"

I just continued to shake my head. Pappa put his arm around Mamma's shoulder. "Let's look for him. He has to be somewhere."

Mamma and I went into the courtyard, and Pappa and Karl looked around the outside of the house. In the courtyard, several women, Cansada and those who worked in the Señor's apartments, leaned out over the railings. Mamma called out, "Has anybody seen Peter? Little Peter?" Nobody had.

The four of us were together again when Baerga came by, sensing, I think, that something was the matter.

"Baerga," Pappa called, "stop a minute, we can't find Peter." He nodded toward the corrals. "Could you ask everybody if anybody has seen him?"

Baerga said, "Sure," and turned back to the men.

Mamma looked at my father and said, "Why don't you go ask them. You're the manager here."

"They sometimes listen better to Baerga than to me. I usually try to talk to them through Mr. Cansado and Baerga. It works better that way. You know that. We'll find Peter. Don't worry."

Mamma wanted to say more, but couldn't.

We watched as Baerga had the men stop work. An uncut calf ran about the corral. All the men looked over at us, then quickly dispersed.

Baerga came back. "No. Nobody has seen Peter, but they will go looking and ask around."

Mamma took us upstairs for lunch while Pappa went to try somehow to intercept the Señor in Machachi to see if he could be of some help. All during lunch, Mamma kept saying, "If they've taken him it's my fault. It's my fault. It's my fault."

I wasn't grateful that it wasn't my fault. I was afraid. A weight sat in my stomach, something like the feeling I'd had standing in front of the synagogue when they were pelting us and taking pictures.

Baerga knocked on the door and stepped in. "Somebody said that they saw the boy."

Mamma almost yelled, "When? Where?"

"Earlier this morning, on the road, on the way to the village."

The village was where most of the men lived, the peons, Indians, and mestizos who worked on the *hacienda*. It was about a half-hour's walk away on a dirt track. I had never been there.

"All right, let's go." Mamma was almost out of the door. "You two can't stay here alone. You come with me."

The dishes were left on the table. I think it took us less than a half hour to get to the village. Baerga started on the road, but Mamma rushed ahead of him. She had to stop very often to wait for Karl and me to catch up. We were out of breath almost all the time, but all she could say was "Hurry. Hurry. Can't you go any faster?"

The village stretched over a large even plain. At the far end of the village, a thin thread of brown led sharply upward toward the macadam highway There were no houses, just several dozen huts made out of wood or adobe. The huts looked a bit like the huts that I had seen out of the window of the train leaving Germany, huts where the tools were kept for the garden plots along the side of the train tracks. These huts were dark on the outside and inside, with wooden slats for walls and a tin or sod roof. Others were made out of adobe, also dark, a gray-black dark, sometimes with smoke coming out through a hole in a roof. The women who stood outside the entrances to the huts had to stoop to get out and stoop to get in. They stood there, often with a child in their arms and a child hanging on to a skirt.

The children were all barefoot. The women all wore the black bowler hats and ponchos and flaring skirts of dark colors. In front of several huts were fireplaces made of adobe. At one, an Indian woman stood waving a fan to encourage the fire. Some of the huts had racks out front on which a brown hide was stretched or an al- most black side of meat.

Somewhere a burro hee-hawed. Soon women were standing in front of every hut we passed. Baerga had started asking about Pe- ter: "A little boy, a white boy, about this high. About three years old. He was wearing blue knee high stockings, black shorts, and a thick blue cable-stitched sweater. Have you seen him?"

They all said no. At the last place we stopped, the woman at the opening to her hut had a baby in her arms and looked younger than the other women we had seen. One eye of the baby was covered by a thick blue-black scab. The mother waved flies away from the eye. Baerga said, "This is my wife, Maria. The baby is Jesus."

It was late afternoon. Peter was still missing. I had to stay away from my mother. She was howling. Horses had been brought down from the altiplano to be broken. I watched, but all I thought about was Peter and the deer whose throat had been ripped.

I followed as the men herded a little black-and-white out onto the road. Once there, the pinto, despite all the terrible weight it was carrying, began to buck. The man leading it quickly pulled it back into the corral. I was still standing on the road. In the far distance, I had seen a rider coming on. I could not make out who it was. At first I thought it was my father, but the horse was brown rather than my father's blue-black stallion, and the rider seemed to be native, I could make out a bowler hat. As he got closer, I could see that he had a package in front of him. As he got closer still, I could see that he had a boy riding in front of him. Some of the men called out to me and pointed toward the oncoming rider. The package in front of him was Peter.

I ran to get Mamma. We stood there at the *hacienda* entrance as the rider came in. He lowered Peter down to us.

"Are you all right? Is everything all right?" Mamma asked.

She began laughing when Peter started to dance a little. Then we saw that he was just in his socks. He was wearing no shoes. Somewhere, someone, during Peter's hours of absence, had taken his shoes. While we were talking to Peter, he had turned around, twisted about, and waved his hand good-bye. We watched him leave for a long time while Mom kept repeating to Pappa, "We have to leave. We have to leave."

Chapter Eleven

We were having a festive meal, a holiday meal. It was the evening before the New Year, Rosh Hashanah.

My father said, "Tomorrow we are going to Quito. To synagogue."

"All of us?"

"No," said my father, smiling, "just you and me and Karl."

Standing on the blacktop, we looked toward Cotopaxi, the high cone that often smoked and rumbled; toward Chimborazo, the sleeping warrior toward whose height the somber, brown, barefooted peons often looked when the loads on their backs became too heavy; toward Pichincha, the slim one whose warm crystal springs bubbled along its base and whose black lakes disappeared among the mists and clouds that forever hid some part of the mountain in whiteness. These three rose over twenty thousand feet and were well known. The lower peaks had names only the Indians knew.

As always, cars were rare, horseback riders frequent. On both sides of the road grew a light green alkaline grass on which sheep grazed. Where a dirt road joined the blacktop, our three horses and a mule waited. Our Pappa was anxious, as always, on his blue-gray stallion; Baerga sat quietly, listening, on his placid mule; Karl and I sat on our squat old mares. This being a holiday, we had on sailor suits underneath our ponchos. Both of us wore broad sailor caps with ribbons down the back and golden letters on the brows saying, "Graff Luckner."

Pappa turned to us and said, "You've both been very good. I'm very proud of you."

Karl said, "I'm not very cold," but I heard his teeth clicking together and saw him shiver.

I had to add, "I'm not cold either."

Baerga smiled broadly and began to reach under his poncho, but Pappa shook his head and said, "It's a tradition that we don't eat before noon on this day." Baerga nodded, then slipped off his mule to check the girth straps on our mares, giving them both a kind pat on the leg when he had finished. As he remounted, he said, "You are wearing good warm ponchos, but anyone can get cold this early in the morning when the wind blows down from Pichincha. You two must have good thick Indian skin."

We both sat up straight in our saddles and pulled on the slack reins of the placid mares, but they barely moved.

Pappa said, "Stay here." He rode onto the blacktop and looked steadily to where it disappeared into the mountains to the south. After a minute, he rejoined our party.

Apologetically, Baerga said, "It's only an hour late."

"I know," said Pappa, and started to smile, "but there are many people waiting for me."

Baerga sniffed the air. His eyes widened in surprise and he called out, *"El Pajaro Azul!"*

Karl and I jumped off our horses and raced onto the blacktop. Pappa followed in a rush, scooped us up, one under each arm, then released us at the side of the road. He was about to swat me hard on the backside when Baerga held up a hand with fingers spread out, and said gently, *"Cinco minutos.* It will be here in five minutes."

My father let me go but began scolding us both, in German, for leaving the horses. "Do you think that you can just leave them? Do you think they'll stay there forever? If they wander into the wheat whose responsibility will it be? And who will retrieve them for you?" We both looked up at Baerga. "No. Not Baerga. They are your horses and your responsibility. And how dare you run out onto the highway!" He continued on until Karl began to bawl.

From the rim of the southern mountains, a loud klaxon mixed itself with Karl's crying, and a small black dot appeared on the highway. The black dot turned into a blue one, and then into the outlines of a blue bus. The horses started to prance nervously at the increasing sound. Pappa found a handkerchief under his poncho and wiped Karl's face. He went to his horse and removed a large soft leather bag that hung by a thong over the pommel. He had to yell to Baerga over the noise: "I will see you later."

"I will meet you here at six this evening, Señor," Baerga said, and turned down the path, leading the three horses by their reins.

The bus seemed to take forever to reach us. For all the noise it made at a distance, it arrived almost soundlessly. The doors opened with a rattle. The driver called out, *"Vamos, vamos,"* then added a respectful "Señor" when he saw that we were European.

The bus was filled to overflowing with Indians and mestizos. All the seats were taken, and from the rear halfway to the front, Indians were seated on the floor. Whole families were traveling on the bus, and seemed to have come a long way, for there was a great deal of food, especially fruit, aboard. On the racks above the seats, along with valises there were whole branches of bananas, baskets of pineapples, and sacks of oranges. There were cages of rodents, too, guinea pigs for roasting. And just about everybody seemed to be eating the wonderful brown chunks of the meat of magnificent odors, wrapped in the usual strips of newspaper, that I was absolutely forbidden to eat.

But as we stepped inside the bus, all the loud and excited talk that that had greeted us became very still. In the silence, we three looked around for seats, and then some child in the rear pointed to the caps Karl and I were wearing and sang out, *"Marineros."* Immediately the bus was again full of talk and laughter, and the word "Marineros" came from everywhere. Seeing so many smiling faces, Karl and I just smiled back at everybody, while Pappa reddened deeply and slipped the caps from our heads — at which the whoops in the bus just became louder.

The driver was skinny and yellow, with a little Hitler mustache. He got up from his seat, faced the rear and screamed out, *"Silencio!"* The bus immediately became quiet. Next, he pointed and spoke rapidly to a seat occupied by two Indian women. The one at the window seemed to be old and wrinkled and quite heavy; the other was still smooth-faced but also quite heavy. The two immediately rose from their seats as Pappa protested, *"No, no, por favor . . ."* But the women seated themselves on the floor despite all the Pappa's protests. With a wide grin, the driver ushered us to the vacated seats. He offered to take the leather bag from Pappa and place it in the rack overhead, but Pappa held on to the bag with both hands and declined with words maybe rougher than he intended. The driver shrugged and returned to his seat. The bus started off. Inside the bus we hardly heard the klaxon.

Pappa settled into the window seat and watched the passing landscape. We two squeezed close to him. It had finally dawned on Karl and me that the laughter and pointing had to do with us, so now we were afraid of all the brown faces surrounding us, and looked down into our laps. Sometimes we looked toward Pappa, but his attention was all beyond the window. For me, there was some comfort in that.

"Cañyo?" A brown hand shoved a stick of green sugarcane under Karl's nose; he had the outside seat. He jumped and shouted, "Pappa!"

Pappa was startled from his reverie. The window steamed over, becoming pearly white and opaque. The old Indian woman offering the sugarcane to Karl kept repeating, *"Pobrecito, Pobrecito."* Pappa saw her concern and smiled back, *"No, gracias,"* over and over. He wiped the window with his sleeve and returned to the outside. Karl loved sugarcane and would gladly have taken it.

"Dulce?" The same woman held a small cake of an amber brown color toward Karl. Her expression was very hopeful. On the seat next to her was an extremely thin brown old man in a black suit and white shirt, who nodded in emphasis to the old woman's urging Karl to eat.

My brother looked to Pappa, who spoke gently to the woman. It took him a while to make the woman understand that he really meant no.

"Platano?" The woman had reached up to the rack above her seat where lay a large branch of small, fat, yellow bananas. She had peeled one halfway down and pressed it into Karl's hand. Karl was halfway to laughing as he looked at Pappa and loudly whispered, "She doesn't know who we are." Pappa, too, had a huge grin on his face as he nodded to the woman and then to Karl.

"Bueno," she said, and pressed the cake into Karl's hand. She then gave me the length of sugarcane. I looked at Pappa, who nodded, and I began gnawing at it and sucking out the juice. Pappa said, "Shouldn't offend them."

Finished with the cake, Karl also took a banana from the old woman. "It's like custard," he yipped, and had just about wolfed it down when he had another in his hand. I kept ripping and sucking the sugar fibers. Very fastidiously, as I had been taught in the case of chewing gum, I would bring my hand to my mouth and spit out the used-up cane. When no one was looking, I dropped it to the floor.

Pappa's attention was still focused beyond the window. The bus scattered a herd of sheep that was crossing the highway. A turn in the road brought the high mountains into view. "Who would have thought it," he sighed, "vote Papen and beat Hitler?"

He looked into the aisle where the two women who had vacated the seats for us were sitting. The younger sat with her back between the knees of the older one, who was running a thumb and forefinger down each long and oily strand of hair. It was a scene all of us had often seen before, in the market, in the park, by the side of the road, in front of a hut; one woman's fingers combing the hair of another, or mothers doing it for the hair of their children. Quite frequently, the older woman would stop, look at her fingers, pinch them together and put them in her mouth. "Lice," said Pappa. I had almost become ill the first time Mamma explained it to me ("A horrible custom of these primitive people"), and I still had not altogether come to terms with it. Since then, she had come to another conclusion and had tried to explain to us that there were several quite rational ideas behind the act: the simple hygiene of keeping the hair clean; the soothing and calming effect in this stroking of the hair; and the good source of protein. Lice were rich in the blood of the people they fed on. Good and nourishing.

We were at the synagogue, a second-story room reached through an outside set of wooden stairs in a white clapboard building. Several men stood on the landing. They were smiling broadly at us and all wearing hats and heavy dark coats. They all spoke German.

"We wouldn't start without you."

"We couldn't do Rosh HaShanah without you.

"So happy you could come."

We reached the landing. One of them hugged me.

"You know, we have the only *shofar* in Ecuador."

It was not a large room, but was full of men in hats and heavy dark overcoats and of women with flowered hats and heavy dark overcoats. My father, Karl, and I sat in the front row.

The cantor began the service. He was old and had a scratchy voice. My grandfather used to do it better.

The room grew warm. The women asked that windows be opened. The men were annoyed at the interruption, but someone opened windows and the door. Through a window I could see the peak of El Corazon. The man sitting next to me smiled and shoved a prayerbook at me, but I was more interested in the clouds that streamed and wrapped themselves around the white shining peak of El Corazon.

Every few minutes, it seemed, the man smiled, poked me in the shoulder and pointed down to the prayerbook I was holding. My father rose from his seat. He held the napkin-wrapped *shofar* in his hand. Bending over me, he took the book from my hands, leafed through it, gave it back and pointed. I read, "To the chief musician, a psalm of the sons of Korah. All ye people clap your hands; shout unto God with a voice of triumph."

My father stood before the whole congregation, unwrapping the *shofar* from the napkin. He handed the napkin to me and smiled. He put the *shofar* to his mouth and tentatively blew into it. He brought it down to his side and looked only at me. The leader of the service called out the words that only the sound of the ram's horn can translate: the short blast, the long blast, the combined blast, the stuttering blast, the immensely long blast. When that last long blast had died, the whole congregation, all those men and women in hats and dark coats called out, with great joy in their voices, *"Yasher koakh!* May you be strong. Congratulations." My father bowed slightly and smiled.

I had seen those sounds, visible *shofar* sounds, sounds looking like sparks, white, yellow, and red. Like sparks that hobnail boots could make on cobblestones. And the sparks all traveled, flew out into the open, through the open window, to the peak of El Corazon, out on this blue sky day to the mountain Cayambe, to Pichincha, to Chimborazo, out over the whole Cordillera that was the spine of the Andes.

Chapter Twelve

We were at the Frisches. We had eaten lunch. The *knödel* were delicious. Sitting on the floor, Karl and I were building houses with a deck of cards. Sophia was reading a book on the couch, and Gerda had taken Peter out for a walk. Pappa and Mr. Frisch sat dividing pieces of a newspaper between them. Mamma and Mrs. Frisch were washing dishes and putting them away. Mamma was saying things I had heard her say a dozen times before, and which always pained me because it felt to be a criticism, now public, of Pappa: ". . .Yes, we always wanted to get to America. Maybe not South America, but anyway it's America. We would have been there years ago but Oscar never wanted to leave, but Hitler taught him to get to the Americas. Dachau taught him. But this is a good place and all in all we are very, very lucky. And we have you to thank. If only my heart . . ."

"The Russians don't seem to be getting very far in Finland," said Mr. Frisch, and my father said, "Mannerheim is a Nazi. The Germans are helping him against the Russians."

"*Jah.* The pact is in the process of being torn up. Read this." He handed Pappa a piece of the newspaper. "Stalin was stupid to trust Hitler."

Mamma called out, "I don't know that. Stalin is playing for time. He knows what he's doing."

"I hope so," said Frisch. "But if Hitler's *drang nach osten* succeeds, and I'm sure he will, the West is done for."

I accidentally knocked over our house of cards, which had reached four stories. We had to start construction over again.

After a while I heard Mamma say, ". . . and they say he sleeps with a pistol under his pillow."

I called out, "Who does? Hitler?"

"Never mind. It doesn't concern you."

"Mr. Castillo does. I know that. I heard Baerga say it."

"You are a real wise guy."

"I know that, too."

Gerda came in. Peter had a little cup of shaved ice with a red syrup in his hand, a Piragua, and Gerda said, "I know, I shouldn't have done it, but he's so cute and he almost started to cry."

"I wish you hadn't," said Mamma.

"You know, the owner of your *hacienda* stopped in front of our door. He was in his car."

"Did you talk to him?"

"He talked to me. He wanted to know if I wanted to see some of the country. Maybe go down to Banios some time."

"A few days ago he asked me, too," my mother said. "He said that he was going to speak to you about going, and if I wanted to go, too. I was just telling your mother about it."

Mr. Frisch turned to my mother and said, "This is something new."

"I know. We have to talk about it."

A week or so later, Mamma and Gerda left for Banios with Mr. Castillo, in his car. When they came back, I heard her tell Pappa how beautiful the trip was, how amazing the landscape. And then she added, "But that man is a pig. A real pig."

My mother now often smelled of valerian. I would sometimes see her in the bathroom with a medicine dropper squirting a tube of the stuff directly into her mouth. "It's my heart," she explained. "The valerian keeps it quiet. It's the altitude. We are very high here. It has to have an effect on the heart. I had scarlet fever as a child and that often affects the heart. The altitude doesn't do it much good, either."

Aunt Irma, Mamma's sister, wrote from New York City urging us to leave the jungles. The affidavits were all arranged, she said; she and others had guaranteed that we would not become a burden to the state. We alkso received letters from Oma and Opa in Germany, in which much of the content had heavy black lines struck through them. We could read, through the censored blackness, that life had become a great burden for them. They now entertained hopes for emigration, but Mamma and Pappa, with sheaves of their letters in their hand, looked at each other and shook their heads with sad, blank faces. They sighed; they held their hands over their faces; nothing could be done for Oma and Opa from Ecuador.

Pappa now seemed to make almost weekly trips to Quito, to the American consulate, to check on our quota number. And for our very slightest transgression, the slaps came quick and hard.

What was happening in Europe became the main topic of talk among the refugees in Machachi. At the Frisches', the newspaper was handed around more often than a bowl of candies. Gerda or I were sometimes asked to translate from the papers. Scapa Flow, a place in England, had been bombed by the Germans. I thought Scapa Flow was such a funny name that I laughed and got a smack from Pappa. "Just read," he said, very loud. Afterward, he gave me a hug and said that he was sorry for hitting me.

Finland and Russia had made peace, but I was still angry. Denmark and Norway had been overrun by the Germans.

Faces now were long and gray. The *blitzkrieg* ran over France, and Holland surrendered after five days. Mamma and Pappa seemed buried in sadness. Over and over they talked about Tante Mina and Pappa's cousins.

It was only after the war that we learned what had happened to them. The day that the Nazis entered Amsterdam, Tante Mina's oldest son killed his two children, then he and his wife committed suicide. Tante Mina's husband also committed suicide; she had come home from an errand and found him dead.

Mina left the apartment just as it was and went out into the street. She found a bicycle leaning against her building. She mounted it and cycled out of the city into the countryside. When her strength ran out, she found herself in front of a farm house. The farmer stood in front of his door. Tante Mina approached him and told him that she was a Jew and that he could either turn her in to the occupation or give her a place to hide. The farmer took her in and gave her a place to hide throughout the war. She told us later, "I always knew what Hitler had in mind for us, but I thought that we still had time."

With most of Europe in Nazi hands, quota numbers for many European Jews were now useless. In tears, Mamma said, "Hitler gave us our quota number."

The time had come for us to leave Ecuador; America held out its arms. But before entering its embrace, there was the question of heads. Pappa was convinced that in the United States there was a market for shrunken heads. He had heard that several of the refugee families who had moved to there had taken shrunken heads with them and sold them at an enormous profit to collectors of such things.

Mamma was very much against the idea. I heard them arguing at night. "It is illegal and I won't let you do it."

"The Sigmunds from Quito, the ones with the two girls, took four heads to New York. He got five thousand dollars for each."

"I don't care about the Sigmunds. If you take them, we'll get caught and they'll send us back to Germany."

"I won't get caught. If Sigmund can do it, I can do it."

"We are not that kind of people. We are the kind of people who get caught. We are lucky in other ways."

"Yes. Great luck. Dachau was great luck."

"We got out, didn't we? We have just about enough money left for the ship tickets. Buy those heads and we'll have nothing when we get to America. It's a waste of money. A pure waste. When did you become a *luftmentsh*? And tell me, just how did the Sigmunds smuggle their heads into America?"

"There were these two Jews . . . "

"Don't tell me — one of Frisch's *shmutzig* stories?"

"There were these two Jews. Refugees in Quito. The one says, "I see your wife wearing all this very nice jewelry. Different ones to *shul* every *shabbes*.' 'Yes,' says the other, 'we were lucky. We got all our jewelry out of Germany.' 'That's really remarkable. How did you get all that jewelry out of Germany, past the SS, past all those border inspections?' 'Well,' says the other, 'I'm reluctant to talk about it but we hid it in my wife's private parts.' 'God,' says the first one, 'I should have talked to my wife. She could have gotten all of our furniture out.'"

"Not one of his best," I heard Mamma say. "Good night. And you really have no idea how to get it through all the customs inspections. Good night. We are not doing this."

Señor Castillo had another *hacienda* near Baños, and sometimes Pappa had to go to there to do something, I did not know what. Baños was the Ecuadorian town just at the edge of the Amazonian jungle, the jungle where those Indians lived, the ones with fierce make-up and wild hair, who practiced the shrinking of heads. They were warrior Indians, and they did not just shrink any heads, only the heads of the enemies they captured and killed. It was a religious ritual.

When the Indians learned that there was a market for their shrunken heads, that museums, scientists, and collectors were willing to buy them, they ventured out of their jungle and hung around street corners and bars in Baños and other towns that bordered the jungle, and surreptitiously offered their wares to buyers. At the time I assumed that these were sellers who had abandoned their religion, because all the Indians I had ever read about were honest and true to their faith; none of them dabbled in business. And there were strong Ecuadorian prohibitions against any traffic in shrunken heads, with fines and jail terms. This was an effort to halt the traffic because there was a suspicion that since a trade had opened up, these Amazonian apostates killed not for reasons of the usual tribal warfare, but now, because it had become a business.

Mamma was packing our steamer trunks when Pappa walked in, "Look what I have."

He sounded very proud. From a satchel he pulled out the rolled-up skin of a snake. It was two or three hand widths wide and when Pappa unrolled it was as long as two of me. The skin, when it was unrolled, shone and sparkled. There were dark scales that changed from black to dark blue, and dark yellow ones and dark red ones.

"They sparkle like diamonds," said my mother. "This will be a nice reminder of our time here."

"And look what else I have."

"You did it. You did it." Mamma slammed a pot she was wrapping into the steamer trunk. "Damn you, you did it."

Pappa pulled out two shrunken heads from the satchel. He held the two by their dark brown hair and the heads gyrated in front of us like a pair of swings. They looked terrible; two men's heads shrunken to the size of tennis balls. The heads were all shriveled and puckered. There were white stripes on their dark hairy brows and dark red paint over their eye sockets. "One hundred dollars each; ten thousand in America."

"For your ten thousand, we'll never get to America. You'll go to jail and we'll be stuck ten thousand feet up here forever. This is so stupid. So stupid. And we talked about it. Oh, Oscar." Mamma began to cry. She walked over to Pappa and held him and put her head on his shoulder and cried.

Baerga had been standing outside our door all this time. *"Pardoneme."* He crossed the threshold. *"Pardoneme, por favor."* He took the shrunken heads from my father's hand. He held the heads close to his eyes and stroked the hair by which Pappa had been holding them. He pulled at hairs around the chin and looked up at Pappa, *"Esos no son hombres."* (They're not men.)

"Not men? Women?"

"Not men, not women," said Baerga, "monkeys."

Mamma grew very quiet, then said, "How do you know?"

"I'm not so long out of the jungle myself. I can tell. I came to give the children a good-bye present."

"Baerga, you're very sure?" Pappa asked.

Baerga smiled. "Since there are all these missionaries walking around the jungle, we don't do this so much any more."

"Not so much any more, but still some?"

"'Still some' is what the men, the sellers in the bars in Baños say, that's to keep the gringos guessing. We are primitive, but we are not stupid. Today, money buys what the little heads can't. But I tell you that these are monkey heads."

Then Baerga gave each of us a tiny crown, perfectly carved from what everybody called a stone nut. "Be well. Good luck." He bowed a little to my father, turned, and walked out.

Once he left, Mamma started to laugh. Once she laughed, Pappa laughed, too. They laughed and snorted and laughed until they started choking. I got water for both of them.

"I guess we'll take them to America," said Mamma. "They can't do anything to us since they're not men but monkeys."

Then Karl called out, "But what if America can't tell the difference between monkeys and men? *You* couldn't."

Before we left, we gave the monkey heads to Mr. Frisch.

Chapter Thirteen

The train ride was all downhill. That's what Pappa said. Mamma would not let him out of her sight the whole time. No more running after trains. He did go out one time when Mamma was in the toilet and the train had stopped at a station for water. He brought in a whole branch of bananas. The bananas were small and sweeter than any I had ever tasted before. I ate one right after the other. Mamma said, "Stop, you'll get sick." I didn't stop and I got sick. When we arrived eight hours later in Guayaquil, I was very sick. We stayed at the same hotel where we had stayed when we first arrived. I threw up all over the mosquito netting.

The next day we were to board ship. Small boats called lighters ferried us through the harbor and out onto the green-funneled *Santa Rosa* of the Grace Line. The lighter wobbled as it ferried us through rough waves. My stomach again emptied itself before we even tied up at the *Santa Rosa*.

The stairs on the side of the ship, over which we had to ascend, seemed mountainous. I hesitated to climb. Pappa picked me up and deposited me on the deck. Once I was there, looking out over the waves to the city, my empty stomach decided to empty itself once more. It would be many years before I would ever eat a banana again.

My relatively brief misery was a terrible introduction to an even greater and longer misery.

I had not really understood all the arguments and discussions between my parents regarding the buying of the shrunken heads. What they really referred to was the fact that we were poor. I did not understand what Mamma meant when she said that we would arrive in New York with just twenty dollars in our pockets. But soon after we boarded the ship, I finally knew.

The *Santa Rosa* was a marvelous vessel, fast, able to do 28 knots on a good day. The two shiny green stacks with white stripes, canted sharply backward, made the ship seem to race even when standing still. It had four decks, three that shone bright and white in the sun, and the fourth that was down and dark. Here were the cargo hatches, covered by dark heavy canvas. From there the masts, hoists, and winches rose like yellow trees to the sky. That fourth deck down, where the cargo hatches were, was the third-class deck — our deck.

Mamma and Pappa had one cabin, and we three boys shared another. It had a strong, sharp odor of some kind of cleaning material. There were bunk beds, one atop the other, where Peter and Karl slept, and a cot for me. But what I saw as the awful emblem of our shrunken fortune was the dining room. No gold-braided captain ate there Not one table was covered with white linen. There were no flowers, no crystal chandeliers, no menu cards on heavy cream paper with red printing that also provided news and the announcements regarding the evening's entertainment. There was no evening entertainment.

There were no great banks of windows lining the dining room that gave access to sun and stars and the broad sea outside. Here were a series of long tables that reached out from the walls. The tables were covered with slick linoleum with a Persian rug design. There were benches on which the eaters, not diners, sat. We were accompanied by dark haired men who glowered and slurped their soup.

The third-class dining room reeked of cooking. The odor of cabbages and cauliflower mixed with the same cleaning smells that soaked our cabin. Over against one wall was something I had never seen before, a low wall that contained pots and containers behind which stood men and women all in white, many wearing high-domed chef's caps. We could pick up a tray and dishes at one end of the low wall and then pass before the white-clothed people who asked, "Would you like . . ." and before one could ask for a translation, they slapped down cabbage or cauliflower onto the tray. "Would you like . . ." and a bowl of soup was handed you. "Would you like . . ." and a little bowl of green Jello was handed you.

I wanted to explore the ship. I tried the stairs from our dank deck up to where the ship's sides shone shiny white. At the top of the stairs there was a silvery chain that forbade entrance to second class. From where I stood, I could see people play shuffleboard and others resting on deck chairs and wrapped in blankets against the ocean breeze. I tried to remove the barrier but I found that very hard. Finally I tried ducking under the chain. When I straightened up, there stood a white jacketed steward before me, glaring. "You are third class. You are not allowed up here. Not even in second class. Where are your parents? Get back where you belong." He spoke English, and I didn't know what he was talking about. I started into German, asking to be allowed. *"Du, dritte Classe,"* he said. *"Nicht erlaubt."*

I was third class. He'd said it aloud, in front of other people. I was third class when a short year ago I had been first class. Only days ago I'd had my own horse, looked into the heart of the Andes, up on my own horse. And my Mamma and Pappa, they were involved in this. My father, a manager of a great Estancia, who rode the great blue-gray stallion that was saddled for him every day, he was involved in this. How had the manager managed *this?* In Germany it was the Nazis, here it was an ugly steward who branded me inferior. How could my father allow this? My mother?

I was leaning over the prow of the ship. The sharp leading edge parted the silver water with a hiss into separate streams of white circling foam. "Look," said my father, his hand on my shoulder, "there, look, flying fish."

I wouldn't look. I looked down at the spinning white ruffs: white waves that looked like ruffs in motion, the ruffs that I had seen on old pictures of old women at an old museum I had been taken to in Amsterdam.

"There they go again. Look."

I wouldn't look.

"Never have I seen so many. Really. This is fantastic." At "fantastic," I had to turn my head. There was nothing to be seen. Another cheat of my father's, another disappointment, like his lack of words to me on his return from Dachau.

Suddenly a squadron of fish surfaced. Soaring like birds, they coasted over the waves while I held my breath. With my exhalation, they dipped down under the water. "Did you ever see anything like that?"

I ran back to my cabin, but I had never before seen anything like that.

My mother was in her bathing suit. She handed us bathing suits. "Put these on. There's a swimming pool on the upper deck."

"They won't let us up there. I tried."

"Ridiculous. We paid our fare."

"They won't let us."

"I got us out of Germany, I can get us into this pool."

"You'll see."

We arrived at the top of the stairs and there stood the same steward. *"Dritte Classe. Nich erlaubt."* Third class. Not allowed. My mother argued long and loud. She evoked Hitler, the Nazis. She never believed that Americans could behave this way to immigrant children; all we wanted was to cool off on a hot day. *"Dritte Classe. Nicht erlaubt."*

While Mamma argued — and I knew that it was she who wanted into the pool, never mind the immigrant children — two men stood a short distance behind the steward listening to our conversation, listening to Mamma practically begging. If we had been on land, I would have run away and hidden out somewhere. The two men came forward and said some words in English to the steward. The steward bowed to the two men the way Baerga sometimes did to my father. The steward removed the chain and then, with another bow, removed himself.

The man with red hair asked in not-so-good German if we would be their guests. My mother said, "Of course," and I wanted to run, but I stayed. We sat on chairs, in first class, in the ship's café while my mother recounted the tale of our miseries in Germany and of our subsequent travels. I hated her telling this story because it sounded so much like begging. She told it because she knew it would create sympathy for us. She told these stories because the red-haired man was Aaron Siskind, and his friend was Jacob Sharp. They were both Jews, they lived in Brooklyn Heights and had been on a vacation and cruise. They were following the situation in Europe very closely. They knew, years ago, what was happening to the Jews in Germany. Jacob had spent a year at the University in Jena. They contributed money to HIAS, the Hebrew Immigrant Aid Society, and to other rescue organizations. The one was a lawyer and the other in advertising, and they both worked for a film production company in New York, but they didn't know Johnny Weismueler or Maureen O'Sullivan.

"Look, if you or the boys want to go swimming? Any time, please, be our guests. If we can do anything else for you, please ask. Okay?"

We went swimming, but I didn't like it. We went swimming almost every day. Every time I went into the pool I felt as if I were betraying something, but I didn't know what.

The *Santa Rosa* crawled up the coast of South America, then through the Panama Canal. The first time we had gone through we had seen just one destroyer racing like a greyhound through the lake in the middle of the canal. This time they were everywhere. They were on the lake, they were in the locks ahead of us and be-hind us. I heard Aaron say to my mother, "Roosevelt wants a war. When he gets it, Germany better watch out."

Chapter Fourteen

We were up early, about to land in New York. Leaning over the rail, we saw a small boat rushing up to the side of our ship. "The pilot boat," said Pappa. I knew pilot boats, he didn't have to tell me. The boat came alongside while we were still moving. A gangway was lowered, and about a dozen men in suits and hats clambered up.

Mamma and Pappa herded us into an enormous hall up in first class; the dining room had been emptied. There were little tables at one end of the room and more little tables on the side, behind which sat the men in suits and hats. Lines formed in front of them. People were presenting their papers. Sometimes someone was waved over to the side tables, where men, evidently doctors, would put stethoscopes to people's chests. While we were all lined up together, Pappa kept on saying, "If anybody asks you anything, just tell them the truth."

They asked Mamma and Pappa all kinds of questions, especially dealing with health. Tuberculosis: Did we have it or did ever have it? They spoke very good German. Finally, one of the men smiled at us and asked if there was anything else, and Karl called out, "We don't have any shrunken heads. We gave them to Mr. Frisch."

At that, several of the men jumped up, their eyes wide. The result was that all our baggage needed to be thoroughly searched.

Mamma and Pappa needed to attend the search, and so missed seeing the Statue of Liberty.

Karl and I saw it, a giant green lady in the middle of the sea. We stood at the railing with Aaron and Jacob, but far more awesome than any green giant lady in the middle of the sea was the sun that we saw reflected in the million windows of Manhattan. The ship slowed down, and tugboats fastened themselves ahead and behind it. "They will take us up river the rest of the way," said Jacob. I knew about tugs but, "What river?"

Jacob's arm moved wide across the blue-gray surface of water. "The lordly Hudson. There are places where, people say, it's as beautiful as the Rhine."

Well, maybe, I thought, *but the orange sun in all those million windows, that must have it over anything in Germany.* "Those buildings," I said, "are higher than the Kölner Dom. Their spires are higher than the Kathedral."

Smiling, Jacob said, "You have to be careful about places where the buildings are higher than the churches." Everybody laughed when he added, "We had enough trouble in places where the houses were lower than the churches."

Everybody thought Karl was so cute. I wanted to change the subject. "Does it have castles, the river?"

"No castles, but some big houses up a ways."

"But you said 'lords.'"

"No, 'lordly,' like grand, like big. It doesn't have lords but it does have some very rich people who sometimes try and act like lords: that's Wall Street over there."

"Wall Street?"

"Yes. In the time of the Indians, the Dutch built a wall to protect their little town from the Indians. A wall of tree-trunks. A palisade."

"But the Indians were friends to the white man . . . like Shatterhand . . ."

"Well, maybe it was to protect the Indians from the white man.

Look, there, the building with that long spire: that's the Empire State Building, the tallest building in the world."

Aaron said, "You know, the Hudson, it begins as a little trickle, a spring, way up north in the Adirondack mountains, you'll see it one day, and comes all the way down here to separate New York from New Jersey. Across there, those are factories, that's New Jersey. And in New Jersey, over there, up, about 125th street, you can't see it from here, is Palisades Park, an amusement park. It has rides and merry-go-rounds."

"Like *kirmesse*?"

"I don't know *kirmesse*, but maybe once you get settled here we might take you there. What do you think?"

I didn't know what to think. Springs and bubbling made the little brook, the Bröl, but in this country, springs in the mountains made this wide ocean of a river that separated states. I didn't know what to think of palisades and lords and rich people and the Rhine without castles, and walls of wood and walls of buildings where all the windows sparkled. How could anybody get in there, through there, those walls and palisades of buildings? It was very confusing, but I loved all the names. Adirondack must be right out of Shatterhand and Winnetou. Before we landed, Aaron and Jacob gave Pappa their telephone number and Pappa gave them Tante Irma's address.

Noise: loud steel bangs, winches squealing, motors rasping. The mid-ship hatch doors opened, fat hawsers were thrown and wound around stubby steel stanchions, with sailors shouting and longshoremen lowering gangways. Sunlight and shadows, long slivers of light. From my point on the deck, leaning over the railing, everyone below was small, rushing somewhere or waving at someone else at the rail.

We stepped off the steeply-canted gangplank into the immense hollow of the shadowy pier. No lighter this time, no bumpy water ride toward land: This time we stepped and stumbled down into an immense, covered pier, where pigeons roosted in the high cross-beams and rushed to daylight with every loud clang. Just at the bottom of the steps, a little lady in a round black hat and a silvery dress was jumping up and down and waving a white handkerchief. Tante Irma! Onkel Theo walked out of the shadows and stood behind her. There were long hugs and joyous crying.

It was decided that Tante Irma would take Karl and me to her apartment; Onkel Theo would stay with my parents while they waited to collect their luggage. I always liked my aunt. She was fun, had smooth skin, and was short and a bit chubby. Already in Germany I had become aware of the family consensus that she was pretty but not very bright, though that judgment of intelligence was related to a scale that began relatively high. After all, Onkel Theo had his Ph.D. in economics, and Mamma ran with a crowd of socialists who thought that they knew everything, and Oma Krämer, after her husband's death, had become the businesswoman who collected every debt, to the very last penny, that was owed the firm of Louis Krämer. Tante Irma was merely apprenticed to a milliner.

Peter remained with our parents, and Karl and I each took one of Tante Irma's hands as she led us out onto Twelfth Avenue. The sun over the cobblestones made them shine like the stones of Ruppichteroth. But this was nothing like Ruppichteroth: Over the cobbles of Twelfth Avenue bounced automobiles and huge black trucks that were propelled by chains in their undercarriages, which jingled, sounding like icicles falling and breaking.

"We take the subway, okay?" Karl and I must have looked dumbfounded, for Tante Irma laughed, then began again, this time in German. *"Schön ist New York am Morgen. Schönsten am Sontag Morgen früh, wenn die Sirenen schlafen."* New York is lovely in the morning, loveliest early Sunday morning when the sirens sleep.

Suddenly we heard sirens. Red wagons screamed past us, one after another. Karl held on to Tante Irma with both hands.

"It's a fire, these are fire trucks. Don't worry. They're going to put out a fire. New York has the best fire department in the world." I thought, *They could have used the fire department in Guayaquil, they had bunches of fires every day.*

We walked longer than we wanted to. We were not used to sidewalks. Nevertheless, every added step produced wonders, mountains of them. First, how the people were dressed: They were clean and walked quickly, women in print dresses, men in hats and suits. After five minutes, the trucks and cars were already passé, but at almost every corner there was a man with a cart. *"Heisse Hünde,"* said Tante Irma. "Hot dogs." Hot dogs were something it would take me a while to understand.

Close to the docks were the foothills of the skyscrapers, buildings of five, six, and seven stories. As we got farther away from the docks, these foothills grew in height. As we got farther, too, the sidewalk became harder and walking became more tiring.

"Oh, don't slow down, don't slow down," Tante Irma said, "you are my champion of the ping-pong games, champions don't slow down. I want to show you something. There." She pointed. "That's Macy's, the largest department store in the world. Some of the hats I make are sold in there. Come, I want to show you something else." We walked past Macy's windows. The manikins were dressed for summer, the women in halters and shorts. Karl whispered, "Don't tell Pappa we saw this."

Tante Irma stopped us in the middle of the block and pointed again. "There, look up there: That's the tallest building in the world, the Empire State Building." Our heads tilted upward, and I wanted to say that Aaron had already told us, but I didn't. The gray building with its millions of tiny windows extended upward farther than my eye could reach. I thought the building was alive. It was rooted in the ground, yes, but if it really wanted to, it would move. It touched the sky so easily; no Andean condor, I thought, could ever fly that high. Manhattan was a rock. Only on hard rock could one stand like that and reach so high. People rushed by. I didn't know anybody.

I had heard of New York's subway trains, which ran under the ground, trains that tunneled underground right through the rock. Now Tante Irma took us there. Steps led down right in front of windows where the manikins wore shorts and halters. We heard the roar before we were halfway down the steps. We were in a darkness eased by puddles of light from ceiling lamps. Tante Irma inserted a coin at the turnstile and walked through. She had us crawl under the turnstiles.

"It's all right, children are allowed." I felt uncomfortable. I wasn't sure that children like us were allowed. We reassembled, and she kissed us. "Now we're here, now we wait."

I saw a Negro man carrying several bundles. The only other Negroes I had ever seen were in Guayaquil. I watched a man wearing a hat who was reading a newspaper. He held it in front of his nose and, reading in that manner, he walked up and down the platform in straight lines. He seemed not to see anyone who might have been in front of him, yet he avoided everyone and still walked in those straight lines. *A circus man: he must be from a circus. How could he do that and still stay away from the edge of the platform?* I wanted to look down and over into that pit at the edge of the platform, but Tante Irma always pulled me back. A train blasted and roared into the station, several tracks over across from our own. It screeched to a halt. Red sparks shot out from the braking wheels.

"Would you like some chewing gum? You have been such good boys." Karl jumped up and down for joy, shouting, "Yes, yes, yes." I pulled at his sleeve, shook my head at him. Mamma and Pappa were in my head. I knew how to behave, that if something were offered, a cookie, a piece of chocolate, from anybody, even an aunt, you refused three times even if your teeth ached, your mouth watered, your stomach screamed for the offered delicacy. The rule was that the goody was to be extended three times, and then, with averted eyes, a fake grin, and dissembling modesty, you refused three times. Your heart beat fast, joining all the other organs to call for the fourth proffer; only then might your hand reach out.

In Germany, chewing gum was unknown to us. Chewing gum had entered our cosmos only in Ecuador, where it was used at the Frisch's as a treat for the girls. Their screaming delight when the white pills were handed out to them had infected us. We wanted that joy and became avid for the white pill, especially avid since our parents had drummed it into us that chewing gum was a disgusting habit. At the Frisch's, our parents would relent, but if we were alone, they could talk for long stretches about how really disgusting the habit was. If we pleaded for gum, the short answer was always, "Cows chew. Are you a cow?" Clearly we were not, yet the deep yearning remained.

Tante Irma turned to a yellow machine at the rear wall of the station, and I edged closer to the edge of the platform and looked down. I saw a rat scurry across the rails, but I had seen many of those poking around the corrals in Ecuador, looking for grain. I looked toward the dark curving hole that was the train tunnel. A sound seemed to reach out from within. At first it was faint, but then it began to sound like the distant drumming of a herd of horses running on the high llano. Then a large swatch of light appeared on the far side of the curving tunnel. The bright swatch seemed to extend itself and to slide continuously over the far tunnel side. Then light silvered the tracks in front of us, which had been black until then. The roar grew louder. Lit by stripes of light, the first car suddenly appeared, and a hand grabbed my shoulder and pulled me back from the platform's edge.

"That is so dumb, so stupid. You can get hurt. What would I tell your mother if you got hurt? You get no chewing gum. Didn't I tell you to stay where you were? Didn't I? Karl gets gum. You don't get any gum."

We entered the subway car and sat on slick, yellow rattan seats.

I watched as Karl gleefully chewed away. And I was supposed to be her hero, her ping-pong champion.

One six two. I saw the numbers on the wall of the subway station where we got off. Tante Irma then lived on 162nd Street between Broadway and Amsterdam Avenue in Washington Heights. We entered her building, and then an elevator. It had no attendant, but was routed, magically, by the push of a button, up to the floor of one's choice.

We entered her apartment, walked down a long hallway toward the living room. I smelled coffee, and suddenly the room danced with faces.

"How is Melli?"

"How are you?"

"How was your trip?"

"How was it in the jungles?"

The many faces were vaguely familiar. I must have seen them in Frankfurt, maybe seen them in Mamma's picture album. There were Tante Irma's in-laws, who, we soon learned, lived with her. There were cousins from Frankfurt, and several old friends of Mamma's.

"I know you don't know me but your mother and I went to school together. We always had such fun. How is she?"

When the ring of familiar and strange faces finally parted, there stood my Oma, Mamma's mother, the Oma of aches and pains. Her arms were wide apart and Karl and I rushed into them. The arms were soft as always, with the familiar odor of 4711 cologne and lilac powder. Oma took us into the kitchen, where there was coffee and plum cake.

When our parents and Onkel Theo tumbled into the apartment with their luggage, there was a cheery mumbling from the assembly. Mamma just stood out in the hall until we ran and hugged her long and hard. Then she smiled, pointed to us, and announced to the waiting friends and relatives: "Here you see our fortune — that, and the forty dollars in Oscar's pocket."

I wondered where we were going to sleep, but Tante Irma had already figured it out: I was to sleep with Oma in her bed; Karl was to have a cot in Tante Irma's bedroom; Mamma and Pappa, along with Peter, were being put up in a cousin's apartment on the same floor. Karl and I lived with this arrangement for two weeks, but our parents were shunted instead to the Rosenbergs, who lived on the second floor of 542 West 159th Street, between Amsterdam Avenue and Broadway.

Mr. Rosenberg was tall, somber, and square-faced, with a white mustache. His wife was Katinka, oval and short. I don't think it was her real name — how could Katinka be anyone's real name — but for as long as we knew her, and that was for many years, she was Katinka. Katinka was a great baker. Her specialty was plum cake. There were three sons: Heinz who became Henry, and was perhaps two years older than I; Walter, a good deal older; and one other who quickly disappeared, said to have gone to St. Louis.

After a ten-day stay at the Rosenbergs, a two-bedroom apartment became available in the same building on the fourth floor. Thus we were all regathered in apartment 4A. The rent was $28 per month, but we had been given a concession of three months for free, three months in which my parents could find work.

Except for us and the baggage that made it out of Germany and across the Atlantic to the *hacienda* and on to New York, the apartment was empty. There was a box of cutlery that Pappa had carried under his arm, some presents scavenged from friends and cousins who had arrived in New York before us. Otherwise the apartment was dark and empty. If someone spoke, there were echoes.

We wandered through it, examining each room: the one small bedroom over to one side, the slightly larger one next to the living room, which looked out over the street; the kitchen with its yellow-brown wooden-sided ice box with brass handles and fittings;

the bathroom with its flush toilet. Karl got the first licking in the house for repeatedly pulling the chain.

The doorbell rang. In came Katinka Rosenberg, large and round, carrying a blue enamel coffeepot and a bottle of milk. Behind her came Henry with a cardboard box full of dishes, and behind him, Walter Rosenberg, carrying a box of matzohs, for we were in the last few days of Passover. When the Rosenbergs left, we all sat down on the kitchen floor, crumbled matzoh into our cups, poured sugar and coffee and milk over them, and feasted. Many years later Mamma would tell me, "It was wonderful, all of us sitting on the floor, and I said to Pappa, that I knew we Jews had been freed from Egypt." She added, "Now we're in the promised land? I don't know that, but we are free from Egypt."

Chapter Fifteen

We were desperately poor. Onkel Theo had given Pappa a slip of paper that read, in English, "I am looking for work. I have three children to support." Advice came from friends and relatives, "Go here, go there," and quite soon Pappa had his first job, as a relief-elevator operator in an apartment building where the regular operator had become ill. Onkel Theo had gotten him the job.

At first Pappa was afraid of taking it. "I don't speak any English, how can I . . . ?"

"You know one, two, three, four, don't you?" said Onkel Theo.

"I know five, too."

"Then all you need to learn is six, seven, eight. The building has eight floors. Somebody gives you a number and that's where you take them. You can do that."

Pappa nodded yes. Onkel Theo gave Pappa a slip of paper which he was to present to the building superintendent. When the super looked at it said something about speaking English, Pappa smiled and started to count, "One, two, three . . ."

He started at $8 a week. Quickly he was almost fired, when a tenant asked him to hold a package for her and deliver it to her apartment. He became confused and didn't understand her instructions. When he attempted to make the building superintendent understand his confusion, the super, seeing how much English

Pappa lacked, said "Don't come back after today." At the end of Pappa's shift, as he was changing out of the elevator man's uniform, the super came to repeat the message: He couldn't keep a man who was unable to help a tenant. Tenants come first — but they would try one more time. Should anything like it happen again . . . He slapped Pappa on the shoulder, smiled, and yelled at him as if he were deaf: "English, English."

Everything went well for a week or two until, one evening, Pappa began to shake and shiver. He was suffering from a recurrence of the malaria he had caught in Guayaquil. This had happened perhaps twice on the *hacienda*: the fever and the shivering would last for two or three days, and then he would be perfectly well again. But this time, the illness made my mother almost insane. While Pappa sat in his pajamas, wrapped in all the blankets we could find, Mom combed our house and then the neighborhood for an unemployed refugee who might perhaps substitute for the few days that Pappa might be out. She ran from one relative or acquaintance to another trying to find a substitute. She found no one. The following morning she took the subway and presented herself to the building superintendent, but to no avail. Pappa was fired. It would be three weeks before he recovered.

Pappa's next job was unloading barges on one of the East River docks. As far as I was concerned, it was the best job he ever had. Each day there came a barge from the Messing Bakery up in the Bronx. Messing sold cakes and cookies in just about every grocery store with which we were familiar: plain cakes, cakes with chocolate and vanilla icing, cookies of all kinds, plain and chocolate-covered donuts, and pies of all descriptions. These baked goods were only one or two days old but, to our great astonishment, in this America, they were old and could no longer be sold. So they were consigned to a dog food factory.

"Americans are very spoiled," said my father. "One day only, or even two, and they can't eat them any more, it's a shame. Such a waste, if only Oma could see it. In her store it would stay on the shelf . . ." — he silently counted on his fingers until all five were spread out, then looked at us and laughed. "Maybe they know better in this country."

Rather than waste such good things, Pappa would somehow stash away whatever he could, retrieve them at the end of the day and bring them home. Thus began the delicious and long-lasting Hess custom of finishing off breakfast with cake, pie or donuts of just about any kind.

Mamma, meanwhile, went to work as a cleaning woman. She washed dishes and scrubbed floors for twenty-five cents an hour. There was a lady in the Bronx who told her, "Come to work for me and you'll get thirty cents an hour." So Mom gave up a twenty-five cent job in Manhattan and journeyed to the Bronx. The first day lasted twelve hours. Included in her functions was to clean this woman's silver. Mamma cleaned it as well as she could, but she had difficulties reading the instructions on the jar that said to wet the sponge first. In the evening, when the woman came home and it was time to pay, the woman told her, "I can see that you're not an experienced cleaning woman. The silver hasn't been cleaned properly. Also, you did not fluff the pillows on the couch. All I can really give you is twenty-five cents." When Mamma told this story she would end with, "What could I do? I was glad to get even that."

On another occasion, she was employed by a very distant relative who had arrived in New York sometime in the 1920s. Mamma was now pregnant with our youngest brother. She suffered terribly from heartburn, and it was difficult for her to bend over. In the evening, when Mamma suggested that she was finished working, her relative said, "I don't know if you should come back. You didn't get down on your knees, you didn't do the corners."

An early job for Mom was for one of the young Gaertner men who had left Ruppichteroth in the middle 1930s and was now married and living in Queens. Mamma was to come once a week and clean their apartment, but Pappa had very strong objections. "What will it look like? After all, they worked for us in Germany. Now you have to work for them?"

Mamma prevailed; we needed the money. After five weeks of work in Queens, however, she was again asked not to come any more. They then received a letter from Opa in Germany. He was terribly upset: Was our situation in America so bad that Mamma had to work as a cleaning woman? And if a cleaning woman, how could she work for these people who had always worked for us? She then realized that the only reason she had been asked to work was in order that a letter back to Germany might say that, "There are Hesses who are now working for us."

We walked up and down Amsterdam Avenue to furnish our apartment from a number of stores that sold old furniture "for only a few dollars down." Although the war in Europe had begun and the American economy had taken a turn for the better, remnants of the Depression still existed. Those who now were doing better sold their old furniture, and there were many others who still sold their furniture because they needed to.

A set of twin beds was delivered and pushed together in the larger bedroom where we three children would share them. An old, dark brown, tufted pull-out couch was delivered and set up in the living room; that was for Mamma and Pappa. In all the apartments we ever lived in, we would be shy one bedroom. (One bedroom always went to Oma Krämer.) As long as the children lived at home, Mamma and Pappa slept on a pull-out in the living room.

We also acquired a white enamel-topped kitchen table and several rickety kitchen chairs upholstered in dark red vinyl. But of all our furnishings, Mamma was very proud of two: the brand new linoleum on the living room floor, for which cash, $12, was paid, and the tall, narrow china closet that she called a "vitrine" ($6).

The top section of the "vitrine" had a window of sliding glass, and the sides had an inlay of a lighter-colored wood. The "good dishes" were kept in the "vitrine," as well as the pewter plate dated 1802, which came from a revered ancestor on Oma Krämer's side.

It always amazed me that we had only these few steamer trunks and valises, but out of them came dishes, a set of silver cutlery acquired at marriage, crocheted stoles, and feather beds. There seemed to be an endless supply of things needed for daily living stored in these leather cornucopia.

Our daily china, one set for meat, the other for dairy, came as presents from Tante Irma and the several cousins who had arrived months earlier and whom Pappa, once he had gotten the hang of English, called "our Yankee relatives."

Not long after the apartment was established, we children began to itch and scratch. On our arms, legs, and chest appeared small welts and little red pockmarks. Mamma carefully examined us and our beds before calling Katinka Rosenberg for a consultation.

Katinka went to our beds and pulled at the mattresses. She folded over folds, flicked a finger at the tufts, put her nose down onto the seams. "Bedbugs."

"Never in my life did I have bedbugs. Not even in Ecuador."

"Don't worry, I had roaches," Katinka told Mamma in a quiet voice. "I got this powder at the Woolworth's."

"Did it do any good?"

"It got rid of most of the big ones. On the package it said it's also good for bedbugs. I have some left over. You can use it."

Mamma boiled our bed clothes in a large tub over the stove, then rubbed them in the kitchen sink over a corrugated wash board, then hung them up in the bathroom. When there was not enough room in the bathroom, she hung them out on a line that was connected from behind the kitchen window to a tall pole in the backyard. After this was done, she took the powder, and carefully dusted every seam, every tuft, and every fold of the clothing. That night we slept on the floor, a blanket beneath us, a blanket over us.

After we returned to the bed, our itching began again — and Mamma and Pappa were soon scratching as well. Again, Katinka was consulted. "I can't understand it. When we had them, the powder got rid of them." Again she put her nose to the mattress and then to the couch. "I can't understand it. I don't see anything."

Next Mamma consulted, with what I sensed was shame, additional experts, Tante Irma and the cousins, "We never, never had anything like that in Germany" was repeated over and over again. What they told her I don't know, but when she was able to make herself understood by the building superintendent, he told her, "Sulphur candles."

It was a Sunday afternoon when Mom placed several large water glasses around the apartment. Inside them were large yellow candles. One went in our bedroom, another in the living room where the offending couch rested, and another in the kitchen. She lit them, and a smoky yellow stink filled the apartment.

"Okay, now we have to hurry and get out of here," she said. "The smoke isn't good to get into our lungs. We are going to the Kino."

There had been no movies since Guayaquil, but she gathered us together — Pappa must have been working, since he was not with us — and off we went to a movie house on Amsterdam and 155th Street. This was the era of double features, and to my great delight the first one on the bill was the same Tarzan that I had seen in Guayaquil. Once again I was treated to the wonderful Maureen O'Sullivan swimming in the nude. In the second film, somebody threw a coat out of a window and that started a lot of chasing and even more talk, hardly any of which we understood. We children grew restless and wanted to leave, but Mom insisted we stay until the end "because the sulphur has to work."

There was a newsreel. To the extent that we understood, there was going to be an American election, and there were pictures of President Roosevelt.

The newsreel made me very afraid when it showed footage of Hitler, smiling, in an open car, driving down streets filled with cheering people. Next were battleships, their guns firing. Then German paratroopers tumbled out the open doors of airplanes, and the screen was soon filled with white, blossoming parachutes. I understood that they were raining down on Norway. I walked home very afraid, thinking about Germany in triumph, with clods of mud thrown at me, people cheering, and fire exploding from battleship guns.

We soon heard the far away sounds of fire engines, and as we neared our street, the sounds grew louder. Turning into our street, we could see firetrucks and flashing lights halfway down the block. Children were running toward them, and knots of people stood in the street and on the sidewalk, all looking upward. As we neared our building, we could see gray smoke streaming from a high window. Firemen in black slickers and funny hats were running with axes while others pulled hoses from the backs of trucks. A policeman, his arms held out wide, was saying, "Git, git, git. Back, back, back. Off the street."

The axe men were running up our stoop and inside. Mom now started running there, too, until Katinka came towards her, waving her arms.

From the sidewalk I could now see the smoke pouring from a shattered fourth floor window.

"It's your apartment," yelled Katinka.

Mamma ran across the street into the arms of a policeman. She pointed up to the window. *"Mein, bitte, mein, mein, mein, bitte,"* she repeated over and over again, trying to force herself past him. Then her voice quavered, and she began to cry. Karl ran to her, held on to her and called out, "Please, please." Finally, after a long pleading, the policeman holding her back let her go.

With Mamma in the lead, we rushed up the stairs. Firemen on the way down passed us, carrying axes, with thick black hoses slung over their shoulders. At our landing, we saw our apartment door fallen inward, off its hinges, with broad gashes. Mamma paused at the door, then crossed the threshold. The smell of ash was everywhere, and the bones of smashed chairs lay about. Every window was smashed, and drafts flooded the apartment. Suddenly she called out, "My vitrine!" Her china closet lay on the floor, its back broken, with glass slivers and white china shards lying near.

She beat her fists against her head. "The Nazis couldn't do it better."

A fireman stepped out of the kitchen, a crunch with every step. He started to speak to Mamma, who had her hands out at her side: *"Nicht verstehen. Nicht verstehen."* Henry Rosenberg appeared and began to translate for the fireman: "Sorry for the mess. Somebody called us. They said there was smoke in your apartment. We couldn't get in, so we had to break the door down. There was so much smoke and we couldn't see where it was coming from, so we had to search all around and do it quickly. Sorry for the mess." Then he left.

"At least he was sorry," said Mamma.

The super stood in back of her. "The super said that front door is very expensive," said Henry.

When Pappa came home, he said, "That was a very expensive movie." I saw the muscles on his cheeks moving in and out. For the next several weeks, while the apartment was reestablished, all of us were again distributed among relatives in Washington Heights.

Chapter Sixteen

Henry Rosenberg was my first teacher of English. Henry was older than me, and he and his family had been in America since 1938. Henry was a marvelous ballplayer and a Yankee fan. He could make the pink rubber ball called a "Spaldeen" do tricks. He would throw it at one of the six steps of our stoop, and every time it would hit the very edge of one of the steps and fly out to be caught. In time Henry would become the best stoop-ball and curb-ball player anyone had ever seen in Washington Heights.

During the war, there were very few cars on the streets, so it was easy and almost safe to use them as our ball fields. Curb-ball was a variant of baseball. Home plate was on one curb, second base was directly across from home on the opposite curb, and first and third were placed in the middle of the street, wide apart and across from each other. To "hit" was to bounce the ball off the edge of the curb. If it hit the house across the street on the fly without being caught, it was a home run. If the ball bounced rather than flew, normal base-ball rules were in effect. Henry could, all too often, get his home run, but adept as he was at hitting, his finest accomplishment was as a fielder. From somewhere he had acquired a fielder's glove. He had removed all the stuffing from it so that it was extremely pliable, and with that glove he could pluck almost any ball out of the air with the ease of a hawk after a field mouse. His range was phenomenal.

Everybody wanted Henry on their side.

One day in spring, Henry said "Let's go for a walk down to the river." The river was the lordly Hudson, and to venture from 159th Street down toward water was to encounter a geography very different from the blocks toward the east. There was Broadway to cross, its center divider green with strange yellow shrubs ranging about the borders. There was the steep walk down the 158th Street. Along Riverside Drive were great multi-storied buildings, some with doormen. Here Riverside Drive was fully as wide as Broadway, and to the south rose high, daunting "elevator" buildings, which looked something like my Oma's in Frankfurt: solid, and substantial, made of gray rock. I knew that anybody living in there would never have to scrounge for furniture in the second-hand shops along Amsterdam Avenue or light sulphur candles to eliminate bed bugs.

Then there were the rust colored brownstones that followed the downward slope of 158th Street, with more yellow bushes in their front yards. At the bottom of 158th, I saw the viaduct of the West Side Highway, cars buzzing north. Most remarkable of all was the long, green, dizzying, cascading steel staircase to the Hudson shore. Henry raced down those steps. Very slowly, holding on to the railing, I followed.

From the bottom of the stairs I could see a pier stretching out into the river. Its wooden beams seemed old and smelled of tar. About half a dozen men, all of them black, were throwing fishing lines into the river, and one was letting down a rectangular wire basket into the water. We walked over to him. He had a tin bucket at his feet. Smiling, he said some words, reached down into the bucket, and pulled out a large blue crab, its feet clawing at the air. Offering me a look, he reached it out toward me. I ran, frightened.

Henry caught up with me. "They fish here all the time. You can't eat crab, you know. They're not kosher."

I knew that. They served crab salad on the *Caribia*, and Mamma had said that she so very much wanted to eat some (lobster, too), but couldn't because they weren't kosher.

We walked north along a black-topped path, the river on our left. In the far distance I could see this immense bridge. "George Washington Bridge," said Henry. "The father of our country, George Washington." I couldn't understand how one man could father a country, but by that time we were at a large playground. Still, I couldn't stop looking at the bridge: the pylons so tall and massive; the crisscross webbing of the steel supports so powerful; the roadway so delicate and thin. The girders at first looked black, but as I kept looking I saw that they were a very dark blue, a blue with something of the sky in it. Clouds flew in back of the great spidery columns, which felt like lords from knighthood stories. The longer I looked, the more afraid I became, thinking of those giants in black standing on their balconies in the newsreel, arms outstretched, while below them a black-booted mass marched in review.

Henry yelled, "Come, I'll teach you English." The playground had swings, slides, a sandbox, seesaws, monkey bars. There were children climbing on each. Henry named each of these strange objects for me and made me repeat their names several times. "Now," he said, "you have to go over to that boy," and he pointed to a tall, broad-shouldered boy who was, in an aimless fashion, pushing a swing with nobody on it. "You have to tell him, in English, 'I beat you up.'" He made me repeat "I beat you up" several times, then pushed me over to this young man.

I said to him what Henry had instructed. The boy's eyebrows narrowed as he took in my words, then he punched me in the nose so that I bled. I had my first English lesson: Know what you're saying and to whom you're saying it.

Mamma started making me read a small, soft leather-covered English-German dictionary that opened with "aback" and ended with "zwieback." Several days later, along with Aunt Irma as translator, she took Karl and me to Public School 46 on 156th Street between Amsterdam and St. Nicholas Avenues. The building looked like a castle, with massive walls of piled gray stones, but it couldn't be a castle because its windows were so very large and displayed sheets and sheets of multi-colored drawings.

Children were streaming toward the building. They were all black. We entered with them through massive double doors into a large entrance hall, cool and dark and filled with children. Suddenly, a huge man in a gray suit moved toward us, cutting through the mass of kids like a ship's prow knifing through water. He was white. With both hands, almost carelessly, without looking, he moved children aside.

"Yes?"

"These are new children," Tante Irma said, "from Germany, from Ecuador."

We were escorted to an office. There was a nice lady in a white cardigan, brown hair piled on her head and eyeglasses hanging from a string around her neck and swinging in front of her bosom every time she moved. Mom handed her some papers; the lady took a book from her desk. It was *Grimm's Fairy Tales*, in German. She had Karl and me read from it. The verdict was that I was to go to class 3B-1 and Karl to 2A-1.

Mom and Aunt Irma left.

I was amazed at how bright my classroom was. The desktops reflected a shiny golden honey hue. Sun streamed in at the windows. The children smiled when I was ushered in and seated in the middle of the room. The teacher smiled, then wrote her name on the blackboard in large block letters. Each time she lifted the chalk from the blackboard she smiled at me, then returned the chalk to the blackboard with a crash. Lift, smile, crash: Mrs. Rubin. She was tall, with a long face and sharp jaw, brown hair, and wearing a rust- colored cardigan. In a peculiar German, she somehow made me understand that the boy behind me spoke German and would translate for me. Through much of the week, though, after every one of Mrs. Rubin's explanations of something, she would sidle up the aisle toward me and whisper, *"Verstaist?"*

The boy sitting behind me, Gerhardt Salmson, was a very good translator. He came from Dresden, and had been in America for six months. He didn't look like Chino, my translator in Ecuador.

"She is Jewish," said Gerhardt/Jerry.

"Who?"

"Mrs. Rubin."

"No. Can't be."

"Yes, she is."

"No. Jews can't be teachers. That's not allowed."

"They can't in Germany. But here they can. She speaks Yiddish."

"What's Yiddish?"

"I don't know."

On Friday of that first week, we were told that we had to go to an "assembly." The class hurried out of their seats and stumbled down two flights. Piano music and song were coming from somewhere. A door opened up, and a blast of full-throated singing by what seemed to be hundreds of seated black children came at us. A teacher in front waved a little baton. I stood there with the rest of the class while the singing continued. Jerry, behind me, translated the words, "Go down Moses, way down in Egypt land, tell old Pharaoh, let my people go."

Standing in this doorway, with my class half in and half outside the auditorium, I began to cry. Wasn't my Opa named Moses, and wasn't he still in Egypt, while I was here, a place where they had Jewish teachers? I knew that Pharaoh was Hitler. And then the song ended.

Each word was carefully enunciated, slow and loud from these several hundred throats: "Let my people go." And I knew for certain that they were singing about me, they were singing for me.

After about four months, once I had acquired some fluency in English, I received another name change. My new friends, John Harmon, Don Seralls, Josh Dickens, Jack Williams, all those with whom I was invited to play handball in the school yard, whether they came from Edgecombe Avenue or down on Broadway, had a hard time pronouncing my name. Sometimes it was Wolf, or Woolie, or Gang, or Woolgang.

Late in the term, just after lunch, I went up to Mrs. Rubin and told her that from now on my name was no longer Wolfgang, but that it was Walter.

"Even if your name on the register is still Wolfgang? Has it been officially changed.?"

"No. Yes, really. Please."

Mrs. Rubin smiled, then had me stand in front of the class and pointed at me with her glasses: "We may not any more call this person by his real name. From now on he has an alias, and we will all call him by his new alias: Walter."

From then until just about the end of the term my friends called me "Alias." It wasn't until the next term that everybody in school started calling me Walter.

And I started calling my parents Mom and Pop.

We knew we were poor, Karl and I. Some children we knew could buy bubblegum with flip cards in the package, and others could afford the ten cents for a pink spaldeen, or ten cents for a comic book, or nine cents for a Saturday matinee at the Costello movie house on Fort Washington Avenue, or the dime for a matinee at the very grand Loew's Rio where the films were only on their third run while the Costello got them on their fifth or sixth. Karl and I, for entertainment, would often go into the Woolworth's on Broadway and spend time at the toy counter just looking. Maybe we would fondle a spaldeen or examine a package of crayons or pick up one of the little toy cars and run a hand over the wheels simply to hear them spin. It was hard, after picking up a toy, to then return it to its place, but we had no money to buy any of them.

One day, Mom walked past a carpenter's shop somewhere up on Audubon Avenue that was about to throw out some short pieces of wood. She came home that evening with a large, heavy bag and spilled these bits and pieces of wood onto the living room floor. "Here, you can build things with them. Look! A house. Look! A bridge. It's lots of fun." She was sitting on the floor, putting the pieces together. We sat down, too, looked at the pieces, handled them, then stood up and walked away.

"You two are spoiled," she yelled after us. "Since when did you get so spoiled? We don't live in a rich elevator building like some people." She stood up and gathered the pieces. That bag of wood stood in a corner of our bedroom for a very long time.

Karl and I were in Woolworth's one afternoon, after school. Karl was fondling one of the toy cars, making its wheels spin. The salesgirl was at the other end of the counter. Suddenly Karl put the car in his pocket and walked out of the store. I was anguished by his theft and awed by his courage. Silently, I walked home by his side. The next afternoon, alone, I walked into Woolworth's. I walked up to the toy counter, picked up a red toy car and made wheels spin. A salesgirl came over and asked if I wanted to buy it. I said, "No, I'm just looking." The salesgirl walked away. I saw her talking to another girl at a far corner of the aisle. I picked up the red car, put it in my pocket and walked out of Woolworth's.

It was Saturday, after synagogue, after lunch. Karl and I were in our bedroom with the door was closed. Our shoes off, we were on our bed, and had puffed up the great featherbed quilts and made rills in them so our toy cars could run down the long slopes.

"Why is the door closed?" It was Pop. "What are you doing?

What do you have there? Let me see."

Full of a terrible shame, we each reached out an arm with the stolen toy in our hands. Pappa took up the cars and examined them, turned them over, looked at the wheels, hefted their leaden weight. We were going to get a terrible whaling. It was justice.

"Where did you get these?"

"Woolworth's."

"Where did you get the money?"

"We didn't . . ."

"Didn't what . . . ?"

"Buy them."

It felt like a scream, but there was no scream. "You stole them from Woolworth's?"

Karl said "Yes."

Pop's face was dark. "Here." He gave the cars back into our hands. We began to cry. We were in a great and terrible pain.

"Put on your shoes. I want you to come with me." We passed Mom in the living room, and she said, "Where are you going, Oscar, you said you were going to take a nap?" He pulled at our arms. "I'll tell you later," he said.

The wind on the street dried our tears, and we wouldn't cry where others might see us. Pop held us hard by the hand, one of us on each side. Women were looking out of windows. Each one looking knew that Karl and I were thieves. The people we passed on the street knew that Karl and I were thieves. They looked at Pop, and they said to themselves, "That man has thieves for children, what kind of a person must he be?"

We were inside Woolworth's. "Show me. Where." We led him, still holding his hands, to the toy counter. We stood at the counter. A salesgirl walked by.

"Miss! Miss. Lady." She stopped across from us and smiled.

"The boys . . . Show her." He pulled at our arms. We each held up our stolen car. "The boys took these cars and didn't pay."

The girl looked at us with her wide, shocked eyes. "They stole them? I'll call the manager."

The manager was going to come and take us down to the 152nd Street police station and register us as juvenile delinquents. Pop said, "No. I want to pay for the toys. How much?" The girl held the two cars, one green, the other red. She looked sharply, angrily at us, as though we deserved to be walked down to the police station.

"These are forty-five cents each. Ninety cents."

Pappa went into his pants pocket and slowly pulled out his leather change purse.

"Ninety cents?"

"Ninety cents."

He opened the change purse and, nickel by nickel and dime by dime counted out the money onto the glass surface of the counter. With her palm, the girl retrieved each coin, making a scratchy sound on the glass countertop and letting them fall into her other palm.

"The toys, please." She handed the cars to Pop. He turned to us and handed us each one of the cars, then wordlessly took our hands and walked us home.

I felt terrible. My stomach hurt. I wanted to cry but I couldn't. He, of course, had bathed for the sabbath, but I smelled the odor of his sweat as when he came home from work and bent down to receive my hug at the end of the day. I was a betrayer of that sweat, and of our mother's day labor. I was a terrible person. I heard the coins sliding on the glass countertop again.

After several months on the East River docks, my father began work as a dishwasher at a restaurant, the Café Eclair on 72nd street on the West Side of Manhattan. The Eclair then was a bit of old Europe, the kind of coffeehouse one might find in Vienna or Berlin or any large German city. While American-style sandwiches were, of course, on the menu, the real reason for its existence was its many varieties of cakes and pastries, all overflowing with whipped cream, chocolate, and custards. There was the atmosphere of an Old World café where one could linger over coffee, read a newspaper, meet and chat with friends. That the Café Eclair was located so very near West End Avenue and Riverside Drive, the heart of settlement for the more affluent immigrants, was certainly one of the elements for its long-lasting success. So in a place that on another continent he might have frequented, Pop now washed dishes and was glad of it.

It was the mid-afternoon before Yom Kippur, Kol Nidre eve, and and as Pop was observant and needed to prepare for the holiday, he had arranged to leave work early. His day begun work at 6:00 that morning, and just before leaving, the boss handed him a box of desserts to deliver to a customer on West End Avenue at 98th Street. Pop understood the chore, since it was customary to have a large and elaborate meal on the evening before the long day of fasting, but he fell asleep on the subway, awakening at our station.

Now he stood in front of Mom with the package in his hand, not knowing what to do.

She took over. She had Pappa prepare his bath and got him something to eat. (We did not have a large and elaborate meal that year.) "Don't say anything," she told him. "When you and Oma are in synagogue, I will take the children and go down and deliver the things." Pop's silence signaled his agreement. Oma Krämer, Mom's mother, was living with us, and she was extremely observant. Our mother's plan would have brought down immediate rebukes from her.

Mom was now very pregnant. With 4-year-old Peter at her hand, we went off to make the delivery on West End Avenue. We children could very well have remained at home by ourselves, and often had, but Mom probably thought that arranging for a pathetic gypsy scene might temper any anger at the late delivery.

We arrived at the door of the house on 98th street and a lady in a dark dress and pearls opened the door. "Wait a minute," she said as she took the package. Mom smiled at us: "Wait, we get a tip."

The lady came back holding the opened box. She was furious. "I have twelve guests for dinner and I ordered twelve petit fours. One of them is broken. Now there are only eleven, and I have twelve guests!"

Mom tried to explain, but the lady interrupted. "Tomorrow I'll go to Eclair and tell them." She slammed the door. Mom pleaded through the closed door, "Please no, please no, we need the job." This went on for a while before we turned around and left.

Mom didn't tell Pop what happened, but when he returned to work after the holiday, the boss told him, "Don't bother changing, you're fired."

Years later when Mom would recount the story, she would say, "*Nebekh*, I was pregnant, I had one kid on one arm and the package in my hand. Maybe the package got bumped. The lady said, 'I invited twelve people,' and now she only had eleven and three quarters. You know, when I invite twelve people I have at least thirteen pieces, not twelve." She would end the story with a shake of the head, "West End Avenue Jews . . ."

Oma's boat had arrived from England just days ahead of ours. She had stayed with Aunt Irma for a few weeks, but as soon as we were settled in our apartment on 159th Street, she had moved in with us. She had been wealthy in Germany, and had given each daughter a large dowry. She was proud of her five brothers who had achieved much as traders and exporters of grain, and she was even prouder of her Hess parentage. There was a certain air of superiority that she carried with her. Although she never said so explicitly, she was certain that her side of the family was far superior to Pop's cattle-dealer side, even though the cattle-dealer side and the wealthy merchant and rabbi side were actually distantly related. Rabbi blood coursed through Pop's veins as well as Mom's. I marveled at Pop's composure when Oma would bring up the rabbis from Würtenberg and Bavaria and the books they wrote. If I sometimes cautiously brought up the subject of family proximity with her, she would brush it aside with, "Ach, how can you compare the two?"

Why she was living with us rather than with her son Theo or her daughter Irma, both of whom had been in the States longer than we and were marginally better off? "Well," Mom would say, "Irma's in-laws are living with them, so of course . . . and Theo's apartment is a little small . . ." If pressed on the subject, Mom would say, "If she lived with them they would kill each other. Only Pappa has the nice temper so it doesn't affect him too much."

One Friday afternoon, Mom was late coming home from work. Oma paced. "Soon it's *shabbes* and she's not home yet. There's no *shabbes* dinner." Her pacing made everyone more nervous. Mom was on a job, cleaning, in Queens. Every half hour I would run up to the 162nd Street station, wait a few minutes, not see her, then run home. Pop would go down to the 157th Street station and do the same. An hour and a half later, Oma was still pacing. After two hours, she went downstairs and stood at the building entrance. Three hours after Mom should have shown up at home, she appeared down the block. She walked slowly; she was pregnant. When she smiled sadly as she neared Oma, Oma hauled off and slapped her hard in the face.

Mom had fallen asleep on the subway and had ended up in the Bronx. From there she became confused, received many confusing directions, and long hours later arrived home to this reception from her mother. Yet Mom and Pop never wondered, at least out loud, whether the five dollars, monthly, that each of Oma's other children contributed to her lodging and upkeep was worth it.

Oma recited poetry, much of which I could not understand, since it was in a rather high-flown German.

Ich hatte einst ein schönes Vaterland

155

Der Eichenbaum
Wuchs dort so hoch, die Veilchen nickten sanft.
Es war ein traum.
Or:
Kennst du das land, wo die Zitronen blühn
Im dunkeln Laub die Gold-Orangen glühn,

The recitation I liked best began:

Über allen Gipfeln
Ist Ruh,
In allen Wipfeln
Spürest du
Kaum ein Hauch
Die Vöglein schweigen im Walde
                    Warte nur! Balde
Ruhest du auch.

I memorized it without understanding it, simply for the sounds.
Much later did I learn that the first poem was by Heine: *I once had a lovely fatherland. There the oaks grew tall, the violets beckoned gently. It was a dream.* It was titled, "In Exile."

One grandmother was here with us in New York, but there was another Oma and an Opa still in Germany. America was not yet at war, so letters could still be exchanged. When they arrived from Germany, I would recognize them not only by the red stamps with Hitler's picture but also by the fact that they would lie on the kitchen table, unopened all day until Pop came to open it. He would sit in the kitchen, there would be a long silence, and Mom would stand behind him, both her hands resting on his shoulders as he opened the letter.

Every four or five weeks, I would accompany Mom to the post

office on 165th Street. With a $20 bill, she would buy a money order and send it to Oma and Opa in Germany. This week the day was sunny and windy, and as she mounted the steps to enter the post office, the $20 flew from her hand.

Mom jumped off the steps to root frantically among the bushes. She was a mother I did not recognize, on her knees, shoving branches aside, and demonically screaming, "Oh, God! Oh, God! No, no, no, no!"

I was beside her, my hands between the bushes, too, looking, looking. "Twenty dollars," she cried, "twenty dollars." Then she raced inside the post office, rushed to what seemed to be a guard, a gray uniform and a wide leather strap across his chest and a wide leather belt with a gun hanging from it. "I lost it, my money, I lost my money," she repeated over and over, as if the guard could do something to help. She started next in German: "My parents-in-law, my parents-in-law. It is for my parents-in law. We have no money. No money. My parents-in law in Germany."

I was embarrassed by her German. The guard turned away from her, saying, "I don't work here." Sobbing as I had never heard her before, I joined her in tears and we rushed out to dig again through the shrubbery. We found nothing. By the time we rose from our searching, Mom's arms were all scratched up. Her crying had stopped. "What will I tell Pappa?" She took my hand, and as we walked home, she kept repeating, "How could I be that careless! How could I be that careless!"

I don't think that Pop ever gave up on getting his parents out of Germany. Almost every day he read newspaper reports of restrictions placed on Jews wanting to emigrate. With the same silence as when he read the letters, he would hand a report to Mom, and she would, perhaps with a fist slammed down on the table, call out, "Bastards, bastards, bastards." Country after country closed its doors or fiercely limited the numbers of Jews that they might accept. The extermination of Jews then already taking place in Poland and to its east were not yet common knowledge.

Then a letter came that made it seem possible that Oma and Opa could be rescued from Germany. An affidavit and $1,000 were quickly needed: a thousand dollars for ship fare and an affidavit that would assure America that the immigrants would not become a burden to the State, that whoever provided the affidavit would be responsible for the care and feeding of the new arrivals.

I wanted very badly to have my Oma and Opa with us, and whenever the talk turned to something having to do with their possible emigration, I would circle about, keeping out of my parents' way but trying very hard to listen. Aunt Irma had provided an affidavit for us, but she was wary of providing another for another group of old people. "Well, yes," she said, "if nobody else is there to do it, okay, I will do it, but you have to ask others first."

All of them repeated the same "well, yes, but . . ." As for the task of raising $1,000 on their $8-per-week, 25¢-per-hour income, one might just as well have been speaking of millions. Nevertheless, they tried.

Pop's brother, the veterinarian, had immigrated to Canada in 1937. By 1940 he had, according to his own modest estimate, established a "nice" practice in Kitchener, Ontario. I sometimes heard Mom saying that she felt puzzled that Pop had to carry the burden of trying to get his parents out of Germany when it seemed to her that Uncle Albert, who had been established in his new country for a good long while, did not expend the same energy. They decided to write to Uncle Albert, let him know of the situation, and ask him for $500 — about which they wrangled, Mom wanting to ask for the full thousand, Pop holding out for just five hundred but letting Albert know that a thousand was needed.

Mom wrote the letter, as Pop wanted.

There was one other avenue that promised hope. Mom had an overwhelmingly wealthy set of relatives in New York. She had never before applied to them for aid either for herself or for family but now, on behalf of her in-laws, she did. We took the subway downtown. Mom had the address on a slip of paper. Mom said, "If I pinch you, you can start to cry."

In the late 1890s, Mom's father, Louis Krämer, and a half-brother, David, had come to the United States together, to New York. When a severe economic depression dimmed their American prospects, Louis had returned to Germany but David had stayed. By 1940 David had died, but not before establishing a flourishing business in notions — small, lightweight items for household use, like buttons and pins. His two sons, Herbert and Monroe, now ran the business.

The elevator to their offices seemed built out of a fantastic erector set. It had neither walls nor roof, only an open iron skeleton through which one could see, far up, a sky-ight. One could see, as well, through the steel mesh openings as we rose, the vast ranging floors that contained row after row of immense white tables where on all sides men and women were bent doing something. Most remarkably, no button needed to be pushed on this elevator to indicate the floor: There was an attendant who pulled on a braided metal rope that extended all the way up to the skylight. A pull and the elevator began to rise; another pull and the elevator halted.

This floor, too, contained the two vast rows of huge white tables. Large, green-hooded lamps extended down from a high ceiling, and again, around each of the tables, an enormous number of men and women were bent. As we got closer, we could see their fingers moving over pieces of paper as if they were practicing over silent piano keys. But there was no silence, only a crunching, rustling sound coming from the tables, as if one were walking through fallen leaves.

Halfway down the aisle between the tables stood two men in white shirts and ties. They seemed to be of about the same age as Mom and Pop. Mom smiled and as we got closer and held her arms out as if to hug them, but they retreated a bit and extended their hands for a shake.

"You look just like your grandmother," Mom said. "Wait a minute." I had seen her in many moods, but never one like this: nervous, rummaging through her bag, repeating, "Wait a minute," two, three, four times. At last she pulled out a photograph on stiff paper, brown with age, of a woman with a tall head of hair and a very serious expression.

The man to whom she handed the picture looked nothing like the woman in the photograph. He was short, slender, and bald, with a mustache and glasses. The other man had shiny black hair that was parted in the middle. Mom reached into her bag again and drew out a small soft blue bag. It was something that I had seen often. I was handed her bag to hold and Mom then drew out a golden watch on a long golden chain from the soft blue bag.

"This is your grandfather's watch," she said in German. "I don't know if you have anything to remember him by, but I thought that maybe you would like to have it."

I was never more ashamed of my mother. I knew she was going to need to beg, but I did not know that she was shamefacedly going to bribe as well. I had seen her, in Germany and in Ecuador, from time to time taking that watch, with its Roman numerals, out of that blue bag and running a soft cloth over the gold casing; she would make a point each time of saying, "This is the only remembrance I have of my grandfather. One of these days one of you will have it."

The bald one took the watch and smiled. Then each took turns holding it in his palm, seeming to weigh it. We stood there in the middle of this vast room, and nobody spoke. There was just the rustle that came from the tables that came from the workers and their nimble fingers.

"Come, you're pregnant," one said. "Sit down in the office. We'll get you some coffee." We sat in an office at one end of the floor. It had a large glass wall that looked out on the workers. Mom told her story about the terrible situation in Germany, "Everybody knows about it, I don't have to tell you, I wrote you about Oscar's parents, these good old people. Religious, good people, they don't deserve to suffer, there are people here in America who could help maybe save these two old people. All we need is a thousand dollars."

"A thousand dollars?" said the two of them, almost at once.

"I know. It's a lot of money. You know Oscar and I would do it but Oscar works so hard for just his eight, sometimes ten dollars a week, and I don't sit on my *tokhus*. I get twenty-five cents an hour for scrubbing floors. The rent is forty-eight dollars a month and we got three kids." Mom put her arm around my neck and pinched me so the others wouldn't see it, but I refused to cry. Her begging recital made me too angry. "Anything you can do to help us, we would pay you back when we get on our feet. And we need somebody to provide an affidavit."

The bald headed one got up, looked down at his brother, then faced us. "How long are you in this country?"

"Why? Months, I guess."

"How can you afford a forty-eight dollar apartment when your husband makes only eight dollars a week?

"Did I say forty-eight? I meant thirty-eight. Thirty-eight. When he gets ten, we still got two dollars left over. And I work, too."

"You're not here even a year and already you're pregnant."

Mom looked down at her belly and stroked a hand over it.

"I think it's very irresponsible," said the slick-haired brother. He stood and faced her. "Very irresponsible. How can you think of having children when you have no money, when you have no real work, nothing that gives you a real future? You have a lot of re-sponsibility; three children to take care of. A hard time at home . . ."

"Not so hard like you think. Money isn't everything," Mom said.

"And then you're hardly in the country and you have another on the way. That's what I call irresponsible."

"I'm sorry that you think so. But I'm glad I have these children and I'm glad we have another on the way." Mom pinched me in the neck again, but still I refused to cry. She got up from her chair. "Oscar got out of Dachau, we got out of Germany, we got out of Ecuador. Do you think all that is for nothing? Do you have children?"

They both shook their heads.

"I don't want charity," Mom told them. "I'm not asking for that. I would never. This is for two old people in Germany. I didn't really want to come and bother you, it is really hard for me to come and beg, but I thought that maybe the lives of two old Jews are really important and that blood is thicker than water, than dollars even. And people help each other when there is trouble."

"You know," said the slick-haired one, "the blood isn't even so thick between us as you say. Your father and our father were step-brothers, not even real brothers."

Very quickly, and more loudly, Mom replied, "Weren't they raised in the same house, one next to the other? I can't believe it."

Then the egg-headed one said, "With somebody as irresponsible as you seem to be, how can we trust that the money will be used as you say?"

Mom reached for the watch on the desk, her fingers surrounded it. "I can't believe it. My cousins! I would lie to you? I can't believe it! I should have listened to Irma and never have come to you."

The two men were standing now. Mom pulled me up from the chair. "She said you sent her a letter when she asked you to make an affidavit for our brother, for your cousin Theo. Your lawyer told you not to do it, you said. You would be responsible if he couldn't support himself: responsible for a doctor in economics!" Now in English, and very loud: "How many people you got working on your tables in these three floors? How much you making on each one every day?"

We were almost at the elevators. People around the tables were now looking up. They had stopped working. "People like you gave money to Hitler," Mom cried. "They bought suits for the Hitler youth!"

The elevator had arrived. We stepped in. On the way down, she said, very quietly: "Maybe if they had children they would think differently."

The answer from Canada did not differ greatly from that of Mom's cousins, although here a son was involved. Here the request was for a much smaller sum, yet Uncle Albert wrote back, "Do you know how much five hundred dollars means?"

On Sunday, June 22nd, 1941, the Germans invaded Russia. One hundred and twenty divisions struck, from the Baltic to the Black Sea. Mom said, "That's their end; that's Hitler's big mistake," but her face did not look happy.

A few days later, Italy and Rumania, too, declared war on Russia.

On June 27th, 1941 my grandparents, Henrietta and Moses Hess, were rounded up, along with all the other Jews in Ruppichteroth who had not already been sent into forced labor. They were transported to the recently-vacated forced-labor barracks in the nearby town of Much, where all of the older Jews of the surrounding district were being incarcerated.

Sometime after the end of World War II, to my parents' great surprise, they would receive a letter written by my Opa Moses. The letter had been smuggled out of the camp at Much to a farmer friend of his, who had sent it on to us in New York as soon after the war as he could. Translated, it read as follows:

The camp in Much, June 23, 1942,
My very dear ones,
Our end is very near. A thick dark line has been drawn through our lives. Until now, things have gone fairly well — we have been living, for the past thirteen months, in the Camp in Much. Because of the kindness of the local people we have been treated well, may God bless these people for their kindness. But my dear ones, soon we will be leaving this place and our dearly loved Rhineland.

We old ones and all the older ones are being sent to Terezin in Bohemia — the younger ones are being sent to forced labor — among them Aunt Lydia. Uncle Julius has met his end. He was "shot while fleeing" in Buchenwald. If, perhaps after some years, you should see this letter, think of us with kindness and respect. You can't help us but Albert did have the possibility. You know what I think about that. God bless you dear Oscar, all your children, and you dear Melli. And sometimes, on good days or bad, think of us, your parents, now hounded to death.

Of my sisters, only Lina remains in Frankfurt — Uncle Willi has died in Poland. Oma is quite healthy despite the hard labor she has had to do. We have quite a business here in camp. We make rubber leggings and uniforms for the military and Oma sits from early morning until late at night at an electric sewing machine. In January I was operated on, in Cologne, for a bladder condition — it is a pain but not a critical condition. I have not yet fully recovered. And now my dear loved ones, may God bless you and your children — raise them to be honorable and useful human beings and keep us in your memory.

Our good things have been hidden with Joseph Lauf and Johann Haas, and when peace returns you can get in touch with them. I will not be alive by then but in my judgment you should see Oma again. I will be seventy when the war ends. Now, once more, my wish is only for good things for you and your children.

Your Opa and Oma

At 8 a.m. on July 27th, 1942 trucks arrived at the camp at Much and took the last group of its inmates, including my grandparents, to local train stations, where, via Bonn and Cologne, they were transported to the concentration camp of Terezin in Moravia. From German documents, my grandfather's date of death is given as 19 October 1942, and my grandmother's as June 1944. Both in Terezin.

It took some time
to look at all those pictures,
the black and white ones;

to hear those stories once again;
heads nodding toward
her and him;

that book of shadows
when we were kids
who knew enough
to fill in that which happened;
knew to perfection that desire,
no, the need to stay apart,
away from them;

from that which happened
endlessly to those you loved
but not to you.

Chapter Seventeen

There was a synagogue up on Amsterdam Avenue, between 161st and 162nd Streets. It occupied a long hall on the second floor above a supermarket. The Rosenbergs belonged to it, as did my Aunt Irma's family. The congregation had only recently been organized. All of its members were refugees from Germany. To see them walk into the *shul* on a Friday evening or Saturday morning was to see them in suits and dresses, in their best clothes. The services were conducted according to the Orthodox ritual. Hebrew, of course, was the language of the service, but all the gossip was in German, and for our noise, we children were rebuked in German.

To be there, above the supermarket, was to be enveloped by a certain kind of comfort. The chants and hymns were so very familiar; I loved the call and response when chanting a psalm, the singing that accompanied the removal of the Torahs from the ark, and the singing with which they were returned to the ark. I loved the singing that accompanied the repetition of the *Amidah*, the petitionary prayer. The whole congregation sang full-throated, the same tunes that my Opa sang in the synagogue with the red carpeting, the synagogue made of large fieldstones, back home, in Ruppichteroth. When, on a Saturday morning, I heard the order of prayer and, after a long absence, the same melodies my grandfather used, it brought me comfort and continuity.

Even better than the Saturday mornings were the Friday nights when all the congregation, sang *"Lekha Dodi."* Then I had a sense that I was back in the synagogue with the red carpets, with Opa leading the singing and, at the last verse, turning toward the door to welcome the mystery, the sabbath spirit, that waited there outside.

"Lekha Dodi" celebrates the day of rest. Its essential trope compares the approaching sabbath to a bride, though I didn't know that as a child. For me, it was simply the song through which my Opa smiled, and in which his voice rang with a lilt so happy that it seemed to lift the moment to grand heights. Toward the end of the hymn, the congregation stands and turns toward the door and bows, as if honoring an entering guest. Just before standing, Opa would smile at me and wave a little circle in the air with his hand, prompting the thought that someone ought to be coming through that door. But who? Opa's smile promised that some time, some day, someone would indeed enter. This turning away from the front of the synagogue, from the place where Opa always stood, close to where the Torahs were stored, and then the turning back, was always the most strange, mysterious, and joyous moment of the week. There was a turning away; there was a returning.

Now, standing in this other synagogue on a Friday night, above the supermarket, when *"Lekha Dodi.* was sung, I was sure that even in this faraway city on this faraway continent, it was my grandfather who stood on the door's other side — not my grandfather in the flesh, but his presence, made up of his smell, his dark holiday suit, his smile, his bristly, unshaven face and white mustache — and that at some time, not so far from now, that presence would come in through that door.

Joining the synagogue meant attending Hebrew school. My first day was the opening day of the Hebrew school, and it began with a translation of the *Akedah*, the binding of Isaac. It occurred to me that Father Abraham, like my father, must have been really nervous to have taken these kinds of measures to punish his son. Never mind that it was God's instruction to take the one he loved best up that mountain. Abraham must really have been nervous, even more than Pappa, after all that traveling he had to do, all the way from Ur to Canaan. Except that it was God who told him "Get thee out of thy country, and from thy kindred and from thy father's house." That's what Mr. Klein, our teacher, read to us before starting in on the binding story; a good thing that Pappa merely doled out the much-too-frequent whack on the backside.

I discovered Audubon Terrace through Jack Williams, who was in my class at P.S. 46 and he went to the Church of the Intercession and sang in its choir. The church was on the corner of Broadway and 156th Street. We were learning about the history of New York City and Jack told some of us that he knew that Peter Minuet was buried in the church's cemetery, and that we could go down there and look. It turned out not to be Peter Minuet but Peter Stuyvesant, and we couldn't get into the cemetery to see him, so we went to look in on Audubon Terrace.

We looked, and we saw a different country: no fire-escape-fronted, soot-splashed brick, five story walk-up buildings all squeezed together. Here was the immense courtyard, in the center of which was the immense statue of a man on a great rearing horse, his arm lifted high, and, as an extension to his arm, a great pointed flag-wrapped spear that wanted to puncture the sky. At the base of the statue it said "El Cid Compeador."

"Who was El Cid fighting?" I asked Jack. Jack thought it was the Indians because one of the great buildings in front of us held the Museum of the American Indian. "He couldn't be fighting the Spanish in the Spanish Museum." I thought, *That's right. He wouldn't be fighting the Spanish because "Campeador" is a Spanish word. Except sometimes Spanish did fight Spanish.*

"And what sense," added Jack, "would there be in fighting the coins in the Numismatic Museum?" So it had to be the Indians. We walked slowly about the great rectangle that held these immense light-gray buildings, with their many fluted pillars and grand cornices. Although they were not very tall, they looked as if they came out of the books showing Greek and Roman temples, and they somehow seemed to be far taller and larger than any five-story walk-up or even any elevator building on 161st Street. Each was surrounded by a great, wide terrace, and grand staircases led to their doors.

The Spanish museum had large rooms with dark wooden walls and massive dark brown furniture. The names "Velazques" and "Goya" under some of the pictures seemed to impress Mom and Pop when I repeated them at home, and one Saturday afternoon when they went on their *Spaziergang*, their customary walk, they tried to visit the Spanish Museum but found it closed. Still, Mom was pleased. "I bet none of these other refugees ever even put a foot on that place," she said.

It would be the Indian Museum, however, the Heye Museum, that called me back time after time, to take long walks in the echoing halls and explore the glass wardrobes and closets that held scalps, beadwork, belts, and breastplates made out of porcupine quills. There were cases of buffalo skulls, and models of Indian villages from different climate areas: bark and long-houses in the wet northeast forests, adobe and rounded hogans in the dry west. There were shields with colorful geometric designs dotted high along the walls. And there were the names: Pueblo and Cayuga, Arikara and Nikoyan, Cree and Taos and Crow. Perhaps these names were nothing like the ports along the French Channel, nothing like those points on a map where the *Caribia* made port, yet here on 156th Street, I was again carried over time and over cultures.

Aunt Irma made hats somewhere in the Garment District. Her husband Herbert had gotten a job in a "Büro," an office. Uncle

Theo, the Ph.D., found a job first at Klein's department store, then in a factory that tanned hides in New Jersey, across the George Washington Bridge. Oma Krämer crocheted table cloths and doilies and complained about the pain in her wrists.

With the war in Europe proceeding and American factories tooling up to supply armaments to our military and to Britain, and with a draft instituted that further depleted the reservoir of able-bodied young men, some refugees found work in those factories and made what was called "very good money." But Pop had not been in the country long enough to be allowed to work in a war factory. We were still considered aliens.

Through synagogue, Pop had made friends with a group of former cattle dealers, none of whom ever had the experience of working in a "Büro" but who knew enough of cattle excrement never to want to deal with it up close again. They had gotten jobs as house painters with the Rubinstein Company in the Bronx, and when a place opened up, they took Pop along, starting at fifteen dollars a week.

A good number of men who had experience on farms in Germany did become butchers. Butchers, too, made "very good money," especially if they worked in a union factory, but Pop had trouble with the sight of blood. So he became a house painter.

One day he came home whistling. He was a very good whistler, and if he was whistling we knew that he was in a good humor. He told us he had been given his first lesson in painting. Mr. Rubinstein was the teacher.

"Rubinstein told me that there were two ways of painting and two kinds of painters. He showed me. One was the Volga Boat Men, and the others were the Yankee Doodle Dandys. The Volga Boat Men are the guys who dip the paint in the pot slowly, and then slowly, very slowly, move the brush up and down on the wall to the sad tune, like funeral music." Pop whistled a few bars of "The Volga Boatmen." Then there were the Yankee Doodles — he whistled

"Yankee Doodle went to town" — who were happy, and dipped their brushes in the pot quickly, and happily made their brushes move quickly up and down the wall, all the time singing "Yankee Doodle."

"He wants me to be a Yankee Doodle Dandy," Pop said. I couldn't imagine it, but soon he was making eighteen dollars a week.

Mrs. Rubin felt my forehead and sent me home. My tonsils hurt. Mom took my temperature: 104°. It remained high, even with aspirin, and my tonsils still hurt. Two days later, a rash appeared all over my body. I heard Mom and Pop talking.

"Dr. Weiss, he would come. Three dollars I think."

"Dr. Joshua is better."

"Joshua charges five dollars to come to a house."

"Yes, but it's sure he comes and he's better. It's only five dollars."

"Only."

Mom hurried down to the Rosenbergs who were one of the few in the building to have a telephone. She called Doctor Joshua. He came late that evening. He bent over me. Oma, Mom and Pop hovered behind him. He put his hand on my brow. "Stick out your tongue."

I did. Mom said, "It's been white, coated like that since yesterday."

"Open your mouth wide." I did. He mumbled, "Forchheimer."

"What? What? We need a specialist?" asked my mother. "What kind?"

"No. Forchheimer spots. I have to call the health department."

Mom, who was not far from giving birth, yelled out, "What is it, what is it?"

"Scarlet fever." He took Mom by the shoulder and pushed her out of the door.

In the morning, an ambulance came. Two men in white coats and a stretcher entered the room. They didn't know how they were going to get me down those steep stairs on a stretcher until one of them suddenly picked me up and threw me over his shoulder. We clattered down the stairs, with women peeking out of their apartment doors, wondering, as we went by.

The back ambulance door was open, with a stretcher lying in front of it. I was plopped down on the tan canvas, and as the men in white picked the stretcher up I saw an arc of children watching me. I thought, *It must be a holiday*, there are so many kids outside and not in school.

I soon sat on a cold marble countertop in an examining room, while a nurse wearing a white mask took off my clothes. Then I was on another stretcher, on wheels, a stretcher that felt soft and was covered with a stiff, starched white sheet.

Then I was in a large cubicle, surrounded on three sides by glass. A number of white-coated men stood at the foot of my stretcher. They were nothing like the two from the ambulance. They had dark pants under their white coats, and their hair was nicely combed. One of them had a hypodermic needle in his hand. There was a silver tray at the bottom of my stretcher. More hypodermic needles lay in it.

"We're going to give you some shots. It won't hurt, just don't move," said the one holding the needle. He moved forward, lifted the gown the nurse had dressed me in, and stuck the needle into my groin. I screamed. He had lied; it hurt greatly. He made a face by pressing his lips together. He repeated the injection into different parts of my groin, five times. I kept screaming.

I was in the Willard Parker Hospital for Communicable Diseases, a massive red brick hospital that stretched for three blocks, downtown from 15th Street, along the East River. Here, children were brought from all over Manhattan, children with scarlet fever, polio, tuberculosis, anything and everything that might spread within a population at a time when there were no magic bullets to prevent or cure any of them.

I was in a ward for young boys. The ward seemed infinitely long, and the ceiling was very high. I lay close to the door, near the top of two great rows of beds arrayed the length of the walls. At the far end, windows looked out over the East River. There were windows, too, with large, heavy panes, behind the row of beds across from me, through which I could see men and women all dressed in white marching up and down. Sometimes they pushed the stretchers on wheels; sometimes the stretchers ferried people, and sometimes they had what looked like people on them, but they were covered by a white sheet.

We were visited by nurses whose faces were almost always covered by masks. We hardly ever saw their faces. The nurses might come with an alcohol rub to ease a fever, or bring a tray with food, and then I would see their raw, red hands. However she might tend to me, one nurse, on leaving, would always say, "I've got to go and wash my hands. I've got to wash my hands a million times a day." I wondered if the nurses washed the books every time we gave them back, since every few days they would come with little carts containing books. These were my entertainment all the five weeks at Willard Parker. Here I was introduced to some very wonderful new reading matter.

The books I liked were the "Twins" books, and there were a great number of them: twins in Alaska, in Holland, in Japan; American Indian twins and Indian Indian Twins; twins all over the world. I found out how life was lived in an igloo and how to skate on a frozen Dutch canal. The twins had names like Kit and Kat, Nip and Tuck, Toro and Take, Jean and Jock. The authors of my books had wonderful names as well, mouth-filling names, real American names, three-names-at-a-time names, like Lucy Fitch Perkins, who wrote all the twin books, and Albert Payson Terhune who wrote the True Dog Stories about Lad and Bruce and Buff. All truly great Americans had three names, like Franklin Delano Roosevelt. Three-name Americans all came over with the Mayflower; two-name Americans came from poor immigrant families who couldn't afford a third name, like Fiorello LaGuardia.

The best author of them all was John R. Tunis. I understood that the R. stood for a name, but one that he didn't want everyone to know, and that the fact that it was only an R with a period maybe meant that his family had arrived on a ship a bit later than the Mayflower. In any case, he was the very best. Because of John R. Tunis, I irretrievably bonded with the United States of America. *The Iron Duke* was the book, and Jim Wellington, long-distance runner, was its hero. The book featured Harvard College, where all the Mayflower descendants went to school, and it had courageous Jim at the 1936 Olympics, where he showed up Hitler.

I never read on Sundays. Sundays the books were underneath my pillow. Sundays I watched and waited. From waking to late in the day my eyes were on the wall of windows across from me. Parents, grandparents, brothers and sisters would appear there, smiling and tapping on the glass — other children's relatives. People mouthed words, and from my side the most common response was, "What? I can't hear you. What?" And then tears.

Pop did come, every Sunday, but usually quite late in the day. Until he appeared there was always the question: Would he? Several times Oma came with him and once, Aunt Irma came. But why didn't Mom ever appear?

Five weeks at Willard Parker, and then on a Sunday I was released, and Pop took me home. Walking to the bus, he said, "We have a surprise for you at home."

I wanted no surprises. What I wanted I did not know, but I wanted something as recompense for feeling abandoned and alone in that great brick pile surrounded by masked nurses with lobster-claw hands. On the long trip home, Pop kept smiling and asking, "So. Are you happy you're going home?" But I was in no mood to answer. "Just wait until you see the surprise." I wanted no surprise. Pop's cheery talk simply clamped my lips tighter. If I wanted anything it was silence and maybe a coffee ice cream cone.

We walked up the block toward our building. I saw Mom in front. There was a baby carriage in front of her. She waved. She came closer, pushing the carriage. I stopped, making her come toward me. She rumpled my hair. "Look. Look. Look what we have." I didn't look. Pop said, "Isn't this a nice surprise?" I shrugged. Mom kept saying, "Just look, he's such a pretty baby." I started toward the stoop steps. "Oh, don't be mad like last time."

"What last time?"

"In Ruppichteroth, with Peter."

I ran up the steps toward our apartment. I waited in front of our door until Mom and Pop came up. They came, Mom carrying the wrapped baby. "You didn't even ask his name. It's Franklin. That's the name of our president."

"Everybody knows that."

"Well, I asked the nurse in the hospital, what was the name of the president, and she told me. Look what I made for you." We were inside the apartment. On the kitchen table was a bowl of vanilla pudding. "We even got some raspberry syrup for you, special." Pop went to the ice box and put a bottle of raspberry syrup next to my bowl of vanilla pudding. Then he went downstairs to lug up the baby carriage.

I sat to eat the pudding, which I loved. I also loved raspberry syrup on vanilla pudding, but I refused to touch the bottle. I let it stand there. When I was finished with the vanilla pudding I licked out the bowl, something Mom hated us to do, but this time she said nothing except a low, "But we bought it especially for you."

Pop came up with the carriage. He was out of breath.

"Before the baby came, Aunt Irma gave us a carriage," Mom said. "We kept it behind the stairs, downstairs. Somebody stole it. Then Pop went to some of the supers in the buildings where he works and he asked them if they had any old carriages for the baby. He got six carriages from them!"

I looked around for them.

"We sold them all," Mom said with delight. "So we have some extra money."

I started to laugh at the thought of all the baby carriages filling the apartment, but then stopped myself. "Money to buy raspberry syrup?"

"That's right."

"But no money for stamps?"

"What do you mean?"

"Kids on the ward got mail all the time."

"There was so much going on here with the baby, the hospital."

"When was he born?"

"Two weeks ago. May twenty-first."

"Last week was my birthday. Twenty-sixth."

Then I ran down to the Rosenbergs and asked if Henry was in, but he wasn't.

Chapter Eighteen

One day, a large, shiny black car stopped almost in front of our house as Henry was teaching Karl and me about curb-ball after school. Home plate was right in front of our building, and the car, although it had a found a fine parking spot, kept rolling forward ever so slowly until we were forced to move our home plate further down the block. Henry had the chalk out of his pocket when a man in a dark suit and tie and shiny black shoes stepped out of the car that had made us move. Henry quietly cursed them, but then Karl ran up to the man and called out, "Aaron! Aaron!"

I would not have recognized him. Mom had given him Tante Irma's address on the ship, and through her he had learned where we lived. We took him upstairs to Mom. He kept looking around wide eyed as we clattered up all four stories.

Mom was waiting at the door. Aaron had hardly opened his mouth before Mom waved her hands in front of her as if to shoo him away. *"Wass will er?"* she said, what does he want?

Aaron laughed. *"Vass vill er?"* I can still speak some Yiddish. I have to go now, but after lunch on Sunday Jacob and I will come by and we'll have an outing with the boys."

"Outing? Outing?" Mom had never heard the word. "What is outing?" I translated. When she went shopping, she would point to the article and say, "That." When the total was rung up she would look sad and say, "So much?" I was embarrassed for my mother when we went shopping, and I was embarrassed for her now, standing in front of a man who was wearig a suit, white shirt and tie.

"I thought we might take them to Palisades Park."

"*Ja*. There." Mom pointed to somewhere across the Hudson. She looked at us and saw our faces. " *Ja, gut*. Okay."

"Good. Okay. We'll be here around one. Be ready. Goodbye."

We sat in the back seats. There were straps on each side of us, and Karl pulled himself up by it first, and sat with his feet under him so he could look out of the window. I followed.

"Just be careful," saud Jacob. "All this must be new to you. That's the Hudson over there, all that water."

I was about to say that I knew, but Karl looked at me with eyes wide and shoulders raised, so I clamped my mouth shut. "

"And over there, ahead of us, that's the second largest suspension bridge in the world. We're going to go over it."

The car veered from the highway and spiraled up a ramp one way and then another ramp another way, and we were on Fort Washington Avenue. A sharp turn, and then very quickly the great iron pillar, a huge arch with a great open mouth in its middle, appeared in front of us. We streamed through the open space and found an even greater wonder: the great silvery wave, the tube from which metal braids, silvery strings, descended. The great pylon that I had been looking at these several months just held the roadway steady, but it was this silver tube, the inverted wave, and the strings from which the concrete hung that allowed our smooth passage high above the water.

The first thing we had to do was to eat, said Aaron, but the first thing I wanted to do was to just walk around and look. In Ruppichteroth we had Kirmes, the annual fair. That's when they set up a merry-go-round with gold and ivory horses, and giant wire boxes on metal strings that once you entered them became swings, and carousels on which you sat in a giant clam shell or on a white swan poised at the end of a long red girder. There were booths where you could get mugs of sweet cider. But after a while, we Jews were not allowed to attend Kirmes.

Now we were at a Kirmes that was a million, billion times bigger than the one in Ruppichteroth, and Karl and I could go onto any of the rides and stand up in front of any of the booths.

"Food," said Aaron. "This place is famous for food. I go here just for food." We were both very quiet while people streamed past us and around us. The idea of food was good, but what we really wanted was to try some of the rides. Did they really bring us out here just for food? We walked through an area where people threw balls at objects and girls walked past us with giant dolls. Very hesitantly Karl asked, "Can we go on one of the rides?"

"Of course, of course, that's what we came for. I've been coming here since I was your age, here and Coney Island, but this was closer to your house. I was just saying that because I remembered the food!"

Jacob was laughing. "He was just kidding," he said. "These days we go downtown to very fancy restaurants when we want to eat, but we remember some very nice things we had here when we were your age. Maybe you'd like them too."

That's how we got cones of white paper filled with French fries with vinegar on top. I thought the fries were delicious but Karl almost threw up after the first taste. Instead he got this huge slice of vanilla ice cream stuck between two huge waffles. He slurped the ice cream and while most of it dripped on his shirt, Karl didn't care. He was happy.

The first ride — "We just have to do this," said Jacob — was the Ferris Wheel. There was something like it at the Kirmes in Ruppichteroth, but this was as different as a Kodiak Bear and a mouse. (We had just learned about Alaska in Geography.) In Ruppichtheroth, a man strained to turn a crank, which made the whole

Ferris wheel turn, and when the man got tired, the whole contraption stopped and you got stuck somewhere in the air until he could begin turning again. Here, a motor hummed somewhere and a man took your ticket before you entered your car. The ride started. Aaron pointed, "There's the Fun House, there's the Whip, there's the Saly Water Pool. That's the Roller Coaster."

We had passed the Roller Coaster and heard the metallic clicking of the chains grabbing a car. Moments later, the train of cars was pulled skyward, and the riders screamed as it careened down to earth. I had seen people exiting from the ride, some of them wobbling as if drunk. Jacob thought we might give the Roller Coaster a try; I thought I would wait until I was older.

Our Ferris Wheel rose up and I looked out over this great American Kirmes. What caught my eye were reflections that seemed to flash from everywhere: momentary bits of white from silver papers, white cups, mirrored semaphores that wove in tune with the happy murmurs from the crowds below. The Ferris Wheel came to a halt when we were at its highest point. Karl asked if the man who turned the crank had gotten tired and stopped. All I wanted to do was look, but I had to explain it wasn't a man but a motor. The view from the top was miraculous. We looked out over the Hudson toward Manhattan, and we saw practically all of Manhattan over to the East River. Ferries crossing the Hudson at 125th Street left silver wakes. There was Grant's Tomb. Jacob said, "Right there, that's Columbia University; we both went there."

I could not decipher one set of gray buildings from another. A train snaked northward along the Manhattan shore. The cars seemed so small. The sight led me toward the George Washington Bridge again. In the afternoon sun, the pylons looked dark red, and what was silver shone a bright white.

"There, there's the Empire State Building, the one with the spire, the tallest building in the world. And down there is the RCA building, Rockefeller Center, we're going to work there."

The rest of the afternoon was spent in bumper cars. I wanted to go and try other rides, but Karl didn't want to leave the bumper cars. I thought that Aaron and Jacob, too, wanted to stay with the bumper cars. They were laughing and whooping and bumping into each other all the rest of the afternoon.

Two weeks later, Aaron and Jacob came again in their shiny black car. This time they took us to a movie. The RKO Colosseum was on 181st Street. It was the largest theater we had ever been in. I must have been nearly stupefied. Jacob hit me on the back. "Take a breath. You can walk in now. Here." He handed me a small package that rattled.

There was gold scribbling on the ceiling and gold scribbling on the side walls. There was a high and far-away balcony. We looked for a seat in the orchestra. "The best seats are right in the middle. That way you can see everything," Aaron said. We made our way toward the middle of the great curving row of seats. "In the middle is where you see best because that's where the best focus is. The sides . . . ' Aaron waved his hand. "Eh, it's sometimes a bit blurry."

An organ was playing, pumping out, "Happy Days Are Here Again," over and over again.

Jacob pointed to our packages. "Try it. See what you think. It's what I always used to get." We opened our little boxes. Mine had chocolate-covered raisins. Karl had "Good and Plenty."

The organ stopped. The theater grew dark. A film came on. A little black girl sang, "A Tisket, a Tasket, a Green and Yellow Basket." Her name was Ella Fitzgerald. A slide came on. Tuesday night, dishes would be given away. The film then started. It was *Fantasia*.

We always had music in our house. Whatever happened, from morning until night, happened to a background of classical music. The radio station was mostly WQXR though in the early evening it was important to hear the news and the news was brought by Gabriel Heater with his signature "Ah, yes there's good news tonight." More often than not, as far as Europe was concerned, the news was bad. Then, later in the evening, WBNX came on, a German-language station all the way at the end of the dial. This station was much more important than WQXR. Its main theme was a waltz from the ballet "Coppélia," and all its ads were for restaurants and furniture stores in Yorkville, the German section of Manhattan. When the "Coppélia" theme sounded, we knew it was quiet time. The evening meal was over, Oma did her crocheting, Mom did her repairs on torn clothing, and Pop read *The Aufbau*. The station played, operetta music mostly, interspersed with Beethoven's overtures to "Fidelio." There was contentment in the living room as the familiar language and the familiar music played, but the listening became intent, with closed eyes and clenched lips, whenever the tenors Joseph Schmidt or Richard Tauber came on to sing their ballads. Mom's and Oma's faces showed thoughts to which I was never allowed entrance.

These pleasant, lulling tunes made me angry, although I never said anything. How could they fawn over German? How could they even listen to this language of people who had thrown them out, who had jailed them, who had burned their synagogues, and who had made abject and powerless the people you loved most?

"*Fantasia*, yes, that's nice, I heard about it. Classical music, like on the radio. How was it?" asked Mom.

Karl couldn't contain himself. It was Mickey, Mickey, Mickey, when all I wanted to talk about were the dancing Hippos.

"Mickey puts on this costume . . ."

"No. It was just the pointed hat."

"And he becomes the wizard . . ."

"No. He pretends, just pretends . . ."

"And then he makes this broom move . . ."

"No. First he makes it stand up, then . . ."

"He makes the broom hop . . ."

"The Hippos hopped . . ."

"Shut up. He makes the broom have arms and feet like fish . . ."

"Feet like flippers, like seals. Seals aren't fish."

"He makes the broom get water in buckets and fill this huge tub. And then he falls asleep."

"You're a fish."

"And then there's a huge flood, and he wakes up, and he tries to make the broom stop."

"You should stop."

"And the broom walks all over him and keeps on working. Then he gets an axe and chops up the broom and each piece of the broom becomes another broom and that broom carries two buckets of water . . ."

"What happens is they become a disgusting army rolling over everything, just like the German army rolling over everything. Mickey can't do anything right. It just gets worse."

"It doesn't get worse. The wizard comes back and the wizard just waves his arms and he makes everything nice and calm. I think the wizard is really President Roosevelt."

"Yes. Then President Roosevelt gives Mickey a swat on the *tokhus* for all the stupid ruins he made — just what he deserves."

Without much conviction, Mom said, "One of these days we'll have to see it."

For several weeks after that, on Sundays after lunch, Karl and I would stand downstairs waiting for the shiny black car, but the shiny black car never came again.

Chapter Nineteen

"I feel weak," Mom would say. "The four flights of steps are hard for me, with the baby. The steps are hard." Then she would breathe in and out quickly, and I would imitate her. "Don't make fun. One day you get old, too."

The weakness turned into pain in her shoulders and knees. One of the Jewish agencies sent a woman to come several times a week to help with the baby.

When she didn't come, it was frequently my job to change the baby's diapers. One night towards the end of summer, I awoke to Frankie screaming in his crib, and found neither my parents nor my grandmother at home. I went to a window facing the street and repeatedly yelled out, "Mom and Pop, if you don't come home I'm going to jump out of this window!" Mrs. Rosenberg heard my screaming and rushed upstairs and remained with us until Oma, Mom and Pop arrived back at our apartment. Evidently, there had been a birthday party for one of our relatives.

To Mrs. Rosenberg's questions regarding their leaving us alone, Mom replied, "What, are we, monks or holy sisters to stay inside all the time?"

It was afternoon, I was on my way to the synagogue for something when somebody yelled down from a fire escape: "The Japs have bombed Pearl Harbor, the Japs have bombed Pearl Harbor!" Kids playing curb ball on the street stopped and listened to the call, then went back to their ball game.

Mr. Klein was the first person I saw at the synagogue, "Walter, this changes everything," he said. "This changes everything."

Pop stopped going to work. He sat in the apartment all day, in the same chair, in his dark green pajamas, with his hands clasped in front of him, never saying anything. Mom said that Doctor Joshua had been there and that it was another attack of malaria, and a very bad one, but usually when Pop had a malaria attack he lay in his couch-bed with a fever, tossing and sweating. He did not sweat now. I was afraid. I didn't know what was happening, but I didn't really believe Mom.

We were taken to the orphanage by subway, Karl and I. It was the last station on the A train, Far Rockaway. Years later, if I mentioned the orphanage to my mother, she would say, "Ach, you shouldn't say that. It wasn't an orphanage. It was like a camp. A summer camp. A camp on the beach. And you came back. We got you back, you and Karl."

"If it was a camp, why did we go to school there, all of 5A?"

"So you went to school there. Was that such a bad thing? School? We couldn't do anything. Pappa was sick. I was almost sick. I couldn't go to work. We had no money coming in. Frankie and Peter needed me all the time. What could we do? You want to make me feel bad?"

I think I did. I know I did.

There had been nothing to prepare us for the place. One morning, Mom simply took us both by the hand, and Aunt Irma came along. She had the address and directions in one hand, and in the other a large paper bag containing some clothes. It was a very long ride.

We arrived at the orphanage on the day that the *Scharnhorst* and

Gneisenau, great German battleships, made a break out of the port of Brest and ran the English Channel past a terribly strong British attack and made it clean back to their home base on the Elbe. It was the day Singapore fell to the Japanese. The *Daily News* had it all. Someone had left a copy on a nearby seat. I read and re-read the paper all the way out to Queens.

The orphanage was a very large house, three stories, made of stone, almost a block long, almost a castle. There were turrets at each end of the roof. Dormer windows stuck out between the turrets like sniffing noses. The place was on the beach, and a cold February wind was blowing in from the sea. We walked down a ramp from the boardwalk into the arched entranceway of the building.

Mom bent down to Karl, her hands on his shoulders, her eyes just across from his. "We'll come and visit every week. Just a little while, you'll stay here. This is a nice place. Everybody says so."

I got a hug. When they turned to leave, I don't think either of us cried.

Mom sometimes would come, but not every week. We got postcards. Pop was getting better.

We were taken to a dormitory. It felt something like the Willard Parker Hospital, in that the two rows of beds might have gone on forever if they hadn't been intercepted by a wall with two windows. Each bed was covered either by a brown or a dark gray blanket. Somebody showed us the lockers next to our beds, but we had hardly anything to put into them. Somebody else showed us how to make our beds; we learned about hospital corners.

"It's not a bad place," said the boy in the bed next to me. His name was Arthur. He had a steam-iron kind of face, long, roundish, and coming to a point at his chin. He had a harelip.

"It's all right," he said. "You can look at it. I don't get into fights about it any more."

"You used to?"

"I've been here since I was three. I had a lot of fights." Arthur was eleven, a year older than me. Three times he had been up for adoption, he said once to a family in New Jersey. "Three times people came, but after they looked at me, I guess, they never came back. They have nice social workers here. They talk to you. They've arranged for a doctor at Mount Sinai to operate, and fix it after the school term is over. That's July. Four months. Most people here are really nice."

There was a synagogue in the home, where we went every Friday night and every Saturday morning. But the service was not conducted in any way familiar to me. Familiar meant the tunes that we had sung, the same tunes that my Opa sang and Rabbi Lieber sang and the whole congregation in Washington Heights sang, especially the tunes that accompanied the taking out and returning of the Torah to the ark. In Washington Heights, these tunes came from the throats of everyone around me, enveloping me the way Joseph's colored coat enveloped him. They were signs of favor and inclusion that touched me the way a gentle pat on the head from my father's friend touched me as we exited synagogue. That touch and the accompanying wordless smile said, "You are Oscar's son and I know you." These tunes said I was a part of all that black-suited crowd that flooded out onto Amsterdam Avenue. These others were the wrong tunes. *Va'yehi bin'sabah hoarau* and *Hodo al eretz v'shOmayim*, these were totally wrong.

In this synagogue boys and girls sat together.

We had been in America for almost two years. We were accustomed to America, accustomed to our neighborhood, accustomed to friends and streets for two years: Henry Rosenberg, and the grocery store on the corner, Hebrew school and Mr. Klein. Ruppichteroth and Machachi were memories in which the tough parts were on their way to being forgotten or changed so that smiles were interspersed with recall. Now this: strange songs that came to represent the leaving of every place I had ever left. They returned to me the shape of all those good-byes, in which something good in me had been taken from me, leaving black, dull, and sad feelings that became, after a while, a judgment: that I must have deserved good-bye, good-bye from Oma and Opa, good-bye from Chino, Chimborazzo, and El Professor.

The food in the orphanage was all right. There was lots of tomato soup, and sandwiches of white bread with thin smears of cream cheese or peanut butter between the slices. The bread had the crusts cut off. Friday night was chicken soup. Although it was announced as chicken soup, I always doubted it. Karl brought to my attention that you could see clear to the bottom of the bowl even though the bowl was full. Our mother's chicken soup was never thin and transparent, but dark yellow, with swirls and eddies of fat swimming on the surface. Everybody got a piece of carrot in our mother's chicken soup, and the bottom of the bowl was never visible until the bowl was empty.

The only work that was required of us was to keep the area around our beds neat and clean. In addition, we 10- and 11-year-olds were given a schedule for kitchen duty, to dry the dishes that the older boys washed.

There was a school. I sat in a room with perhaps thirty others, both boys and girls, a familiar schoolroom with blackboards and shiny blond desks. Construction paper of many colors, covered with writing, decorated the walls. The teacher was a man with a thin mustache, Mr. Teller, who read the newspaper *PM*. Every morning, when we came into the classroom, he was bent over the desk reading or writing something, and there was the paper on the left side of the desk.

Everybody in the class was smart. Should Mr. Teller ask a question — and he asked questions all the time — just about everybody, it seemed, had a hand up, except for the girl who sat in a seat in front of me. Her hand never went up, though every time Mr. Teller called on her, and he often called on children who did not have their hands up, she had the right answer.

"Ina, tell me about how we operate on rational numbers."

"By addition, subtraction, multiplication, division. That's how we operate." Her voice was low and had a sneer in it, as if she hated being asked something so very simple. She had straight blond hair that was cut like the Dutch boy in the paint ads. I liked her.

At lunch, when Mr. Teller guided the students out the door, I kept back and sidled up to the desk to try to read something from his folded-up newspaper. Maybe I could catch a headline, maybe there was something happening somewhere besides thin chicken soup and hospital corners. Gingerly, I tried moving the paper with one finger to see if it would unfold.

Mr. Teller stood over me, and I quickly removed my hand.

"Would you like to see the newspaper?"

"Yes. No." I ran out to lunch.

From the time in Germany when Pop set up our shortwave radio so that we could hear the reports about Spain, I knew that news was terribly important. What the radio said could bring Mom to tears and give Pop his very serious face, the one that meant we could not talk to him. I sometimes thought that the voices that came from the radio speaker were like herders of sheep, and we, all of us listening, were sheep shooed this way and that. I imagined that there were other voices behind the voices on the radio, who held knives for the sheep.

People left their homes for other countries because of news. Newspapers and radio broadcasts held information that meant life or death for somebody — somebody we might know, maybe even us, maybe even me. "Did you hear . . . ?" was a very scary phrase. Mrs. Brill in 4B had said that I was the current events kid. I heard her tell another teacher that I was a prodigy when it came to following the news. I looked up prodigy in the dictionary. I was very pleased.

When we had still been on the high seas, on the *Caribia*, we had heard about the Hitler-Stalin pact. I'd announced it to Mom, which was something of a coup for me.

"I can't understand it. I can't understand it."

"What's the matter, Mamma?"

She looked around, then whispered, "Stalin. Stalin signed a pact with Hitler. How could he do it? Impossible. Just impossible."

Later, Pappa had said, "You and your socialists. That's what you get." And for the first time ever, I'd heard Mom shout at him, "He's just playing for time. Just playing for time." Then she'd clamped her hand over her mouth and had begun to cry.

In Ecuador, the men had discussed the Finnish-Russian war with serious faces. We were still in Ecuador when the men, with joy in their voices that they communicated to all of us, had talked about this great warship, the *Graff Spee*, that had surrendered in the port of Montevideo.

We had just about arrived in America when, a few days after Pop's birthday, Denmark fell, then Norway. I read about how German soldiers, who as starving children in the terrible years after World War I had been taken into Norwegian homes to be fed and nourished, were now returning as strutting conquerors. The *Blitzkrieg* had overwhelmed Holland. Where was Tante Mina? She lived in Amsterdam. She had saved our lives, gotten Pop out of Dachau and then saved the rest of us by paying for our ship's passage and giving us money to live on in Ecuador. Pop always prayed that she might be safe, along with his cousins, Tante Mina's children, including my cousin Eva.

I wanted England and France to win, but the headlines of losses and defeats were stamped in big black letters almost every day. In June, Hitler danced his victory jig at Compiégne. But now it was 1942, Singapore had fallen, and the Scharnhorst and Gneisenau were safe.

Evenings, the great entrance hall of the orphanage became a place for recreation. Kids could play board games or cards, or do homework, although very little homework was ever assigned. There were several large bookcases crammed tight with books. Karl would wander around the hall looking at what other kids were doing, and so would I. Some played cards, pinochle or rummy. Chinese checkers seemed to be big, and so was dominoes. I wanted to do something with Karl, play a game, play cards, anything. He had on Pop's serious face, so I knew that he didn't feel happy.

In these early days of just looking around, I would often see Arthur and Ina sitting next to each other on a bench in a dark corner next to the player piano, each of them absorbed in a book. After several days of wandering, peering at what others were doing and getting stares from those I stared at, I wandered over to the bookcases. There were many fat books; a whole row with maroon backs and gold print, all written by Charles Dickens. Another smaller row, with black backs and gold print, was written by William Makepeace Thackery. There was a whole row of the same book: "Bible Stories for the Jewish Young."

Then I came upon a bunch of John R. Tunis books, and another set of my favorites, the Sam books by W. Maxwell Reed. Seeing them, I smiled and felt, for a moment, almost warm and almost at home. I had read *The Earth for Sam* and *The Sea for Sam*.

I was about to pull *The Earth for Sam* from the shelf when Ina, behind me, said, "I wanted that."

"Sorry. I just wanted to look at the pictures."

"Why," she said in a very dull voice, "can't you read?"

"I can read. I've already read this one."

"What's it about?"

"Is this a test?"

"Yeah. What's it about?"

"Well, it's about when the Earth was hot, and how the Earth was formed: mountains, rivers, volcanoes, glaciers, and glaciation." I was rather proud of glaciation, so I went on. "It tells about the different periods, Silurian, Devonian, and Carboniferous, that's when coal was formed, and it goes on with the Permian, the Jurassic and Triassic, and then it goes on with dinosaurs and human beings. There's some nice stuff about seaweed and jellyfish and shells."

"What's the picture you were looking for?"

"I wanted to see the ichthyosaurus, here," and I leafed until I found the full page picture of the massive ichthyosaurus, its sword-like bill and rows of sharp pins for teeth, swimming as if he owned the ocean.

"That looks like Mr. Kadish." This was Arthur, now looking over my shoulder.

Ina smiled for the first time. "In case you don't know, Mr. Kadish is a trustee." She strung out the word trustee as if it were important and foolish at the same time. "He comes once a month on a Sunday during lunch. He tells everybody, 'Be sure to brush your teeth.' And he pinches girls."

"Why, are they bad?"

Both Ina and Arthur giggled. I felt foolish, I didn't know why.

"It's about geology," I said. Ina took the book from me, and handed me the book she had been carrying. "Did you like it?

"Yeah, a lot. What's this?"

"I just finished it."

"What's it called?"

"Oliver Twist."

"What's it about?"

"Orphans." She took the book back and stuffed it between the others in the row with the maroon books with the gold writing on the back.

The lunchroom (it was the breakfast and dinner room as well) was very large. There were many rows of tables with benches attached, at which four or five children could sit per side. Along one of the long walls of the room was the cafeteria-style serving area, and behind that was the kitchen. On one of the short walls was a large bank of windows that looked out over the beach.

Ina, it seemed, was always one of the last to enter the lunch-room, and evidently did that in order to sit at a table where fewest other children sat. Her preference, it seemed, was to sit with her tray in front of her, all alone, on a bench by herself.

The first few days or maybe weeks I would try to sit somewhere with both Karl and Arthur, but then I copied Ina and waited almost to the end of mealtime to see where she sat, and then I would sit near her at the same table. I might try to start a conversation with her about a book or a subject from class, but she never answered me, never even looked up from her meal.

Arthur found my sitting at a table with Ina peculiar. "Why do you always sit with Ina?" he asked one sunny day in early March, as he and I looked for shells on the beach, where we were allowed if we were nicely bundled up and had a scarf around our necks.

"Huh?"

"With Ina at her table, all alone, and she never talks."

"I don't know."

"She hits."

"What?"

"She hits. At one of the movies, one of the older boys tried to kiss her, and she hit him with her fist on the nose so that it bled."

"That's funny."

"He had blood all over him. When we were 6, I think, one of the families that looked at me adopted Ina, but she came back after a couple of months."

"So?"

Arthur had dug something up with his hands, held it in front of him and dusted some sand off the object, then yelled, "A whelk! A whelk!" He ran back to our orphan home.

I continued to sit at Ina's table. After a week or two of her not speaking, she called across the table: "Can't you sit somewhere else?"

"It's a free country."

"Can't you sit somewhere else in this free country?"

"What are you going to do, hit me if I don't move?"

I couldn't tell whether the twinge in her lips was anger or the beginnings of a smile. "Yes," she said. It was the start of a smile that was quickly broken off.

"You can't hit me," I said, "I'm a bleeder. When I start to bleed I keep on bleeding, and it doesn't stop. My grandfather was a bleeder, and my father was a bleeder."

"Until all the blood is gone?"

"Probably."

"Are you related to the British royal family, or is it the Russian?"

"You don't have to be sarcastic."

"How come you're still around? You must have been scratched sometimes. Or at the dentist, people bleed at the dentists."

I remembered a line from one of my favorite radio programs, *Can You Top This?* "We didn't have a dentist, we were too poor."

"That's why you're here? You were too poor?"

"Yes. Why are you here?"

"I'm an orphan, and you're a hemophiliac. I don't want to talk to you any more."

We didn't talk any more, but a few afternoons later, I was doing homework in the hall when Ina brought over a set of Chinese checkers. Without a word passing between us, we played.

I was purposely slow leaving Mr. Teller's room, and when his attention was elsewhere, I fingered his folded newspaper just to get a peek at a headline. This day, at just a touch, the paper unfolded and the headline read, "GREAT BATTLE OF THE JAVA SEA." The first few paragraphs told of our Dutch, English, and American navies sinking great quantities of Japanese ships. This was heart-pumpingly wonderful after the scores of soul-eroding defeats that our side had suffered: France and Poland, the London Blitz and all the burning churches, Pearl Harbor, emigration.

"Something in there interests you?" Mr. Teller loomed over me. I ran toward the door.

"Come back here, you *vantz*." His voice was loud. It made me stop. "Now!" he said.

I wanted to run.

"Would you please come here?" His voice now seemed less harsh. I held onto the door jamb with one hand.

"Please, just for a second. I'd like to talk to you." The voice was now gentle, even kind. Very slowly, I returned to the room. I kept a desk between myself and Mr. Teller.

"It's okay, it's okay. I'm just curious. What's with you and this newspaper? I've been watching you nose all around it. Is there something in the ads you want?"

"It doesn't have ads."

"That's right. Not yet, *PM* doesn't have ads yet. So what is it?"

"The news."

"The news? What about the news?"

"I need to know the news."

"You need to know the news. Why?"

Suddenly I didn't know why I needed to know. I clamped my lips together. Tears began to form in the corners of my eyes. I bit down on my lips.

"You're one of the refugee kids?" I nodded.

Mr. Teller put a hand on my shoulder. "He's never coming here. Hitler." He smiled, "You don't have to worry about that, the Russians won't let him."

"I saw. Smolensk."

"You saw Smolensk?" He almost laughed. "Where'd you see Smolensk.?"

"Somebody left a paper here. A visitor. In the pot with the palm. Last Sunday. I saw about Smolensk."

"So, what do you think?"

"Maybe."

"Maybe what?"

"Things can get better."

"Things can get better? We're getting our *kishkes* kicked in all over the world, and things are getting better?"

I ran around the desk to where the paper lay and flipped it open so the headline was revealed. "Look, the Java Sea. And Smolensk."

Mr. Teller was quiet for a long time, while I just stood there.

"You know," he said, "if you want, you can have the paper. Take it any time. By the time I get to class, I've read it. So you can just take it. Okay? Only thing, when you're finished with it you have to throw it in the trash. You may not leave my *PM* in the pot with the palm. Okay?" Then he walked out the classroom door. I stood, looking in wonder, at the headline about the Java Sea.

"Mr. Teller stuck his head back into the room. "Take the damn paper already. You have to read the whole thing every day, cover to cover. There will be a test on it." Mr. Teller was just joking, there never was a test, except that sometimes he would say, "Make sure that you read this or that." He'd often say, "Read the letters." Many were about the difficulties "Negroes" faced in America, and I thought of all those friends at P.S. 46. But his most insistant "make sure" was the time when he said, with a very sad face, "Tom Mooney died," and then, in a loud voice, "Make sure you read the damn obituary."

I had to look up "obituary."

Tom Mooney had died. Tom Mooney was a Socialist, like Mom. Tom Mooney was for working people. He organized unions in San Francisco. He was accused of setting a bomb that killed six people but it was a frame up. He never did it, and everybody knew it. They protested. That was why his death sentence was commuted to life in prison, and he was in prison for twenty-two years. Reading that obituary, I learned names that stuck with me, mostly of those three-name people: Eugene Victor Debbs, William Jennings Bryan, H.L. Menken, William Allanson White, George Bernard Shaw.

(My mother thought he was a great playwright, which my father pooh-poohed, saying, "Of course, Goethe and Schiller are better. Shaw is too advanced. Like Ibsen," and that I shouldn't read him until I was much older and could really understand him.)

I learned that Franklin Delano Roosevelt had refused to intervene on Mooney's behalf. I was very much troubled by the idea that such an injustice had taken place in my new America.

I looked for the headlines every day, about the war, and I read the stories, but there also was "Barnaby," a comic strip about a little boy who had parents, Mr. and Mrs. John and Ellen Baxter, and an imaginary godfather, Mr. O'Malley, who said, "Cushlamochree." He had a magic cigar for a wand. Mr. O'Malley looked a little bit like mayor LaGuardia, but with wings coming out of his shoulders. There was also a talking dog, and a friend, Jane, and a mushroom, McSnoyd, who came from the Bronx. I think what drew me to Barnaby was the everydayness of the magic, of making the impossible a matter of course. It was an unreal real that had something of the ichthyosaurus, the Jurassic, glaciation and making the needed double-play at the absolutely right time in John R. Tunis' books. "Barnaby" was playful and funny; dogs talked; O'Malley who had to look up his Handy Pocket Guide before he could do a bit of magic.

There was something else: Mr. and Mrs Baxter. To me, they seemed far more magical than Mr. O'Malley. The way Mr. Baxter sat so easily in his easy chair, a pipe in his mouth and the day's paper in front of him, talking so easily to his wife, who sat across from him in another easy chair with a book on her lap, her face relaxed and her eyes large, and who answered her husband so easily — that was true magic. Mr. Baxter always wore a jacket and tie, and they lived in a house with a yard and a front lawn. Nothing ever concerned them except, perhaps, that their child knew something, saw something that they did not. Mildly, gently, while looking at their paper or their book, they might concoct ways for their boy to forget about pixies, but they had no idea of what really went on in Barnaby's head.

Dr. Seuss was in *PM*, too, not that we knew him by that name. That was to come much later. In *PM*, I thought of him as "Quick Henry the Flit," a slogan plastered on billboards everywhere, including the subways. Funny-looking mosquitoes were eradicated by flying Henry and his funny squirt gun.

Other drawings, cartoons very similar in style to Henry, also appeared in *PM*. Hitler was a leering flying dragon, costumed as from a weird Wagner opera, dropping bombs and laying waste English churches. Churchill was the knight in a Spitfire about to lance him. Mussolini was a power who could invade Egypt, but in reality he was a mere janitor trying to dust off the pyramids. McArthur was a hero wiping out Japanese sharks in a shooting gallery. No defeat was so serious that we would not ultimately triumph over it. That was the message. It drew some of the terror out of the terrorists.

Around that time, there was the wonderful British raid on the French port of St. Nazaire. German U-boats that were sinking our ships all along the American coastline were stationed in St. Nazaire. The report said that a destroyer had rammed a dock gate. I didn't know what a dock gate was, but I felt the magnificent courage of the tiny ship and felt the physical force of the crash in my bones. The harbor was blockaded so that U-Boats had difficulty coming out. British commandos took part in the raid, and I told Arthur and Ina that the second front was not far away.

We were beginning to hear about the great toll that U-boats were taking on coastal shipping. We had to make sure that our windows were covered at night so no light might spill out. If it did, the light would make it easy for the Nazi sharks to sink our ships. Block wardens were appointed, and just about every night one could hear somebody yell, "Hey, up there, turn it off." It was also the time, but I did not tell Arthur or Ina, that the Philippines had surrendered to Japan and all that was left to America was the fortress of Corregidor.

One evening the orphanage showed a movie in the large entrance hall. The lady who was the head of the home stood in front of us all and told us that we should be very thankful to Mr. Kadish, who was a trustee and who sent us these films every month from his office where he worked on Lexington Avenue. I sat at the end of one row, near the back, next to Arthur. This was going to be a wonderful film, she said, in color, of the great American novel, by the great American novelist, Mark Twain. It was called *The Adventures of Tom Sawyer*, and we should enjoy it and be grateful to Mr. Kadish.

The lights went out and a stream of light shot out from in back of us, a stream that was thin at first, then grew larger as it met the screen. The screen showed numbers that counted down from ten to three, and with each number there was a loud pop of noise.

Ina was standing next to me. "Move over. I want to sit." I nudged Arthur, Arthur nudged someone else and after a series of nudges there was Ina sitting next to me. I was very aware that Ina had punched someone in the nose while watching a movie.

I don't think I had ever seen anything so wonderful, not even Maureen O'Sullivan swimming in the water. The film was in color, it took place in the country, not in the city, and that it was set a hundred years earlier didn't matter. Injun Joe was a Nazi, and Muff Potter was my Opa. I had to marvel at that air of ease and indifference that Tom shared with the Baxters, and with which Tom got the others to paint that fence: that was American, that was beautiful. Could I ever own that air, that attitude? Tom was heroic, he spoke the truth and saved Muff/Opa from sure death. Was ever a knight battling a dragon more heroic, more honorable? And the reward? The praise of the town, the acclaim of the universe, and a little blond girl. But there was still more, a quest and submission to even greater challenges requiring even more courage: the cave.

The second Tom and Becky entered the cave, both my hands

gripped the edges of my chair. Bats were awakened from their sleep on the cave ceiling and swooped like solid pieces of a black cloud, and I heard Ina drawing a long breath. There were more long breaths when the cave-ins began. When Becky cried for her mother, there was a loud scream from Ina, with words that I did not understand. Everybody turned and looked at her. Ina reached for my hand on the chair and held it, and softly said, "I'm sorry. Sorry."

I whispered to her, "It's only a movie." She took a brief dark look at me, then she took her hand away.

I read that the Battle of the Java Sea had not really been a victory. The news came out bit by bit. British cruisers, Dutch battleships, American destroyers, all were sunk. There had been immense losses of men and ships that led to Japanese victories, first in Java, then in the whole Dutch East Indies.

But then there was the glorious raid on Japan. In the middle of April, Jimmy Doolittle took off from the carrier *Hornet* with his medium bombers, twin-engined B-25's, the ones with the glass noses and the bubble gun turret on top. They bombed Tokyo and other places in Japan. Mr. Teller began the morning by reading the whole story to us. "Hess," he called out, "you ought to get a scissors and cut this story out. Save it for your kids and grandkids. This is history. There are pictures."

On Sundays, many of the children would wait inside near the entrance to the home, though some would lounge out on the boardwalk, hanging over the railing along the beach, looking out into the distance, toward the subway station from which a relative might emerge. Sometimes Mom and even Oma would come out to visit on a Sunday. Karl and I watched for them. When they came near to us, Karl would run toward them, but I made a point of not running. I tried to look beyond them, trying to look for someone else, though he never came. When Karl asked why Pop never came, I would tell him, "He probably has to work on Sundays. He gets overtime on Sundays," but I didn't believe myself.

Although the entrance hall and dining room were set up to accommodate our Sunday visitors, if the weather was the least bit appropriate, Mom always insisted on walking on the beach. We would sit on the sand and Mom would begin, "Isn't this wonderful? Right on the ocean. The air so clean. The waves. The food here is good, I think," and then she would open the bag that hung at her side, place a large towel on the sand and unroll a few packages of food from the wax paper. It was mostly cake, Rührkuchen, a pound cake. From Oma we would each get a bar of Hershey's chocolate, accompanied by the plaint, "The chocolate in this country is not so very good. It was much better over there."

As we ate, Ina would circle our group from a good distance away. Sometimes she would hunker down and watch us. Mom noticed. "Who is that? Do you know her? Is it somebody from the home? Poor child, has she nobody to visit her today? Why don't you invite her to come and sit with us." Mom waved her arms toward Ina and called out, "Come. Sit with us." But Ina quickly jumped up and ran off down the beach.

At the end of our picnic, Mom would take off her shoes and socks, hike up her skirt, and walk out into the water to where the surf hissed, coloring the sand a darker tan. When she returned from her water-walk, she would say, "I could tell you to come in too. The feeling is so nice, but I know you wouldn't. I'm just glad you ate the cake. You are such a thick-head. Let's go back."

Walking back, Karl had Mom's hand. When we were almost at the entrance, she gave a big hug first to Karl, then to me. "Just wait," she said. "You are going to have a surprise."

Over the next several weeks we waited for the surprise, but none came. At each visit, we asked about it, and all Mom would say was, "Maybe I shouldn't have said anything. Pop said I shouldn't have said anything, but anyway, not yet."

Meanwhile Corregidor fell.

I mentioned to Ina that our mother had spoken of a surprise.

"You're going to go home soon," she said and from that time on, she seemed to disappear quickly after class, and there were no more checker games.

For several weeks, Pop came along on Sunday visits. He had on his smiling face, not the serious one, and I was glad for the smiling face. It was I who put on the serious one. I was happy that he visited, but not totally. Where had he been all those other weeks? We all walked out onto the beach. Mom waded. While I sat and watched her, Pop and Karl went looking for shells.

There had been a great sea battle in the Pacific, the battle of Midway, in early June, not long after my birthday. For six months after Pearl Harbor, the Japanese had won a string of terrible victories. All of Asia, all of the Pacific, seemed to be theirs. But at Midway, the Japanese advance was stopped.

It was Sunday, and the great victory spilled happy black letters over the newspapers' front. It was the Sunday that Mom came to take us home. Karl and I stood outside the office where she was filling out papers.

I looked around the entrance hall. There were the usual waves of murmur and silence, of kids talking, scraping chairs, looking into books and writing, studying, playing board games. Arthur stood nearby and waved to us. I saw Ina near the hall entrance. I walked over, and as I did she ran. When I reached the doorway, she was at the ramp down toward the beach. She ran, looked backward, stumbled, and then ran out farther onto the sand.

Chapter Twenty

The usual course from 162nd Street, where the A train stopped, would have been to walk a few blocks south on Amsterdam Avenue and then down 159th Street to our house at number 542. But this time Mom insisted we walk down 160th Street. I was puzzled. Karl said, "Mom, we're going the wrong way."

She smiled. "Now comes the surprise. We have a new apartment."

Walking down 160th Street, we crossed Broadway, then Fort Washington Avenue. As we approached the middle of the block we could see a slice of the Hudson River. The building, 652 West 160th Street, was on the south side in the middle of the block. Apartment 2C was one flight up, and Pappa was waiting for us when we entered.

There was a mirrored coat rack in the tiny foyer, but I was not able to take off my coat because Pop drew me into a living room that astounded me with its shine. There was shiny new linoleum on the floor; a shiny dining-room table at the other end of the room, a couch with a flowered covering along one wall, and a credenza of a dark shining wood across from it, with what seemed to be neatly carved little doors. There was a gold-framed picture above it, a watercolor of a street in Ruppichteroth.

I stared at the credenza and slowly ran a hand over its shiny surface. Pappa leaned against the credenza, looked down at me:

"Well, how do you like it?" There was a small smile on his face, an intense eagerness and an intense shyness. I understood from his look and from the softness in his voice that it was terribly important to him that I be pleased. I understood in some large measure that all the shine was there in order that I be pleased, that it was there to make up for the months that we had been sent away. By the look on his face I knew that he felt terrible that we had to be sent away and at the same time he wanted me to feel proud of him because there was a sense of immense accomplishment in the shine, that in the shine there were long hours of labor and pain, both his and Mom's. There was a pleading in his face: He wanted to be forgiven, excused. What I might say seemed to matter intensely.

I was glad that we had accomplished the crossing of Broadway, even awed by all the newness, awed by all the shine, but I felt totally apart, separated, unconnected to it. I wanted angrily to destroy it, rip it apart, because it had come at the price of being put away, sent away, feeling unprotected by my parents and especially by my father, who had sat there, in his green pajamas, saying nothing, as we were taken to the orphan asylum.

I felt terribly separated from my father, at an immense distance. Never before had I experienced this very real feeling that we were two different, distinct people. Where before my "I" seemed to extend everywhere that my interest or my caring led me, it now extended no farther than my skin. What he wanted so badly from me I could not give him. What he wanted me to acknowledge I could not, because just then I hated him. So I looked Pappa in the face, turned away, and said nothing. I walked around the room touching things.

There were framed pictures, photos of Pappa's parents on the credenza, a crocheted tablecloth on the new table.

"This is a wonderful country," said Pappa smiling, "Nothing down and only a few dollars a month and you can get anything anybody would want." Time payments. Now I had to worry whether these two people with their painter's and housemaid's wages would be able to make the monthly payments. Weren't we sent away because of their inability to manage?

I walked around the apartment. There was a kitchen where we could eat, and a small bedroom just as one came in the door. "That's Oma's room," Pop said. I opened the door and smelled camphor, liniment, face powder, and lilacs, a smell it would never relinquish in all our time at number 652.

There was another bedroom to the right of the living room. A crib in which brother Frank was sleeping sat to the left of the door, and across from the crib twin beds that had been pushed together. I saw a closet, an armoire, and a chest of drawers.

"That's all for you."

"For me?"

"*Ja*, and for Peter and Karl." He pointed to the chest and armoire. "These are not new. We got them second-hand on Amsterdam Avenue, very good and real cheap."

Our Sunday evening meal was of cold cuts and rye bread and tea. Cold cuts were always one of my favorite meals. It was delicious, better than any tomato soup and sandwiches of white bread with thin smears of cream cheese or peanut butter.

"So how is it? We got it special for you," said my mother.

I chewed, and when I had finished chewing my teeth were clenched and my lips were tight.

"Nothing? Nothing to say? We got it special for you."

I remained silent, and I remained silent through the rest of the meal. And I was silent, at home, for a long time after that.

Tobruk fell. Rommel was driving the British out of North Africa. Thousands of good men were captured, hundreds of guns and tanks fell into German hands. There were pictures of long lines of men with their hands on their heads. I had long been following the British and Italians chasing each other back and forth across Libya and Egypt, but now the Germans were involved, and Rommel was driving toward Cairo. He had bypassed Tobruk. His Africa Corps had Tobruk surrounded, and for heroic weeks it held out, but now it had surrendered. The names of Rommel's victories were driven into me: Homs and Misurata, Sirte and El Agheila, Bengazi and Derna, Sidi Barrani and Mersa Matruh. The war was one great geography lesson.

On a Saturday, soon after Karl and I had come back from the orphanage, after morning synagogue, after quickly slurping down the soup of our *shabbes* meal, and over our parents' protests, we ran out of the house to meet Henry Rosenberg in front of our old house. Henry walked us down to the Polo Grounds. From 159th Street it was a relatively short walk to the great Giant's stadium: over to Amsterdam Avenue, then St. Nicholas, where tall gray houses and high elms stood. From Coogan's Bluff we could look far down into the valley where the Polo Grounds stood. We could even see across the blue-gray Harlem River, and then farther yet, out over the distant roofs of the Bronx. Henry pointed. "That's Yankee Stadium, and on a good day you can even see the Long Island Sound."

There was the Polo Grounds beneath us. Even from our distance, it looked so very immense, like a great ocean liner, like the immense black flanks of the *Caribia*. I wanted to stay and look at the giant horseshoe building, which enclosed that patch of green, but Henry pulled me along. "We've got to get there soon."

Now it was down to 156th Street and the 156th Street Bridge, which vaulted the Harlem River, then down from the immense height of the bridge, via narrow metal stairs, to the vast field, far below, which lay like an apron in front of the great building.

At the bottom of the stairs we could see a group of black men distributed over that bare field. They were all dressed in white, and someone was hurling a ball with a peculiar motion at some sticks a good distance in front of him. A large man in white, holding what looked like a shovel, stood in front of the sticks. The hurler pitched, and the man with the shovel hit the ball and then ran back and forth to the sticks. There was great shouting from the men. Karl, very confused asked, "Is that baseball?" "

"No," Henry told us, "it's cricket. Those are men from the Islands, the Caribbean. He pointed toward the great stadium: "That's baseball."

People streamed out of the 155th Street subway station only yards from the stadium, and policemen guided them to their proper entrances. The stream declined to a trickle, and suddenly there was a huge roar from the stadium. "The game's starting," said Henry and motioned us to walk over to one of the heavier policemen who was bent over a car at the curb, yelling at the driver: "No, you can't stand here, don't you see the signs?" He whacked the roof of the car with his billy club as it drove off.

He turned around, and we saw the blue chevrons on his sleeve and the gold badge on his chest. A sergeant. Karl and I both looked at our shoes.

"And what might you two be wantin'?"

"We don't have money."

"Ya don't have money? Well, you have those black nice suits on, but ya don't have money?"

"Well, they're our *shabbes* suits."

"*shabbes* suits, eh?

"We have to look nice for synagogue."

"An' you don't carry money on *shabbes*. Right?"

We both nodded. Then I blurted out, "We don't have money anyway, we're poor. We're from Germany." If we hadn't been looking down at our shoes we might possibly have seen a smile on the sergeant's face.

"Poor refugees from Germany? From Hitler?" Nods. "Some of my Irish friends wanted to play footsie with the guy. But I told them that he's an unholy bastard. Sorry. Look, you just stay over there

—" he pointed to some dark depths near the stadium entrance — "and after the first half inning we'll see where there'll be some empty seats for you."

We waited, as latecomers streamed past. Karl and I both jigged up and down on our toes with excitement, and Henry asked if we needed to pee. The sergeant came by and also asked if we needed to pee. "Inside," he said "you'll see the signs for the toilets. Sorry you had to wait for the end of the first inning." He then ushered us into seats in far right field. "An' if you should come again on another *shabbes*," he said, "just ask one of my men for Sergeant Haase, I'm here mostly on *shabbes*, an we'll see what we can do for a couple of poor German refugees from Hitler." He patted us on our heads and disappeared.

Our seats were way back in right field, but in the first row. The richest green we had ever seen extended right and left and forward. "Look down there," said Henry Rosenberg, "that's Mel Ott." Right below us, we could see him, the great Mel Ott, doing some jigging dance steps and pounding his glove. "Does he have to pee?" asked Karl. I started to laugh. A contemptuous look from Henry followed. "Ott has more home runs than anybody except for Babe Ruth," he said. "And look, the pitcher. That's Harry Feldman, he's throwing to Harry Danning, they're both Jews. I think that's the first time in history that a Jewish pitcher is throwing to a Jewish catcher; and look, on second base, that's Sid Gordon, he's Jewish too. This is history. Today is history."

"History?" said Karl, "they play on *shabbes*?" We ignored him.

It didn't mean much to me, at first, that there was a Jewish battery and a Jewish second baseman. All the players were so small from where we were sitting. If the second baseman were playing third and the pitcher were somewhere in the outfield it would have been one and the same. To us, there seemed to be no distinctions in their uniforms. In the third inning, Feldman struck somebody out, and a great cheer went up from the stands. People rose and clapped. Behind us, all around us, people yelled wildly, "Way to go! Way to go!"

Feldman picked up the rosin bag, and threw it down hard so that we saw white powder puff out from the bag. Feldman turned around to look at his outfielders; he nodded, he grew majestic in his approval. He then turned back toward his catcher, his gloved hand resting on his hip. Feldman nodded to Harry Danning and began his wind-up, and the cheers grew louder.

Suddenly, I seemed to know Feldman. Feldman was Herbert Gärtner, the man who threw me up on his shoulders and carried me, Feldman was El Profesor, my teacher in Ecuador, the man who sat me up in a chair on top of a table and played the guitar in front of me. Now, the man on the mound in his cream-colored uniform was the only one out of all nine on the field that I saw. Feldman, with his high kick, became huge. I didn't see his face, and then his arm came forward and he released the ball, and with the pop in the catcher's glove I thought I saw myself standing in front of our burning synagogue, clods of dirt being thrown at me, a brown shirt with a camera smiling as he took pictures of our fear.

Harry Danning returned the ball to Feldman and Feldman again turned slowly around, his eyes panning the stands, seeming to take in all his audience with this slow turn of his body, and as he turned, and just with his turn, some of that fear that the German cameras had captured seemed to evaporate. A whole stadium had risen up and cheered the Jew Feldman. A great joy came over me. Here was a Jew who was cheered, a Jew who could throw a ball towards a man standing a good distance away, and he was cheered, he was a hero. He was Bar Kokhba, he was a Maccabee.

I started to cry, slowly, just moisture at the corners of my eyes, then more, and a hiccupping, then a loud bawling that seemed to burrow throughout my body. Henry pulled at my coat sleeve, and Karl looked at me, frightened, Mel Ott looked up at the stands behind him and then returned to pounding his glove.

I was happy, I was angry, I was sad. Watching Harry Feldman, I suddenly felt, though it was indistinct, that all my losses of people, of my Oma and Opa, my losses of place, my losses of the approval from adults who had a perfect knowledge of who I was, all those losses had a chance of being retrieved.

Early one August evening, my parents were out, I was in charge, and I was dialing the radio that stood on a small table at one end of the couch. Just about every station now had news "every hour, on the hour." And the news in the excited announcer's words was, "U.S. Marines land on the island of Guadalcanal." We were on the offensive in the Pacific, and I could see Harry Feldman pounding his glove after his strikeout.

A few weeks later, dialing the radio, I stopped and heard Colonel MacCormick announce, "And now, the Student Prince." Seconds into the overture, a voice broke in: "We interrupt this program . . . "

British and Canadian troops had landed in force on the French coast and had struck Dieppe. Naval and air forces, all were involved. The invasion of Europe had begun. I screamed for joy, I ran to the door and shouted out the news. It echoed through the hall and stairway. I kept on shouting, "It's started, it's started." I wanted to run to wherever my parents were for the night, but I couldn't. I pulled my head from the door when a neighbor shouted down the stairs for me to shut up. I was devastated when I heard later that it was all a false alarm. Dieppe was just a raid to test the German defenses. Oma and Opa, their freedom, would have to wait.

That fall, Karl and I started at Public School 169. On the first day, Mom led us to the school and to office ladies wearing yellow or blue sweaters with their eyeglasses on strings around their necks. They asked us where we had gone to school before. Karl said, "In an orphan asylum." Mom said, "No, no." And the lady in the yellow sweater, smiling, her eyes large and her head tilted to the side, said, "How nice that you adopted them, and you're here just how long?" Mom simply shrugged and said nothing. The lady in the yellow sweater, who could bellow down the hall when a child was doing the forbidden running, would always smile and rumple my hair whenever we met.

Public School 169 was on 168th Street and Broadway. From our house that was only two blocks east and eight blocks north, but it was a new geography for me, a new terrain that I had to negotiate. I knew that Manny Kirchheimer, a friend I had met through synagogue, went to P.S. 169, but Leo Levy, Jack Williams, John Harmon, Don Serealles and all the others did not. They were still at P.S. 46. All those dark face and those few white faces were gone; the spirituals were gone. Here the faces were all white, all cross-Broadway faces that I hardly knew.

"We have, all of us, been promoted from 5A1 to 5B1, haven't we?" said Mrs. Hohenstein, smiling. "But today we have a new addition to our group. Walter, please stand up and tell us something about yourself." I mumbled, "No," and shook my head. Then, in the kindest way, she said, "It's all right, you don't have to." It's then that I stood up and mumbled something about Germany and Ecuador and P.S. 46 on Amsterdam Avenue and that now we lived on 160th street and Riverside Drive.

I had lied. I had given the impression that we lived on the corner of 160th and Riverside, when we actually lived several houses distant from the Drive. I was appalled that I had lied to a whole class and to my teacher. But lying was not new to me. Soon after returning from the orphanage, I had again met Manny Kirchheimer, and we had become friends. Sometimes we would play chess up at his house. when he asked me where I had been all these months, I told him, "In Hollywood."

Manny was impressed. "Yes," I continued, "while I was there I became friends with Mickey Rooney. And he took me all over the place, showed me things and introduced me to a lot of movie stars."

Manny was very impressed. The next week, in synagogue, his mother, sitting next to mine, asked her if it were really true that I had been in Hollywood. It was Mom's turn to be appalled.

"When were you in Hollywood?" Mom asked me later. My red face answered for me. "Shame. Shame on you for telling such lies. Shame." She turned away. I wished that she had given me a spanking rather than provoking this burning face.

After lying to my school, the next morning I came very early and found Mrs. Hohenstein at her desk. "Please, Mrs. Hohenstein . . ."

"Yes, Walter." The Walter came with an inflection that indicated that she was not sure of my name.

"I don't live on the corner of 160th and Riverside Drive."

"All right."

"I really live several houses from the corner, and . . ."

She looked straight at me for what seemed a long time. "You've been on a long trip haven't you?"

"What?"

"I mean, Germany, you said, and South America, and then here. That's a very long trip. And you've been very lucky."

"Lucky?"

"Yes. After all the things we read about Germany."

"My Oma and Opa . . . that really means grandparents in English . . ."

"And you're worried about them."

I nodded. "I read all those things too."

"Tell me about what else you read."

I told her, starting with Karl May and Sven Heddin, then going on to all the twin books, the Sam books and on to John R. Tunis. She smiled, wide-eyed at each mention, saying, often, "Really! Oh, really!" in a wonderful, approving manner. But the time I got to *PM*, the classroom was almost full. They had waited while Mrs. Hohenstein and I talked. Now, she raised her hand, a signal for me to stop, and in the kindest voice, a voice meant just for me said,

"You know Walter, in this class facts are really important. I put a great stress on facts in this class, but you know, stories are important, too."

For the rest of the morning I tried thinking about what she meant. Yes, facts. All those facts about the ways the various twins lived, all the facts that *PM* told — but could I also tell stories about living where I didn't live? Lies were stories, weren't they? I was confused.

It took Rabbi Lieber to straighten me out.

He was now teaching my class at Hebrew school. Rabbi Lieber had a club foot and he wasn't a rabbi, he was our cantor. He had a beautiful voice. But the congregation didn't have enough money to pay both a cantor and a rabbi, or people said that the congregation was too cheap to hire a rabbi, it depended on to whom you talked. (After a while, Rabbi Lieber did become a rabbi.)

He announced one day that for our perfect attendance, he would take the class to a play. Perfect attendance was easy — Mom saw to that. Only a fever of 102° or above could possibly interfere with our study of Hebrew. Since no such luck pursued me that year, perfect attendance it was.

The play was "Life With Father." It was my first play since coming to America, and it was wonderful. We came early and sat in a high tier from which we could see the audience entering and find ing their seats. The seats were a burnished rust, and the wooden arch in back of them, running from wall to wall, had the same patina, and even the lighting from the chandeliers bathed the whole theater with this red-copper tint. It was a shine that I have always connected with gentry, and it somehow mocked our unsettled refugee status.

The audience laughed out loud, but we didn't, when Mr. Day came to the breakfast table and bellowed that the New Haven Railroad had suffered another accident. His stocks — his stocks! How I wished that my father might have trouble with the stock of the New

Haven Railroad.

The play, said the program, was based on the book by Clarence Day, Jr. On the subway ride home, I asked Rabbi Lieber, "So what does 'based on' mean?"

At the subway station, he had rushed to ride in the very front of the train, at the front window, to watched it hurtle through the tunnel. I was next to him; the front of the train was also my favorite place. It raced and rumbled, and its light made the tracks shine.

"Well, it's like wood," said Rabbi Lieber, looking straight ahead. "'Based on' is like a tree. You cut up a tree and the wood from it is used to build a house. That wood isn't a tree any more, because now it is a house. So you could say that the house is 'based on' a tree. So: First there was a book that told the story, then there was a play with actors who spoke the lines that came from the book, but it's really not the same any more."

"So it's not a lie."

"Well, even lies have something 'based on' them, something that happened before. Lies don't come out of nothing. There's always something that came before, before somebody lies, and some real reason in the person's mind for his lying."

I didn't know what my real reason was.

"You read books, yes?" he continued. "There are stories in the books. The stories are made up. Somebody makes them up. Okay? Would you say those are lies? Is the Lone Ranger or the Green Hornet a lie? No they're stories that you like. Is *They Died With Their Boots On* a lie?"

"No, I don't think so," I said. "It was 'based on.' Based on General Custer and the Indians. Okay, I get it."

As we were walking down 162nd Street, Rabbi Lieber came back to the subject. "You know, there are all kinds of lies. You maybe heard of white lies? Like, '*Ja*, you look wonderful today.' If you like a person, you might say that even if the person had pink spots and blue stripes all over their face. Lies are terrible if you hurt somebody with them. But you can't always tell if you are hurting somebody else with a lie — and sometimes, maybe, a liar is only hurting himself. So maybe the best thing . . ."

"But what about the Ten Commandments?"

"That is a very good question. We should discuss it the next time in class."

We never discussed it in class, not the next time or any other time.

So if my lies didn't hurt anybody, I was okay? If, if, if, if. But I knew very well whom my lies hurt. Still, "based on," somehow, had possibilities for bandaging the wound.

Chapter Twenty-One

We were reading about Christopher Columbus in class. History was my favorite subject. Our teacher, Mrs. Hohenstein, had the custom of sometimes lending a student a book on a particular subject, and this time I was the recipient, and the book was on Columbus, and this is what I read: He had been questioned, derided, and taken for a fool and all for his belief, his certainty that the Earth was a globe. And he traveled long, a nomad almost, with his son from one European court to another so that someone, king or queen or prince, might provide the money for ships so that he might prove that the Earth was indeed round.

It occurred to me that I could do something "based on" Christopher Columbus. I could write a play, *Columbus!*, about his travels, the contempt and scorn shown him at first, and then his final triumph over those who had derided him. I began walking around with a little pad of paper. On the way to school and on the way home, I would talk to no one. If an idea struck me I would write it down. Mrs. Hohenstein noticed.

"What are you putting in that pad? What's so important?"

"Nothing." Yet I was full of wonder at myself, at what I could do, at what I could summon up with my pencil. Just thinking and putting it down. It was marvelous, a great joy, and it was not lying. When I finished, I transcribed it in ink, and the next morning in school I placed it on Mrs. Hohenstein's desk. Then I waited. For three days in her class, I sat rigid and still, my hands folded tightly in front of me on the desk.

On the third day, just before afternoon dismissal, Mrs. Hohenstein said to me, "Please stay for a minute." It was the "please," that made me marvel at what might come. Mrs. Hohenstein's voice was always kind, with "please" always somehow implicit in her questions or demands, but now the "please" was voiced. I was proud. I felt selected.

"What would you think," she said, "if we put on your play in an assembly before Columbus Day?"

"The assembly? The whole school?"

"I re-typed your play," she said, and waved some sheets at me. "Tomorrow we'll hand them to the class and see who wants to play which part. After that, we'll arrange some time for rehearsal and you can direct all the players. I like the way," she added, "you have Columbus overcome all odds and opposition, the way he achieves his victory."

All I could do was smile, nod, and run off. The play was cast, rehearsed, and presented twice, once for the lower grade, and once for the upper grades. There was a great deal of applause, and a lovely note from the principal home to my parents.

A few weeks later, as we filed out of the classroom for lunch, Mrs. Hohenstein said "please" once more and asked me to wait. "The National Board of Review asked the school to choose three or four students to help review movies for them. We thought you might be interested in doing that."

"Doing what?"

"It means, maybe once a month, to go down to the Paramount Theater . . ."

"Where Frank Sinatra is singing?"

"I don't think it would be on the Paramount stage, but somewhere else in the building. You would go down there, they would screen a film, and then ask you to write down your opinion, what you thought of the film. Do you have someone to go with you downtown?"

"I can go downtown by myself. My mother lets me."

"The principal needs a note from your parents to that effect."

"Sure."

"I'll tell Mrs. Maloney, then, that you'll do it."

"Sure."

I felt washed clean, relieved of some of the fear, the almost constant tension in my belly, the feeling of strangeness in almost every vista, the feeling that everything was temporary and provisional — all those feelings that had been my intimate possession since leaving Ruppichtheroth. On the way home, I looked down at my shoes: no hobnails now. I crossed asphalt and concrete rather than cobblestone. The stores that I passed were familiar — not in the way my blacksmith had been familiar, or my chestnut trees or Harry Regensburger's bakery, but part of my landscape, now, the peripheral backdrop to what now was my home.

Here was the White Tower, where some kids might buy the forbidden food, hamburgers. Here was the Audubon Theater, a movie house where upstairs, in the ballroom, Rabbi Koppel had his synagogue. Here was Estee Chocolate store, which, before Chanukah, would buy the candles that Karl and I sold in the neighborhood. Here was Lieberman the butcher, who did not buy candles from us. Here was Spector's deli, which had a barrel of pickles standing near the door, pickles that were almost as good as my Opa's. Here was the Daitch dairy, whose butter was almost as good as my Opa's. Here was Bernie's candy store, where I might buy a piece of gum for a penny. (I would work there later as a soda jerk. Some of my parents' friends would come in and say, "Ach, Wolfgang give me please a cherry soda." They'd drink the glass halfway down, "Ach, Wolfgang, please, a little more soda." They'd take a few gulps, "Ach

Wolfgang just a little more spritz of syrup. Okay?" Of course okay.

(Bookies gathered in back of Bernie's. One of Bernie's bookie friends had given him tickets to a Giant-Dodger game he could not use. It was a night game, and as I was not working and he was, he gave the tickets to me. It was the night that the Dodgers' Rex Barney pitched a no-hitter. Bernie was so jealous of my having been a witness to so rare an event that he fired me.)

"Mom, I need you to write a permission slip."

Mom did not hear me; she looked down at an envelope in her hand.

"Mom, I need a permission slip."

"Since when are you getting mail?"

"I need the slip so I can go downtown. For school."

"No. You can't go downtown by yourself. Why is General Motors sending you mail?"

Nothing happened in my life or in the life of my brothers which our mother did not make it her business to know. Privacy may have been difficult anyway, given the closeness of our living arrangements, but at least as it pertained to her children, it was a concept with which Mom refused to deal. So it was all the more surprising to me that the envelope that Mom held was unopened. She began to wave it at me. "Since when is General Motors writing to you? Who do you know at General Motors?"

"It's probably a ticket."

"A ticket to where? You got stamps for gas?"

I tried to reach for the envelope, but Mom pulled it away.

"It's probably a ticket to a concert," I said.

"What concert, big shot? You're going to the philharmonic?"

"No. Toscanini. It's at the NBC symphony."

Mom tore open the envelope and looked at the ticket. She seemed stricken. "Toscanini?" she mumbled, then said, with full maternal authority, "No. You can't go."

"Mom!"

"No. You can't go downtown by yourself. You're too young. No. Not by yourself. The crowds, the subway. It's hard for me, even."

"Mom, you can't come along. There's only one ticket. You can't get in. The ticket is for me, not for you."

"Don't worry about me, I'll just stand outside the door and listen, but I'm going along. I only want you to be safe."

My friend Gary Thalheimer knew all about music; his uncle, after all, the one who lived a few houses down from ours, owned recordings of all the hundred and four Haydn symphonies. All of them stood arrayed in yellow sleeves on the bottom shelf of his bookcase. Gary knew a lot about a lot of things. Sometimes, on weekends or holidays, we'd walk down to the playgrounds next to the Hudson River and talk. About music, Beethoven was really the best, Brahms — well, almost there, but not like Beethoven. About politics: I went with the American Labor Party, but Gary was for the Liberal Party. The Liberal Party was supported by the garment unions, and Gary's mother worked in the garment industry. About which was the better paper, the *New York Post* or the *New York Times*. I was for the *Post*, but Gary was for the *Times* even though the *Post* supported the garment unions. About the war: Stalingrad. Oh, God. If the Germans break through at Stalingrad and get to the Caucasus oil . . .

I would keep track, to myself, of how many different topics we might touch on during one of our walks. And we had decided, on one of them, to try to get tickets to one of the Toscanini NBC concerts. Since General Motors sponsored the concerts and General Motors had a headquarters building on 57th Street, why not go down there and speak to someone about getting us tickets? How Gary knew that we had to speak to someone in "public relations" I will never know, but one day after school we went.

The young woman at the desk, just past the great glass doors, said no, they didn't give out tickets to the concerts and that anyway, for tickets, you had to send to this address in Detroit. I thought of Sergeant Haase and began talking about the fact that we were poor refugee kids whose families had fled Hitler and that we loved Toscanini the great anti-fascist . . . The lady smiled, stopped me, and ushered us toward an office where we repeated our stories to a man behind a desk. He smiled and had us give our names and addresses to the young woman and told us that in two or three weeks we would be receiving tickets.

"Gary's mother is not going with him," I said to my mother.

"If Gary's mother does not care what happens to him, it's not my business. I care what happens to you. You are not even twelve yet."

"You don't really care about me. All you care about is getting to see Toscanini!"

"*Quatsch. Ganz falsch.* You are completely wrong. How can you say that? I would never ever say something like that to my mother. You'll see. I will stay behind you. A good distance away. You won't see me. I won't embarrass you. If I see that you do all the right things going downtown, I'll sign your paper."

"It's not my paper."

"Whatever."

The Sunday came, and I dressed in my *shabbes* suit. Mom looked like she was going to meet the president. From somewhere had come a dark coat with large shiny gray buttons, and a gray fur collar. "I got the hat from Irma. Not too fancy, is it?" There were feathers in the front of the hat. I wanted to pull them all out. I just did not answer her.

As we were walking to the subway, she said, "Even in the subway I will stay away from you. Just don't run away to the next car." How could she have read my mind? I hurried out of the subway; Mom hurried after me. At the Sixth Avenue entrance to the RCA building, I said, "Okay, you stay here. You said you'd stay outside."

"In this cold? You're so smart, you know this is November. I hope you don't mind if I stand inside the door and stay a little warm."

"Okay. Inside the door. Here. But that's all." A crowd had gathered about one of the elevator banks. I followed them. Yes, here was a sign, "To Studio 8E." I jammed myself into the elevator full of people, took my ticket out of my pocket and held it in a fierce grip.

Just across from the elevators a uniformed man was taking tickets. I turned around just as Mom came out of the elevator. How had she ever gotten into the elevator and come out in back of me? Mom rushed to the ticket-taker. "We got only one ticket, but I have to be here with my son. He's just too young to be by himself."

"One ticket, one person. No ticket; no person. Make up your mind who's going in."

While people piled up behind her, Mom argued, "My child, he's so young," but to no avail. I showed my ticket and took a step toward the hall.

"Lady, you can sit on that side bench, and wait for your kid."

"It's all right, Wolfgang, you go. It's okay. I'll just sit back here and listen. Don't worry, it's okay."

I didn't worry. I was now inside and Mom was not. Halfway down the aisle I looked back, and through the open doorway I saw Mom gesturing and again arguing with the guard.

Gary was already in his seat.

It was a wonderful concert. I heard the Coriolan overture for the first time. I had a marvelous view of Toscanini, his wonderful animation, his marvelous white head as he turned to us to bow.

The main program was Beethoven's Third Symphony, with that marvelous tune right in the first movement that Pop always whistled. "Everybody around here knows that tune," he would say, "here" meaning Ruppichteroth. Whenever Pop said "here," I had to wait for the whole story before I knew whether he meant Washington Heights or Ruppichteroth.

"You can hear them whistling when they just walk through

the woods, or when they're raking hay. Everybody knows it. That melody comes right from here. They're whistling the Eroica, but if you told the farmers that, they wouldn't know what you were talking about. You know that Beethoven came from Bonn, twenty miles away from us, don't you?" And Humperdinck, he came from Siegburg, he got his tunes from "here," too.

The concert over, I sat for a moment longer, after all the applause, to watch the musicians stand, collect their instruments, and leave, or simply stand and chat with each other. When I turned to leave, and there stood Mom in the rear of the auditorium, smiling.

"He let me in. He was such a nice guy. I asked if there were any empty seats and he said yes, a few, and he let me in. Please don't be mad. We can tell Pappa about the Third and that nice tune he whistles. Wasn't Toscanini wonderful? Please don't be mad. Gary, wasn't Toscanini wonderful?"

Mom had stopped working as a cleaning lady. She now had a job as a cook in a kindergarten just a few doors down from our house. The kindergarten had been established by one of the newer refugee organizations, by upper class West End Avenue and even some Park Avenue ladies. Mom called them the "*Shutz-Juden*" ladies. The "*Shutz-papier,*" a letter of protection, was given in the late Middle Ages until the 18th century to Jews who, in one way or another had been helpful to the reigning authority. The papers could also be bought.

These letters of protection were no patents of nobility, though many with such a document seemed to have adopted the manners of nobles. Passed from one generation to the next, the papers granted their possessors privileges that were far and above what the rest of the Jews were allowed, and in modern times, a woman with such a history might often become Lady Bountiful.

One day, while making tuna salad for her charges, Mom went to mixing all her ingredients in a huge bowl with her hands. Suddenly several of the *"Schutz-Juden"* ladies appeared behind her. In a voice shuddering with indignation, one of them said, "Mrs. Hess, I'm appalled! Really appalled! Stirring the food with your hands?"

Mom, thinking that the best job she'd had in America was about to be lost, held up her tuna-covered hands. "I was only thinking of the children, Madam. I was making sure there were no fish bones anywhere."

"*Ach, ja.* That's wonderful. Thinking of the children. Very nice, very nice."

"And they went off muttering," Mom reported, "about that wonderful Mrs. Hess."

While Mom may have been wonderful to the children at her kindergarten, to her sons she was often less than wonderful. While other kids were playing outside, we were indentured to inside work. "I don't have any girls," she would say, "so the boys have to do the job." But not boys, only me! Karl had outside work as a delivery boy for a drug store in the afternoons, and gave Mom part of his pay every week. Therefore I had the job of scrubbing the kitchen and bath every Friday afternoon and laying down newspapers on their floors so they wouldn't get dirty so quickly. On other days, after school, I helped Mom with "homework" consisting of cleaning zippers and, somewhat later, inserting toothpicks into white beads for costume jewelry.

It was wartime, of course, and whatever factories had made metal zippers in peacetime were now fashioning the tools of war, so some enterprising soul was collecting all the old and discarded pants he could find, tearing the zippers off their fronts, and giving bundles of them to women who, with a single edged razor-blade, could separate the pants' cloth from the cloth in which the zippers were bound. Sunday was the day that Mom made her trip to somewhere in the Garment District and returned groaning with heavy sacks of zippers. For the rest of the week, and except only for my school homework or truly unusual causes, I would sit and separate the stinking pants from the stinking zippers. It was stupid, hard work to which attention had to be paid, since we were working with sharp objects. I still have a long scar on my right arm that was the penalty for a wandering mind.

Mom joined me in the work in the evenings. She was paid pennies for each zipper cleaned. Later, shortly after the war, when zippers for men's pants began to be manufactured again, a neighbor entered the fringes of the costume jewelry business. It was his job to prepare recently stamped-out white plastic costume jewelry beads for their baths in colored paint. To prepare them, toothpicks had to be stuck into the holes. Now Mom was paid pennies per gross of beads. Everybody in the house participated, from Frank, the youngest, to Oma. The work was just as boring, but less dangerous than zippers.

Henry Rosenberg introduced me to more than the New York Giants and the English language. On the west side of Broadway, between 159th and 160th Streets, up a long flight of stairs and down a long hallway and just before one reached the local pool hall, there was a huge loft that stretched over the ceilings of several stores and had a wide bank of windows that looked out over Broadway. The loft was the center of the Maccabi sports club for immigrant youth, an Jewish organization that a number of refugees who had arrived in the 1930s organized. Its aim was to provide a meeting place and a facility for recreation and sports for young immigrant Jews. There were similar organizations created and led by earlier arrivals, such as the New World Club and the Prospect Unity Club on 158th Street, but ours was Maccabi.

The vast room had two ping-pong tables, a scattering of tables and chairs where one could sit and perhaps sip a 7-Up — bought at the canteen of the billiard parlor with tips from running errands.

Henry Rosenberg was a brilliant ping-pong player. From five, six feet away from the table's edge he could hit a vicious backhand slam that intimidated every opponent. His cutting delivery of shots that he retrieved, it seemed, from nearly under the table brought gasps from onlookers. After a while, Henry was forbidden to slam either forehand or backhand because the force of his stroke often dented a ball. It was wartime after all, and ping-pong balls were extremely hard to get. After a while, to get anyone to play with him, Henry was made to play with his left hand and spot opponents anywhere from five to twelve points.

Henry was also the star right wing of the Maccabi men's soccer team. It was soccer, really, that formed the matrix of all our belonging. Maccabi had a junior soccer team to which I and all of my friends belonged.

The league in which we played was — we all felt the irony — "The German-American Soccer League." It was impossible for me to understand how we could play in a league that had the word "German" in it. There was even a team called the German-American Club. There was also the Irish-Americans, the Italian-Americans, the Czech-Americans, the Hungarian-Americans, and the Pfälzer, who were Germans from the region of the Palatine. Why Pfälz had no "American" appended to their name was always a mystery to us.

During the fall and early winter, the Maccabi juniors would play home and away games with about a half dozen of these hyphenated Americans. Interesting to us was that all of these hyphenators seemed to live in parts of the city that had large open green spaces and parks nearby where our opponents were able to practice their soccer morning, noon, and night. We Maccabi, except for Dicky Strauss and Frankie Spiegel, were a group of flabby kids, mostly parent-driven bookworms, whose only soccer practice was the half hour warm-up before games.

Dicky was our brilliant goalie, Frank our hugely athletic center-forward. Every year we came in last in the league standings because we lost every game we played. But if Dickie could hold the opposition to no more than three goals, or if Frank could put at least one of his bullets into the net, we would count that game as a victory, and the senior Maccabians who chaperoned us would, after the game, treat the whole team to sodas.

My great dread, each year that I played soccer, was the trip into the wilds of Queens, somewhere under the Throgs Neck Bridge, to play the German-American boys. A group of the senior members of our club, those who had cars with a sticker on the windshield that allowed them to purchase gasoline in wartime, would drive us out to the field. We would see our opposition, already on the green turf, booming shots from mid-field, it seemed, while others, in a file, raced around the field's perimeter singing — *the Horst Wessel song,* I thought, which, of course, it was not. The game would begin, and all thoughts of attack were gone as we were instructed to play defense. I tried keeping up with their striker, this 12-year-old who could run and at the same time keep the soccer ball magnetized to the toe of his shoe. Their whole front line, in fact, their whole team, had legs like young birch trees, and while they ran with ease, never seeming out of breath, we panted and hoped for the whistle that would end the game.

It did end, five for them and zero for us, and we slowly dragged ourselves to the locker room. On the way we had to pass a gauntlet of our opponents' parents, who smiled at us as we passed. One of them patted my brother Karl, just ahead of me, on the back and said, "Nice game."

Karl turned and screamed at the man: "I'm practically blind and I can read better than you can!"

Chapter Twenty-Two

I cried when I heard Churchill in November. His words, rumbling from that great belly, were broadcast, it seemed, almost every hour. "This is not the end. It is not even the beginning of the end. But it is, perhaps, the end of the beginning." The words thrilled me, as they came in the wake of the great British victory at El Alamein, where Montgomery had beaten Rommel and the Africa Corps. Still greater, Americans were invading North Africa and had landed in Casablanca and Oran. There were battles in the Pacific, too, but what was happening against the Germans was of overwhelming importance to me.

For many weeks, Churchill's words were replayed in the newsreels. If I put my ear to the unattended back door of the Costello movie house on Fort Washington Avenue, I would hear the sounds from inside the theater. My ear was often at that back door, and one day I was struck with an idea. I ran to the ticket-taker wailing, "Please, please, I have to pee, I have to pee. Let me in to the toilet. Please, or I have to do it right here!" He let me in. I stayed, slumped in a seat all the way up front to see Churchill twice make his speech.

A bit later in the year, Pop came home from work one evening and said, "I heard a terrible thing on the radio today." He was washing himself, stripping himself of the paint on his hands.

Mom was setting the table, "What terrible thing?"

"From the Warsaw ghetto." Pop came out of the bathroom, drying his hands. "They are sending people from the ghetto to Treblinka."

"What place is that?" asked Mom.

"It was on the radio, from England. A man, Murrow, was saying it from London, that an Englishman in Parliament said there were two million Jews killed in Poland and Russia."

Mom slammed dishes down. "Bastards, bastards, bastards! And we don't give a damn. Nobody gives a damn."

In selecting me for the Young Reviewers, Mrs. Hohenstein gave me a great gift. The films I saw, all of them, were American war films, anti-Nazi. They told me that my country was aligned with me in my anger, my fear, my hope, and that no matter what happened, ours would be the victory. They told me that we were good, and so I was good.

I saw the films in a special screening room at the Paramount Theater, the Paramount with its wonderful stage shows and its prices that my family could not afford — the Paramount, where bobby-soxers went wild over Frank Sinatra. I sat in a private screening room, the beam of light shooting over my shoulder to project these wonderful dramas onto the white screen. The best of them was *Sahara*. Bogart was the tank commander, not even an officer, simply a sergeant. In the early part of the film, he collected a ragtag crew for his tank, black and white, French, Italian, British, a melting pot of justice, a noble joining of shining knights set against evil. Bogart was fair and just and wise; he was Roosevelt and Wallace and LaGuardia. He was Moses. He joined foresight and courage in a desert world in order to find water for his people and to guard that water because it was life. And with a knight's bravery, he denied that water-well, that life, to the enemies of life.

There was *Five Graves to Cairo* with Franchot Tone, Anne Baxter, Erich Von Stroheim and Akim Tamiroff. Von Stroheim was a magnificent Rommel. There was fright in this film, and there was, at the same time, lightness and even humor in the struggle. Tone told me that whatever the burden was, it need not be an impossible weight. Here, again, as in *Sahara*, all the people of the world, whatever their station, were united with me in the fight against the Nazis.

Two other films presented more difficult problems: *Hangmen Also Die* and *This Land is Mine*. These two were full of moral dilemmas and turned on choices that very ordinary people needed to make. I didn't know, then, that these were called "moral dilemmas," but I knew about the ache in the belly and the wool in the head that some people experienced when they were forced to consider for whom to make out an affidavit for America. A beloved aunt or a sister? And did one have the courage to appeal for funds to a well-off distant relative, to beg and to grovel for the twentieth time for maybe just one more affidavit?

Charles Laughton was a schoolteacher in *This Land is Mine*, who saw himself as a coward but was forced to bring himself to behave with courage. *In Hangmen Also Die,* Brian Donleavy was compelled to choose between his own life and those of many others. Both films pointed great red arrows at Germany, at all those good people who avoided choices or made the wrong choices, all those people who came to watch while we were being photographed in front of our burning synagogue.

Mrs. Hohenstein's gift had another dimension as well: It began to shape in me the impulse that guided me to my future career in film.

In early February of 1943, we heard about one of the great victories of the war: The German Sixth Army was broken, the siege of Stalingrad was over. The numbers of casualties were enormous. We didn't always believe Russian announcements — that is, Pop didn't. "They exaggerate. They always exaggerate."

Mom, who was ironing, gave Pop a dirty look. He smiled and

added, "But in a war everybody exaggerates."

Three hundred thousand German soldiers had been killed; a hundred thousand were made prisoners. Four hundred thousand Italians, Rumanians, and Hungarians had been killed, four hundred thousand were captured. "Anyway," Pop said, "Tim O'Shenko did a great job."

"No, Pappa," I said, "It wasn't . . . and his name is Timoshenko. It was General Chuikev that did it."

"Irish, Russian, what's the difference? We won."

In May, as I began my *bar mitzvah* studies, the Germans in North Africa surrendered to the British. In June, Pop came home with the *Post*, and before he took off his painting clothes or even washed, he lay the paper on the table and called everybody to come see. Mom, Karl and I peered over his shoulder. "Look at this! Cohen captured an island, a whole island. My God, *borukh habo*. Look at this and read."

I read, and was filled with a real whooping joy that Cohen had captured the island of Lampedusa, a tiny island in the Mediterranean near the island of Sicily. Sergeant Cohen was an RAF flyer who had crash-landed his plane on the island. When he walked away from the crash, the whole Italian garrison walked toward him with their hands up."

Mom smiled at Pop, "Good thing that you are 4A."

"What's 4A?"

"Pappa's draft number. 4A means that he's too old to be a soldier. I think he feels he wants to be like Cohen. Good thing he's 4A."

That Saturday the whole synagogue was all buzz and smiles, "*Nu*, what do you think of Cohen?"

"We need Cohen to land in Italy, to land in France. They hear Cohen is there, and they all come out with their hands up."

"The war's over: Cohen did it."

"Thank God for Cohen. Cohen, the king of Lampedusa."

As American and British forces invaded Sicily, a brand new list of joyous names entered my vocabulary: Agrigento, Trapani, Palermo, Ragusa, Catania, and Messina — all Allied victories. In early September, the Allies invaded the Italian mainland in Calabria, and soon after, Italy surrendered to them. One down.

In the American landing in Anzio, a young man from our congregation was killed. Herman Kahn had volunteered the day after Pearl Harbor. The Kahns lived on Fort Washington Avenue, and whenever we passed his building, someone would say, "That's Herman Kahn's house." I never passed the house without a sense of awe. He was someone I hardly knew, but had sometimes passed in the street, or had seen being called up to observe the first Torah reading because he was a Cohen. A very quiet man with large furrows in his brown face — he had been killed fighting the Nazis. One Cohen was master of a whole island; another was killed fighting the Nazis.

It was a Friday when we heard the news. That evening, the synagogue was more crowded than on any holiday. At the end of the services, all the men passed in front of Mr. Kahn, Herman's father, and with awfully serious faces, shook his hand and nodded in understanding. The women, all of whom sat in the rear half of the synagogue, passed in front of Mrs. Kahn, nodded and shook her hand. There were no tears. A large red bordered flag with a gold star was added to the front of the synagogue. Before the war ended, two more gold stars were added to the flag.

That fall, I began Stitt Junior High School 164, on 164th Street. between Edgecombe and St. Nicholas Avenues, on the edge of Harlem back then. Stitt was supposed to be a "rough school," which we all understood meant that it was primarily black.

Most of my class from P.S. 169 was now in 7AR (the "R" stood for "rapid," because at some point we all were going to skip a grade), but not everybody came; a number of parents, not many, had moved heaven and all the connections they had to have their children enrolled in a more light-complected school up in the hundred-and-seventies on Fort Washington Avenue. Still, while I missed some people, I was now reunited with some of the friends I had made earlier in P.S. 46: Leo Levy, Jack Williams, John Harmon, Don Serralles, Harvey Groppa.

From Groppa I learned about bebop; from Seralles, in our arguments and discussions, about British colonialism in India; from Williams, about singing and Welsh song. Leo Levy is my friend to this day. John Harmon saved my life.

At Stitt I encountered a remarkable set of teachers, as I did throughout my school career. It seemed that at each new stage of learning, I was provided with someone to give me what I needed. At Stitt there was Mr. Pressman, with English and *Julius Caesar*. Mr. Pressman had a thin black mustache and wore a different suit every day, each a different shade of dark blue. There were stories that he told off-color jokes and pinched girls. So we all sat there waiting for the jokes that never came.

Before Mr. Pressman, Shakespeare was a name in quotation marks. The name existed somewhere, close to that space where also lived the names of Theodor Herzl, Heinrich Heine, and Albert Einstein. But now Shakespeare became real, and *Julius Caesar* became real.

My joy, however, was clouded right from the opening. There was Shakespeare's wonderful punning, awl in all. But the deriding of the commons in *Julius Caesar* was something I thought shameful. Did we not live in the time of FDR and democracy on its worldwide march (except for the Nazis and fascists, of course)?

What was *Julius Caesar* like, Mr. Pressman asked. And he guided the answers. It was like politics, like Tammany Hall, like Sicilian gangsters, and somebody called out, "like the numbers game." Who were the good guys? I needed good guys. Disturbingly, Mr. Pressman did not even leave Brutus with any kind of nobility because

Brutus has to lie to himself to make himself believe that Caesar is a "serpent's egg." Mr. Pressman didn't seem to know that I was in a war where there were good guys and bad guys — and everybody knew who they were. Mr. Pressman seeded our 12-year-old minds with doubt about the motives of many in this world, but it was his real intention to have us search deeper than the surface.

There was not a black child in our class who did not understand the nature of race in the United States. There was not a refugee child who did not understood the stakes in the war against Hitler and fascism. Mr. Pressman's *Julius Caesar* became for some of us a vaccine that inoculated against facile questions and easy answers. And with all that, there was Shakespeare's music: For several days, we wanted to speak in nothing but iambic pentameter.

Mr. Stitt's foil was Mrs. Morton, who became our homeroom teacher for several terms. Circling her room above the blackboards were oaktag signs with the large black letters, MYOB, Mind Your Own Business. Mrs. Morton was small, wore a yellow-brown wig, and every once in a while had me take clothes of hers to a cleaner down on Broadway. One day, at dismissal, she bent close to Leo and me, and in an intimate tone, one that an aunt might have used with her nephews, she said, "Listen, I see you always talking and playing with all these *schwartzes* in the class. And you have spin-the-bottle games? Do you have to do that?"

We both looked at her face. How she learned about spin the bottle, I didn't know, but without hearing another word, Leo led our way out of her room,. Not then or ever afterward did we speak about the incident, and never again did I carry Mrs. Morton's clothes to the cleaners, nor was I asked to.

Often, at lunch time, a number of us would play in the school-yard, where the lines for a handball court had been painted against one of the school walls. They were two-man games where the winners would stay on the court and the aspirants hang around the edges, waiting, and while waiting talk about everything in the world. At one of our playground, sessions Don Serealles broached the idea that after we all finished high school and college, we would again join together and start a company that would manufacture chains. Chains would somehow become terribly important after the war. So our group, black and white became "The Chain Corporation." And indeed, once or twice, at someone's house where both parents worked, we had interracial spin-the-bottle games.

My long preparation for *bar mitzvah* was about to end. I had labored long over a Torah passage that I thought mostly boring. The passage I wanted to read would have dealt with Joseph, my hero, the greatly loved child who made it big in his exile, his new refugee home. But the section about Joseph was read in cold wintry weather, whereas my portion was read in spring, determined by my birthday, was called *Naso*, from Numbers 7. It was full of picky details such as who was to carry the furniture of the Tabernacle through the desert, how to tell if a woman was unfaithful, and the contributions of the splendid utensils given by the rich princes of the people to the Tabernacle.

Rabbi Lieber was very displeased with me when I expressed my feelings over the portion: that making a special group to carry the Tabernacle furniture reduced people to slaves. If carrying the furniture even of the Tabernacle were such a great honor, I said, it should have been distributed to all the people.

I said nothing about the testing of the strayed wife, though my mother thought that it was grossly unfair that a suspicious husband could initiate a test for the wife while nothing was said about a suspicious wife having a husband tested. But as for the rich princes making donations to the Tabernacle, they seemed to me like the rich ones in our congregation making contributions and so purchasing honors for themselves. When I repeated as my own something my mother said — that not merit but money made distinctions in the synagogue — the rabbi, with some heat, answered that we were created to try to understand God's word, not to judge it.

There was one other Torah portion that made a great deal of difference to me. It was a section that dealt with the laws concerning the Nazarites, who abstained from wine and consecrated themselves to God. This section in the Torah fetched an additional reading from Judges, the section concerning the birth of Samson.

Manoah was Samson's father; the name of Samson's mother is never mentioned. An angel, announcing the birth of Samson, appeared directly to the mother, but Manoah waited in a field until the announcing angel neared. This image of a man standing in a field, the grass ankle-high, somewhere a barn, somewhere cattle on a green hillside, the man waiting and still waiting while from a far distance a man, maybe an angel, approaches, filled me with expectation, an expectation without anxiety. It made the boring parts of the Torah seem bearable. The image of the angel arriving had a golden aura surrounding it.

On the day I became a *bar mitzvah*, I read my portion, synagogue was over, and we hurried, practically running the three blocks, to our apartment to prepare for the rush of my parents' friends who would come soon after the midday meal, for the obligatory congratulations, the *schnapps* and cookies. Soon after returning home, I turned on a radio. Whatever it was that I was listening to was interrupted by a bulletin, and I could hear the excitement in the announcer's voice.

"It has been reported from London that the invasion of Europe has begun. British, Canadian and American troops have landed on French soil."

I was quiet for a good while, amazed that this epic event was coupled with my *bar mitzvah*. Saturday, June the third: Hitler was done for, Oma and Opa might be retrieved. I announced it to my parents, who were in the living room putting liquor bottles up on the credenza. We had to have a drink, Pop said, a toast to the success of the Allies. To my amazement, he asked me what I wanted.

I asked him what he was drinking, "Slivovitz." "Me too, Slivovitz."

The afternoon was noisy. All our visitors could talk about was the invasion, and there were loud toasts to the invasion. I was glued to the radio. Later in the afternoon, with the visits over, there was a special service in synagogue for the success of the invasion. I remained home, stuck to the radio.

At about 7:00 p.m., the radio told of official denials from Washington and London: No invasion had taken place. My day had been uncoupled from the epic event, and I was uncoupled from great joy. Three days later, however, on Tuesday, June 6th, the invasion of Europe did, indeed, begin. The gratitude I felt, the joy in this immense effort, was the same as if it had happened on the day of my *bar mitzvah*.

Much later, in film footage of the invasion, I saw the same shots repeated, from inside the boat, the hatch opening, the troops pouring out into the water and onto the beach, some falling or stumbling into the water — and then the shot from the land, toward soldiers running onto the beach. They run, some stumble, and one man, just as he reaches dry land, is toppled instantly. I would eventually see those shots over and over again in my career editing documentary film, and that I would come to mourn that soldier as I do my friend Willi, as I do my grandparents.

I was not only a poor soccer player but a terrible athlete. In any of the street games I was usually the last one picked.

We were playing stickball, and it was my first time at bat, I had one strike. Suddenly, windows from buildings on both sides of the street were flung open, and children, mostly my friends, began yelling down to us, "President Roosevelt is dead. President Roosevelt is dead."

We rushed to our houses, to our own radios for confirmation. I heard funereal music interrupted by confirmation. I wanted to stay at the radio but could not — I worked as an errand boy at a local drug store and was already late. It was a three-block walk, and all the way to the store, from window after window, people cried out that the president was dead. Soon after arriving at the store, my boss sent me home and closed up.

Arriving home, I saw Mom in a chair in the kitchen, crying. "They killed him. They killed him. Just like Rathenau, the same thing, exactly the same."

Pop was standing over her, bowing over her, his hands on her shoulders. "No, that doesn't happen here. Things like that don't happen here. This is America; it's a different country, this isn't Germany."

Mom just kept on crying. Pop opened some cans, and we had soup for supper and nothing else.

At school the next day, Friday the 13th, we were called to an assembly in the auditorium. The hall was packed, and my class stood in the aisle. Our principal walked onstage. He was a very small man, Mr. Fitchhandler, bald and stooped. All he said was, "This is for our dead president," and he went to the piano that always stood on one side of the stage and played the funeral march from the Chopin B-flat minor sonata. We had the record with Rubinstein playing it.

Almost every night after supper, Pop spread a map of Germany on the dining-room table. "How far are we from Ruppichteroth?" he would ask, and in black ink scratch the advance of the Western armies toward our Rhineland town. In early March, he was in a jubilant mood. "Look here. They crossed the Rhine on the Ludendorf Bridge. The Remagen Bridge. You crossed the bridge already when you were a baby. I crossed it lots of times, lots of times."

One Saturday morning, toward the end of the service in synagogue, someone posted a list of Jews near the exit door, maybe two thousand people who had somehow been transferred by the Red Cross from the concentration camp at Buchenwald to Switzerland. Even before the service ended, there was a mad rush toward the door for a look at the list. There was a pushing and shoving, loud curses and loud cries of pain.

Pop stood at the back of the crowd. He found a bench and sat, holding Peter's hand. The rush went on, with perhaps a hundred people all trying for a look at the list while Rabbi Lieber continued with the service, his high baritone cutting through all the noise.

With the end of the final hymn, Mom, who always had sharp elbows, emerged from the crowd, sat next to Pop, took his hand and shook her head.

Not long after the end of the war, Leo Baer visited us. He was still in his uniform, a major's oak leaves on his shoulders. Leo was a distant cousin of Pop's and came from Nümbrecht, a village close to ours. He sat on our couch, relaxed, smiling, his outstretched arms resting on the back of the couch. All of us sat around him in a circle while he told his story.

Leo had enlisted early in 1942, and had received a battlefield commission in Africa. I wanted to know what he had done to achieve it, but he just smiled and went on with his story. Because of his fluency in German, he had become a translator in surrender negotiations with the German army in Africa, then later, after the invasion, for the 7th Army in France. Like Pop, Leo was anxious and excited about the progress of the war and went every day to check the maps at Army headquarters that would tell him how close the leading units might be to our old town. Once the line nudged close, he begged the commanding general to allow him to lead the first troops and the first tank into Ruppichteroth.

As Leo told his story, I was with him. I saw his head sticking out of the lead tank. I saw the tank rumble up past our house, past our synagogue, past Gustav Gärtner's butcher store, past Aunt Lydia's house, past the kiosk where I would read who I was and who I was not, to the street where the lead Nazi, Löwenich, lived. Leo had ordered Löwenich arrested and thrown into jail by the special occupation troops that accompanied him. Then he'd gone down to the Willach factory, which made guns and machinery for Hitler and his army. He found hundreds of dead slave laborers and a thousand other bodies on the factory grounds. He made the villagers come out of their houses and give burial to the dead and bring food to the starving survivors.

He found one of the Willach brothers hiding in the basement of his mansion. The man broke open his basement wall and uncovered a small, hidden safe. He opened the safe and dragged out gold coins and jewelry. He offered the lot to Leo, just to be left alone. Leo beat Willach to a pulp and turned him over to the occupation troops.

Not long after the war, early in 1946, Mom and Pop began receiving letters from several families in Ruppichteroth with whom they had been close. In the letters were indications that food was scarce. Almost immediately Mom and Pop began sending them packages of food that included instant coffee, sugar and cans of Crisco. I would not take or accompany either of them to the post office to mail these packages.

"If it hadn't been for some good Germans, you wouldn't be alive today," said my mother. "If Hitler had been against bicycle riders instead of the Jews you would have put on the nice brown uniform and marched with the rest."

Usually, on those occasions, I did not answer her because there was a softness in her assertions, a softness that told me that despite everything, leaving Germany had been an enormous loss for her. Although we were all alive, and perhaps life in America was better than what she might have had in Germany, there were still associations, an intimate history.

Not long after Leo's visit, I saw Pop on the street, six floors up, in his painter's clothes, painting a fire escape. He had recently gone on his own, formed his own painting company, with four or five employees, but still, every day, he went out on painting jobs. I thought of our time on the *Caribia* when he had grown dizzy, almost fainting, from looking down onto the ocean from a high deck. Now he was earning our living on those spidery slim steel stairs six flights up in the air. Did he dare look down? Had he overcome his fear of heights? The thought struck me that I had always thought of my parents' whole generation as weak. My father in his paint-smudged clothes, my mother on her knees cleaning floors, were now silently shaming me, and I began to cry, understanding how truly strong these two really were.

Chapter Twenty-Three

Miss Seidl taught English at the George Washington High School in upper Manhattan. Actually, it was a writing class. She was tall and slim, with dark hair piled up high on her head. As no teenager is capable of judging age, Miss Seidl was at various times deemed to be 30, 40, or 50. As far as I could tell, she was not quite as old as my mother, who was then in her late forties.

Miss Seidl wore makeup, pewter earrings, and soft corduroy suits. Her face was both stern and questioning, hard and soft at the same time. Before she asked a question, she would look up at the ceiling for what seemed a long time, and think. Her eyebrows often grew together when she was listening. When she spoke, it was abrupt, soft, and energetic, with a conviction that no rabbi I had ever heard could summon. She hardly ever sat at her desk, but walked back and forth in front of the blackboard, or up and down the aisles between seats. Yet there was nothing nervous about her movements or gestures, only control.

While other teachers might read the tabloid *News* or *Mirror*, and many, the *World Telegram*, and some had the *New York Times* on their desks, Miss Seidl read the *Herald Tribune*. Just as one could practically determine somebody's class and ethnicity by knowing which New York baseball team they rooted for, a somewhat similar determination could be made by knowing which New York newspaper they read. If you read the *News* or *Mirror*, you were working class, the *Times*, intellectual, *World Telegram*, civil service (it carried news of teacher job openings or Board of Education tests for higher job categories). The *Herald Tribune* spelled WASP, but what kind of a WASP name was Seidl, and what about the "Miss"?

One beautiful spring day, Miss Seidl stood at the front of the room and commanded, "Everybody out of your seats and get over to the windows. Tell me what colors you see."

Puzzled, we all looked at one another. While Miss Seidl often sounded both kind and peremptory with her requests, her voice seemed a bit harsh this time. Nevertheless we all crowded to the bank of windows that flanked one long side of the room.

There was a broad lawn beyond the windows. Bordering the lawn were young sycamore trees, and at about the middle of the lawn, perhaps twenty yards away, was another stand of trees. Beyond them were several more that guarded the red brick walls of an old-age home, the only other building on St. George's Hill.

"So what do you see?"

From twenty or so voices came the loud reply: "Green."

"Look again," Miss Seidl said.

There were loud whispers, astonished and questioning. "It's green," various of us repeated.

"What else? The tree trunks?"

A girl turned to her and said, "There are shades of green."

We all turned and saw, standing next to the wardrobes, Miss Seidl with a great smile on her face. "Wonderful. Just wonderful. You saw. And just how many shades of green do you see?"

For the rest of the hour, many shades of green were seen. My favorite was "baby green grass." For many days after, we saw the many differing shades of color on our classroom walls, on the walls of houses, on lawns, on the leaves of trees, on faces, on the surface of the Harlem River, in the blue sky. We saw shades in each other's faces and in the faces of strangers on the street. We saw shades in our reading and in our discussions. Our eyes and our minds had suddenly become conscious.

Everyone who went through one of Miss Seidl's classes read *Queed*. *Queed* was written by Henry Sydnor Harrison, a three-name person with a very strange middle name. *Queed* had been among the top ten of bestsellers in the year 1911. What initially captured me about the book was Miss Seidl's intense interest in it. She did not gush, but at the same time we all could feel that this book was of supreme importance to her.

Queed was a comedy shaped out of a diction that was, with the exception of some of Miss Seidl's usages, foreign to almost all of us. It was the decidedly upper-class sound and tone that we assumed Mrs. Roosevelt used when speaking to her friends, or that the president used when speaking to his Groton and Harvard chums. In *Queed*, the writing seemed to be toying with its own condescension. Yet it also modeled the kind of language to which, once melted in the melting pot, all of us might aspire.

Miss Seidl's intention for us to speak properly, like Mrs. Roosevelt, was the least of it, however. *Queed* is set in turn-of-the-century Virginia and its capital, Richmond. A young man in his early twenties, the autodidact of all autodidacts (he has never been to school), is on a quest to find the one guiding principle that will unite all the sciences. To that end he is writing a book on "evolutionary sociology." Queed is a physical type that Woody Allen somewhere describes as a "homunculus." In Richmond, he is on an Odyssean journey of self-discovery and a Telemachean search for paternity. The book's other main character is a marvelously courageous young woman, a "new woman" in 1911 terms. Sharlee Weyland is *Queed*'s Athena — a guide, an instructress, ultimately Queed's partner, all in the guise of a daughter of "the new South." She is one of the Southern elite who has come down in the world, and that descent has been of immense use to her, making her strong and richly human. The novel, without belaboring the point, has her incorporating the spirit of both feminism and Teddy Roosevelt's progressivism.

There is a third character, a "leading man" type, foil for Queed and beau for Sharlee: three-named Charles Gardiner West, charming and handsome, well born and ambitious, acknowledged by all and sundry to be a certain success in life. While the evolution of these three characters spans the narrative, at the center of the plot is that wonderful subject: money. Queed, owning higher ideals, is indifferent to it, Sharlee understands its human uses, and Charles Gardiner West, in many respects a model for teenagers, is ultimately corrupted by it.

While negotiating the book's moral labyrinth, we were given new words and phrases to play with: "eleemosynary," "ruminative," and "your cosmos is all ego," were among our favorites. Beyond expanding our vocabulary, the book wrestled with issues that weighed heavily on many of us. Clearer than any biblical exposition, *Queed* outlined for a group of 15-year-olds in 1946 what an honorable life might be, should be. Even today, when I mention *Queed* to one of my old classmates, a ruminative smile will break on his face and he will say something to the effect that yes, *Queed* and Miss Seidl's labors are still something against which they judge themselves.

My father said, "You're good in history. Be a history teacher. Teachers have a good life. School is out at 3:00 and you have the whole summer off."

Indeed, I was good in history; in my graduating class at George Washington High School, I had one of the highest grade averages. I was also good at chemistry and biology, so my mother said, "A doctor maybe? My boy a doctor?" But my first course of college chemistry permanently settled the doctor notion, so history it became.

At age 18, I registered for the draft. The notion of being drafted then, in 1949, seemed ridiculous, but toward the end of June, in

1950, that all changed.

I was working as a bus boy in "The Mountains," the Jewish Alps, the Catskills, at the Mountain Glen Hotel, owned and run by Messrs. Stern and Liebenstein, German refugees all. The hotel catered mainly to German refugees. Frau von Halle was on my station, a widow, the hotel's only guest for the full season. She came from one of those few Jewish families who had indeed achieved the status of nobility somewhere, Austria, or Bohemia, or Germany. She was in her mid-fifties, large and delicate at the same time. It was a pleasure just to watch how delicately she buttered a cracker at lunchtime. She was the only guest at the hotel to have, in the cool of the basement, two large cartons filled with wine — white with lunch, red with dinner — and it was part of my job to see that the proper bottle rested on her table before her entrance to the meal. Sitting at her window seat, an elbow resting on the white linen, she would spend time just looking at the green mountain landscape. Then, her face lost in thought, she poured herself a glass of wine.

I did not care for red wine then, but white, especially from the Rhine or Moselle, was something I had come to appreciate at my father's table. Bringing the white back and forth every day from the kitchen refrigerator to Frau von Halle's table began to arouse a certain curiosity in me as to the taste of that white wine. After a few weeks of serving the lady, I decided try the wine myself. In a nook on the way to the kitchen where no one could see me, I uncorked the bottle, raised it to my mouth and took a slug. Cold, a bit thick and a bit sweet, it was the best wine I had ever tasted. On following days, greedy, I would take not one slug but two and then three — but never more than three.

One sunny day, Madam von Halle, always at the same table where she sat alone, here table next to a window from where one could see green mountains stretch into blue distances, called me over to her. "Walter, please come here."

Dutifully, smiling, my napkin folded over my right arm, and with a slight bow, "Yes, Madam?"

"You are a very nice boy."

"Thank you, Madam."

She smiled. "What do you think of my wine? The white."

"I don't know much about wine, Madam."

"I do think you are a 'Geniesser' — that's not all bad, so you can tell me."

I wanted to sink through the floor, but I shrugged.

The smile went. Her lips were pressed together, her brows almost joined, and there was a hard ridge of skin between them. "Look here—" she held the bottle in her left hand and with a knife in her right pointed to a straight scratch that had been made on the label —"You see? I made a mark."

I saw.

"How do you explain it? Every day after you take it and return it, the level in the bottle seems to be closer to my mark."

"Madam . . ." But before I could confess, she said, "Just tell me how you like it."

I was saved. "It's wonderful. The best I have ever tasted. Better than Eiswein."

"Fine. Now, at least, you are honest." Her smile had returned. "You can, please, get yourself a bottle of my wine from the basement. One bottle! That's all! That will be yours, but no more drinking from my bottle. You understand?"

I nodded. I understood. It would have been a short summer for me in the mountains had I not.

The next morning at breakfast Madam Von Halle stood at her table and called to me before sitting down. "Walter, have you seen this?" She unfolded her copy of the *New York Times*. The headline told of the North Koreans having invaded the south. "What does this mean for you?"

"I don't know," I replied. "I don't know."

"Do you think the Chinese or the Russians also have the bomb?"

There was now a new geography to learn and a new set of anxieties to acquire. The names were easy: Pusan perimeter and Inchon landing, Seoul, Yalu River, and 38th Parallel. The fighting was hard: Pork Chop Hill and Heartbreak Ridge. It was Truman's War and McArthur's, and we'd be "Home by Christmas."

Some of our older friends appeared in khaki and the question of deferments arose. They were given as long as one attended college full time. At the City College of New York (CCNY), we took Selective Service tests and filled out forms to make sure our deferments lasted at least until graduation. I needed to keep my grades up. Outside the dean's office, a posted notice told us that if we became fluent in the Vietnamese language, the deferment could be permanently continued. Rather than study Vietnamese I concentrated on history.

In the summer of 1950 I was 19, at home and working at a factory. I could not make enough money setting tables and collecting tips in the Catskills. I had worked about twenty hours weekly in my freshman year, giving a portion of my earnings to my parents, and I didn't want to work that hard again as a sophomore. So I lied to the foreman, telling him that I was through with school and looking for something permanent, and I was moved to operate the drill press, for good money.

One Saturday night, I got sick. The pain began in my stomach. I lay on the couch in our living room, moaning. My father came over and asked, "You don't have any place to go?"

His question made me angry. "I'm not feeling well, Pop."

Everybody always said that my father looked like Spencer Tracy. He had that same white hair and that same genial craggy face. When we were younger, and if we begged, he would play Jekyll and Hyde for us, Tracy's role. He would turn his back on us and then, very slowly, turn to us again with a sweet, benign, almost ethereal visage: Dr. Jekyll He'd then turn away from us again and return with a mean, cold, blank face — and then, to our delicious fear, his features would slowly melt and rearrange themselves into the hideous Mr. Hyde. One year, a movie company was promoting a new Spencer Tracy film with a Tracy look-alike walking around Manhattan. If you walked up to the look-alike and said, "You're Spencer Tracy," you would get a free ticket to his movie, and one winner would get a free vacation in Hollywood. Everybody was walking up to my father and looking disappointed when he had to tell them, "No. I am not Spencer Tracy. I'm sorry." He almost got into a fight with a man on the subway who kept on insisting that he was, indeed, Spencer Tracy and that he wanted his ticket to the movie.

"What's the matter?" he said to me.

"It's my stomach."

"You have a fever?"

"I don't think so. It's my stomach."

"Ach, no fever, then it's nothing." He went over to the combined radio-and-record-player console, the shiny ebony Dumont console that I both hated and felt proud of — hated it because it made me terribly anxious that we could not afford the payments, proud because I knew that none of the other refugees in Washington Heights, those cheap refugees with all that money they made with their overtime in the war-time factories, would never in all their lives even think of laying out good money for an object that day by day brought what our mother called "lovely culture" into our apartment. ("It's as good as a subscription to the Met, and it plays both thirty-three and seventy-eight.") Pop opened the doors to the console to pull out his favorite long-playing records: "La Traviata," the complete opera, with Richard Tucker, Robert Merrill and Licia Albanese. Tucker and Merrill were both Jewish.

The console had been my mother's achievement. She had first seen one several years earlier while working as a cleaning woman in the house of a doctor in Queens. "It's wonderful. It's wonderful. Such sound. And you should see, after a long day with patients, the pleasure he gets from such an object. The relaxation. And Mrs.

Emanuel, too. The kids. too. They all stay home at night and listen to records, to the best music. It will do good for everybody. Pappa can relax just like Doctor Emanuel." My mother and father had argued for most of a year over the acquisition.

The next year we got our television, the first one on the block. Now, on many evenings, Rabbi Lieber would come to our house. He loved to watch wrestling.

"I think I may have fever," I said.

"How much fever?"

"I don't know. I haven't taken my temperature."

"Why don't you take your temperature?"

"I can't get up. My stomach hurts."

"No, no. You can get up. Let's see. Try."

There must have been something on my face, my lips in a curve of pain as I tried to lift myself from the couch, that worked to convince my father that, yes, I was hurting. He put his hand on my brow and nodded.

"You feel hot. Where does Mamma keep the thermometer?"

"In the bathroom. The cabinet."

"I'll go look."

My mother was not at home. Had she been home she would already have been on the phone to Doctor Mayer, but she was away, recuperating, up in the green country, Westchester County some place, Hartsdale, from what she called "nervousness." I always thought of Hartsdale as a camp for adults that our mutual insurance company made available to refugee women who had had enough of hard work for little pay, enough of children, enough of arguing, enough of being refugees.

My father smiled. He gave me the thermometer to read. *"Wie viel fahrenheit."* It was an old refugee joke, a bilingual pun that translated to, "How many will leave today?" Leave by boat, by train, by plane. How many people will you let out of the concentration camp, out of Germany?

"One hundred and one."

"What's that in Celsius?"

"I don't know. Forty? Forty-one? I don't know." I was hurting.

In 1950, doctors still made house calls. "Yes, I know it's Saturday night, Dr. Mayer," my father said on the phone. "Yes the fever is over a hundred and one . . . A lot over, Oscar?

"A little bit over."

"No, it's not yet a hundred and two. . . .I should call you if it's over a hundred and two? . . . Fever is an infection, maybe penicillin? I should call you if it's over one hundred and two? Okay."

"What did he say?"

"You heard. I should give you some tea. You want tea?"

It was about then that I began to throw up. I threw up until all that was left in my stomach was a bitter green bile, and when that was gone, I still retched. My father had gotten a basin because I could not negotiate the trip to the bathroom. He had gotten a washcloth and repeatedly wiped my face. He put his hand on my brow and shook his head. Every time he put his hand on my brow I would see that they were never free of traces of paint. There was paint in the creases of his fingers in the folds of his hands, beneath and in the corners of his fingernails. No matter how long he washed or how hard he scrubbed with Lava soap and with turpentine, he never seemed to be able to get rid of that paint. We sometimes begged him to take out the flute he had brought with him from Germany and carried all through our long trek to the United States, and there were rare occasions when he did, but most of the time he would look sad and pained, wiggle his fingers in front of us and say no, he couldn't.

Mom always said Pop was too nice. She repeated it often after he started his own business: OSCAR HESS, PAINTING AND DECORATING. "You are not a real business man. You are too nice, too easygoing to have your own business. You let all those damn landlords deduct, deduct, deduct, from the bills." And then she would add, "Oh, if only I were a man."

It was true. He was too nice. He'd go into some apartment to give an estimate, "Okay, sixteen dollars a room." And if the lady of the house made a sad face, he'd start going down two dollars at a time. "Okay. Ten. But I'm losing money."

Everybody loved my father, who looked like Spencer Tracy.

"Yes. I know it's Saturday night, Dr. Mayer. After eleven, yes, I know, but you said to call if it's a hundred and two. It's over. He threw up on the tea . . . What time in the morning . . . Ya, all right, but he's hurting very much . . . Thank you Dr. Mayer. Thank you."

By 1:00 a.m. the fever was almost 104°.

"I know it's after one, but you have to come now, please. It's almost a hundred and four."

My father called again at 6:00, and Dr. Mayer's wife answered the phone. He came at 8:00 in the morning. He pressed my stomach. Wherever he touched I screamed.

"It's the appendix."

Pappa suddenly, started to cry. He tried to wipe his eyes, there was no sound, but the tears kept coming. The tenderness I had always felt for his hands now enveloped the rest of him. In all my life I had seen my father cry only once before, and that was when in 1946, after the war, out of the blue, he'd received a letter from his father, my grandfather, which had been smuggled out of the collection camp where all the Jews of our village had been taken. A friendly German farmer had first received the letter, then sent it on to us after the war. There were red and blue stamps with Gothic script on the envelope. The stamps said Deutschland and our address was rendered in Gothic. How had they gotten our address? Oh yes. My parents, right after the war, had sent some packages with canned meat, with sugar and instant coffee to old friends in our old town. I remember sitting with them in the living room, my father on the couch silently reading and silently weeping, and my mother standing in back of him, stroking his hair, "We had to leave. You know we had to leave."

"Oscar, I don't think it's perforated. I'm calling the hospital. Siegfried Steuerman is the best surgeon there is."

"My brother died of an appendix," my father explained.

My arm was around his shoulder. He held me, carried me, to a taxi. In the hospital elevator, I looked at my father's wet face and thought, *Who is he crying for, me or his brother?*

At CCNY, I took every course that Hans Kohn taught. Professor Kohn was a historian. When I listened to him lecture, I had the sense that I was in one of those great gothic lecture halls of an old European university, Salamanca, Heidelberg, Cambridge. From behind his desk we were showered with both knowledge and wisdom. His classes were always full, and each one of us understood that we were in the presence not only of a great teacher but of a great tradition: Seneca and the Stoics, Heloise and Abelard, Parcifal, Wagner. The Enlightenment loomed large in his lectures, as did Nietzche, and Schopenhauer. It seemed as if he knew the French philosophes as well as he knew his Prague friends Max Brod and Franz Kafka. And while he was attached to Enlightenment hopes, he understood, and had us understand "better than the Enlightenment did, the infinite complexity of human nature and history, the inherent limitations of all human knowledge, the uncertainty of the human condition. . ."

He understood — and that understanding gave me goosebumps — that the role of the historian in the 20th century was akin to that of the poet, in that both of them made meaning of the present and of the past. Kohn taught me how little I knew and how much there was to be known, and I loved it.

He taught courses on nationalism and European intellectual history, but his nationalism was intellectual history, and his intellectual history was nationalism. His understanding of nationalism derived from personal experience: Having lived in Bohemia, he had seen the shattering of the Austrian Empire by nationalistic passions, and experienced the fascination among Germans, Russians, and French with myths of race and peoplehood, which resulted in the horrendous agony of a new thirty years war, 1914-1945.

Kohn's ideals of governance rested in the examples of political compromise that allowed the people of Switzerland and the people of his beloved England to live in peace.

He sat and just talked, never looking at lecture notes or rehashing the reading he had assigned some days before. There was in his voice the sort of melancholy sweetness that I found, sometimes, in those who remembered both the greatness and the great fall of the Hapsburg Empire — and that accent I knew, of the German speaker who somewhat late in life had made his transition into English.

Kohn had made many transitions: from journalism to teaching, from Zionism to its disappointments, from soldier to prisoner and long years in Siberian exile. And he had made many stops among many nations: Czecoslovakia, Palestine, France, Switzerland, England, America.

By my last year at City College I had completed all my required courses and so had the pleasant choice of taking almost any offering in the CCNY catalogue. In 1952, the college was one of the very first in the United States that had a filmmaking department. My friend Manny, who was majoring in film, told enthusiastic stories about his adventures, and what could be bad about a course in which one just sat and watched the classics of film unroll on a screen and listen to one of the great personalities of the 20th century? I thought, and I was not alone, that Hans Richter, the famed surrealist painter and filmmaker who joined the CCNY faculty in 1941, was just that. "Many opportunities, but no jobs," he would say of the film industry, in his heavy German accent, making students laugh while at the same time rubbing a bit off the glamor off the profession.

Sidney Meyers taught a course in film editing, which would change my life. Once again I stood in the presence of a master. Many years later, working as a film editor, I encountered some remarks by the novelist Clancy Segal, who had once been an assistant to Sidney during the making of Sidney's great film, *The Quiet One*. Segal's description felt right: "He had time to spend with me, a film newcomer, and we spent many afternoons discussing life, art and politics, sometimes just horsing around, and occasionally he let me watch him cut. He was . . . a master. I'd never before seen such playful competence. At first it was terribly confusing to me because I never knew what was supposed to be serious and what was a joke. Later I learned that this was Sidney's method of instruction, to break down the distinction. I learned practically everything I know about the cutting technique from him, as I imagine many other people did. . . . I always felt sure of Sidney when he was talking about movies or pictures or books, sure that he had felt what he was saying . . . And you know, he made me laugh more than almost anyone. Not that the jokes were good; they were part of his playfulness, the artist's kind of playfulness, that was very dear to my heart. I felt I was being allowed into his own private playground when he trotted out yet another one of those surreal . . . jokes of his."

In one of his notebooks, Sidney wrote, "We all of us live our lives with certain loved figures hovering over us. Whatever we do, whatever action or moral stance we assume, we ask those figures what they think of us, and if we behave unworthily, we hope they were not looking."

Sidney was and is for me one of those loved, hovering figures about whom he wrote, and I have often asked myself, in varied ways, what, he might think of me at that moment — and yes, if I behaved unworthily, I hoped that he was looking elsewhere.

There was a war raging in Korea. During most of college, whenever he was looking at the TV news and there was a report about Korea, Pop would quickly glance at me and then quickly return his gaze to the screen. We saw the war in the pages of *Life* magazine and on the evening television news. In black and white we were given heroes, without feeling much triumph. It was an uncomfortable war, like the whole of the Cold War, because I could not summon up the enthusiasm, the anger, the mourning, or the joy that had accompanied me during the "good war." Ten years earlier, General MacArthur had been a hero, and now he was a villain because he differed with President Truman on Korean war policy. Spring, summer, and fall they fought in Korea, while in winter both sides talked — and the result of their talking was to agree to continue fighting while their talks went on. Had I missed a class of Hans Kohn's in which he explained these things?

In June of 1952 I would be a college graduate. What would happen then? Everyone now seemed to own a shiny car with ballooning fenders, and every apartment in Washington Heights now had its own private phone, no more party lines. Korea lay lightly on most people's psychic map, but Pop kept glncing at me. In the spring and summer of 1952, despite the talks, soldiers were being killed. The maps in the *New York Times* showed the back and forth movements, in millitmeters, it seemed.

I had taken all the tests the army gave to allow me, as a college boy, to receive my deferments. Now the letter arrived in late July: "Greetings." There was no reporting date, which would arrive later, but once that first letter arrived, after taking a long breath, Pop began asking me, evenings when I went out, where I was going, something he had stopped doing a long while before.

In late October, I received my two weeks' notice to report for induction into the Army down on Whitehall Street. That evening, in a low and serious voice, Mom said, "Pappa asked if you could please stay home in the evenings until you go in the Army." Her voice had a tone that might have been used in synagogue, as in,

Please get me that book of prophets in the German translation that they have in the back. The last time I could remember hearing it was the evening of my graduation from junior high in 1946: There had been a vase of cut flowers in the center of our table, and it was the first time since our arrival in America that we ate steak. I had sat on the couch while others cleared the table, and Mom sat down next to me and said, in a low and serious voice:"You didn't say nothing. How did you like the steak?" In answer, I hugged her around the neck. Now I remembered that tone of voice.

For weeks, on odd occasions — seeming odd merely because I was present — both Mom and Oma had talked of their experiences in the First World War. Mom, for instance, would talk of the lack of food: "It was potatoes, potatoes, potatoes all the time. And when the potatoes were gone, we ate the potato peels. God, I remember the first time after the war that we had chocolate. Oma's brother, Uncle Moritz brought it from Holland."

"What did he do in Holland?" I asked.

"He was trying to get the brothers' grain business going again."

"How do you remember all that? You were just a little girl."

"I remember a lot. I remember every little shit you took in Ruppichtheroth."

Oma, too, talked about food, how she would walk out of Würzburg into the open country and stop at farmers' houses to see if she could get fresh vegetables or maybe even some meat. "Even turnips cost a sackful of money," she said. "The farmers got rich during the war." Mom would then quickly add, "The arms manufacturers got even richer," and Oma would wave Mom away while muttering, "Politics. With you it's always politics." Then Oma would continue: "My brother got killed in the war, got killed early at Verdun. Got killed for the Kaiser and for Germany and where did it get us? Lots of good young boys got killed. Jewish boys. I know a lot of them."

Then Mom would ask Oma, "Did you know so-and-so, he was a teacher. And so-and-so. He was so handsome. He volunteered when the war started. Jews were patriotic. And so-and-so. He came from a rich family." Oma would take my hand and squeeze, while Mom said, "Don't volunteer. Don't never. Just do what they tell you."

They were afraid for me, and I mostly remained home with them in the evenings. Pop was home every night now. There had been many nights when he was not, when he had to prepare for the next morning's work, see that the paint went where it was supposed to go, talk to customers in the evenings when they were home — but now Pop was home every evening. After supper, he would sit in the living room reading the *New York Post*, while Mom sat knitting and Oma sat crocheting doilies.

I sat reading history. I read Francis Parkman's *Montcalm and Wolfe*. One of the things cruising through my mind was to continue in history, to study historiography, the history of history, especially American historiography. Those 19th century American historians were great and wonderful writers, novelists, really, as far as their techniques went. One could read Prescott, Motley, Parkman for fun. Then there were the Adamses, and then Turner, and Beard. There could be an occupation in it, and all it required was reading.

We were all sitting, quiet, occupied, the radiator hissing, the room warm. After a while Pop would walk over to the console, opened the cabinet where the records were stored, and ask me, "What would you like to hear?" The first time he'd asked, I was as-tonished — it was a question never before heard in our apartment. The phonograph was Pop's domain, that and the telephone.

At first, the question made me angry: Banned for so long from the selection of music, I wanted then to kick in the ribs of the con-sole. I was being condescended to, given a present to make every-thing all right. What was "everything"? I thought of being carried to the hospital by Pop while he cried, and being suspicious of Pop, thinking he might be crying for his dead brother rather than for me, groaning in pain.

Pop smiled and asked again, "What would you like to hear?"

I was on the verge of crying. I bit my lip. "Capriccio Italien."

Pop's face grew serious as he nodded, pulled out the record, and let it play. The Capriccio, even more than La Traviata, was Pop's favorite music. He played it so often, it had come to be my favorite piece as well. The music begins with crashing chords, scary, dominating, hard chords — but then the Capriccio becomes a lullaby, gentle, enveloping, soothing. Did Pop need a lullaby? I saw his mother, my grandmother, so often quiet as if in silent, dark-eyed mourning. What did I know as a kid? I knew her silence. Her youngest son was dead; the other, the oldest, had gone to the university and married outside the religion. Mom always said that Pop should have gone to university, been a teacher. But he was needed on the farm helping his father with the cows. In the music I saw a dark shiny baby swinging in a hammock. I saw a dark-eyed mother, happy, singing a lullaby to the baby. What did Pop see? Did Pop need a lullaby? I know I needed one.

Pop said, "When you go, I'll drive you down there."

I said, "There's really no need."

"I know, you're old enough," Mom said, "but the morning traffic is very bad down there. It's Wall Street."

"Near Wall Street."

Mom gave a good-bye party for me, on the evening before my leaving. Pop stayed home. "I'm going to walk you to the subway," he said.

A hard, wintry Hudson River wind was blowing through 160th Street. It was even cold on Fort Washington Avenue, away from the river. We walked past the new synagogue that had once been the Costello movie house. "The ladies in the congregation are going to send you a package to Fort Dix," said Pop. "We'll visit you weekends."

"I don't think . . ." I stopped talking and we just walked. It was cold walking down Broadway. At 158th Street, Pop took my hand. At the top of the stairs to the subway, we stopped and he gave me a hug. He was crying. He remained standing at the top of the stairs, and as I walked down to the trains I felt terrible. I was so very stupid. I had been stupid for years.

Chapter Twenty-Four

At Fort Dix we began our transformation into soldiers, and found that soldiering meant waiting. We waited to get our uniforms, we waited in long lines for meals, and we waited for information: where were we going to be assigned. The scuttlebutt was that if you were assigned to basic training at Fort Dix, you were lucky because there basic training lasted only twelve weeks, and that meant you weren't going to Korea but somewhere else. With sixteen weeks of basic, you were sure to get duty in Korea, and if you ended up taking basic at Indiantown Gap, in Pennsylvania, it was certain that you were going to be sent to Korea because its mountains, the Alleghenies, so very much resembled the mountains in Korea.

After three days at Fort Dix, we were loaded into cargo trucks, now and forever more known as deuce and a half, and sent to Indiantown Gap, Pennsylvania. For two and a half hours, while the truck curved through the eastern Pennsylvania mountains, we were stomping our feet on the truck's floor and complaining, "Fuck, it's cold." The phrase was sometimes adjusted to "Shit, it's cold." Here began the change in my vocabulary. Sentences grew shorter, and in all of them, most of the time, there was an angry snarl. As a friend later said, "If, while in the Army, you can't use either 'shit' or 'fuck' somewhere in the sentence, you're just not getting your meaning across."

The truck drove past long avenues of barracks, a vast cityscape of elongated huts, infinitely repeated. When the truck finally halted, loud voices ordered us, "Move, move, move!" I moved, running after the man in front of me, followed by men running after me, all of us herded off the trucks and into a barrack.

About half the beds in the barracks were made, the other half empty of sheets and blankets but with striped mattresses, many covered by large yellow stains. At one end of the barrack there was a head-high shelf on which a radio rested. Someone fiddled with the radio, and a nasally country-and-western tune blasted through the barrack from a small loudspeaker. near the roof.

A bunch of men had preceded the contingent from Fort Dix. Some were simply wandering about the vast room examining its wooden walls, others were sitting on the beds they had made. One of them had turned on the radio. A head poked through the barracks door: "Get your fucking asses off those beds. Just because you guys come from New York, it don't mean shit." Turtle-like, the head withdrew.

Having dumped my duffel bag in front of a bed, I, too, began to wander about the room, until someone tapped me on the shoulder.

"Oh, shit. Zack!" Zachary Marantis was a high school classmate.

"Morty Zucker is here, too," he said. "I think a GW reunion might be possible."

Before I could ask how he had been, where he had gone to college, was he married, a voice called out: "Walter." It was John Harmon, whom I hadn't seen since junior high. John's family did not live on "Sugar Hill," but somewhere down in the valley where, they said, "the regular colored folks live." Once, at P.S. 46, the teacher had asked the class to vote: "What would you colored children like to be called?" Her voice was cheery. "You white children don't get to vote. So what would you colored children like to be called? Black or colored or Negro?"

John had piped up, "What about Socialist or Baptist? Some people are that kind." I don't remember how the teacher replied to John, but her three categories were the only ones in play. What I do remember is that although the class voted for "Negro," John called out afterwards, "I'm gray. Look at me, I'm gray." He held up a bare arm. "Look at me. My Pappady says I'm gray." Indeed, his arm had a dusty gray tinge.

I felt uncomfortable about what the teacher had been doing, making us conscious of the separation between blacks and the rest of us. Something about it felt uncomfortable. In Germany, there had been Willy and me, and then all of the others, singing, loud German songs while we were silent, with loud anger rattling inside. Now, on 156th Street in New York City, something again rattled inside me, although the teacher's voice was cheery.

"Goddamnn," I said. "Gray John Harmon."

"Here to fight the enemy." He smiled. "Who's the enemy?"

We were interrupted by a blare of sound. "Welcome to the third platoon, Charlie Company of the muffled training battalion of the Fifth Infantry Division USA," screamed the loudspeaker. "You are at Fort Indiantown Gap, P-A. Your address for the next sixteen weeks. See you soon."

Almost immediately a sergeant came through the door and began ripping up the made beds. When he straightened up, I could see a Combat Infantry badge on his chest, and below that a Purple Heart ribbon with two bronze bumps on it.

"I'm Sergeant Fowler. Any ridge runners here?" Yeows came from some of the group that had preceded us. "Won't do you a fucking bit of good. Like the tune, but goddamnn, turn it off. You all are here to learn. For you boys from New York and Boston, tell 'em what a ridge runner is." From behind me came the shout, "West Virginia."

"An' that's right. But the first thing to learn is how to make a bed."

I hated Sergeant Fowler's corn-pone voice. He had a sharp face and a long nose, but his hair was turning gray and it was the gray hair that somehow shocked me. He was old. He must have been in the Second World War, the fight against Hitler. There was that Combat Infantry Badge, and those bumps on the Purple Heart that he wore on his chest. He knew things. I had no real notion of what he knew, but I saw great slow-motion explosions in black and white, and water on a black-and-white beach washing over an army helmet half buried in sand — pictures from old *Life* magazines. The things he knew, the things that I attributed to him, awed me.

Sergeant Fowler ripped sheets and blankets from one of the beds and began to remake it. "Hospital corners. Hospital corners, see." When he was finished, he took a quarter out of his pocket, threw it down on the khaki blanket. It bounced three or four feet up into his hand. "If you can't make a quarter do that on inspection, you will be cleaning a lot of sump pits."

Morty Zucker raised his hand, "Sir, what's a sump pit?"

"First of all I ain't a Sir, the queen has not yet seen fit to give me a knighthood, it's sergeant to you. Second —" and he took Morty to the barrack's door and pointed to a barrack across the way —"See that? That's your mess hall. Get over there and ask the first man with stripes that you see what a sump pit is. Get your ass over there." Morty went.

"Okay. You are all here to learn. Your pal is beginning his lessons. You all are here to learn and you better goddamn learn. Get your minds set. You are all going to Korea. You are the frozen chosen. Listen to what we tell you. Listen, listen, listen. If you don't, you are going to get killed. You are going to die.

"The company commander's name is Captain Bitzer," Fowler continued. "I served with him in doubleyou doubleyou two. He's a good man. On your first payday, he will call a meeting of the company outside his office. There he will give you a talk about the importance of charity. His special charity is the Salvation Army, and he will expect you to come up with some dough for the charity. Don't come to me later and tell me I didn't warn you. The captain is going to ask somebody who can type if you want to be company clerk. Who here can type?" Just about everybody raised their hand.

"Anybody who volunteers is going to get killed," Fowler warned. "Anybody who volunteers is going to die in the snow in fucking Korea. Anybody who is company clerk will miss this great training you will be getting at this fucking university. Anybody who sits and types will not know what to do if he sees millions of hordes of screaming Chinese coming at him. What do you do when you see millions of hordes of Chinese coming at you?" Nobody raised their hand. Sergeant Walker looked around. "Nobody? All you typists don't know? Well that's what we're here for. Teach you. You are Charlie Company, third platoon. Charlie Company third platoon is the heavy weapons platoon." Fowler looked around again. "Nobody asking what's a heavy weapons platoon?" He smiled. "You are the smartest group I've had here in a good while. You guys have learned the first rule of this goddamn army. Do not volunteer. I'll tell you, anybody who volunteered would now be hauling an 81-millimeter mortar base plate around these barracks. Well, you'll all be hauling it anyway in a while. Mess is at 17:30, reveille at Oh six hundred. Today will have been your easiest day at Indiantown Gap. You will be issued weapons tomorrow."

At about 11:00 that night Zucker came in from the mess hall. He spent most of the rest of the night throwing up in the john. Two days later Zucker became the company clerk. How he did that I never found out.

The next day was not so very hard, either. We were issued equipment: "The rifle is your very best friend. Take care of it." There were hours of filling out forms, lectures on General Orders, lectures on the uniform code of military justice; the signing of loyalty oaths. It was day three when I learned about the base plate of the 81-mm. mortar. It is extremely fucking heavy. What did they know about me that I should be assigned to haul this awkwardly shaped, murderously heavy piece of steel? I was a college graduate.

A four-man team was assigned to "serve" the 81-mm. mortar. One "served" to haul the base plate, one "served" to haul the cannon, one "served" to haul the tripod. The fourth man was the mortar "captain," and he also "served" to level the machine and set the elevation. The "captain" carried nothing, just twiddled with a couple of knobs so that the proper coordinates were "fed" into the thing so that when the rounds were "fed" into the pipe they would not fall short and kill people on our side of the line rather than kill people, the enemy, on the other side of the line.

"The 81-millimeter mortar is a smooth-bore, muzzle-loaded, high-angle-fire weapon. The 81 uses four types of ammunition, high explosive, phosphorus, illumination and practice. The ordnance weighs nine pounds, the cannon weighs thirty-five pounds. The tripod weighs twenty-seven pounds. The base plate weighs twenty-nine pounds. The maximum range of the ordnance is three hundred yards — the length of three football fields. You point the barrel, set the elevation, remove the safety, drop it, and get your head out of the way. The entire operation will take fifteen seconds."

In the sixteen weeks at Indiantown Gap, we did not fire the weapon once. We just carried it around all the time. To my twenty-nine pounds was added the normal backpack, which usually weighed nearly fifty pounds. The only time the weapon was ever fired was when the instructors demonstrated. We never, in our whole sixteen weeks at Indiantown Gap, "fed" a live or even a dummy round of ammunition into the pipe.

John Harmon was slight and small, so he got to carry the cannon. Zachary Marantis who was 6'2" and lifted weights in high school, became captain of the mortar crew.

All of us spent many hours of the day lying prone in icy mud or crawling around in it. Lying prone refers to the times the platoon spent either at target practice, or crawling on our bellies while live rounds from 30-mm. machine guns were fired over our heads. Target practice was at either fast targets or pop-up targets, and we practiced from the kneeling as well as the standing position. There was always a great deal of discussion in the evening, in the barracks, as to why we began our shooting in the prone position rather than standing or kneeling, and it was the almost unanimous opinion that neither standing nor kneeling would get us into the cold mud fast enough. Of course, to stand or kneel while machine guns were firing at us would have been silly.

What was not silly was the earnestness with which our training cadre took on their tasks. Their constant, solemn admonition to us was "Do it right or you will die." Several weeks into basic, at the firing range and shooting from the prone position, a young first lieutenant, we did not know his name, hardly older than most of us draftees, walked up and down in back of us. "Get your asses down. Get your asses down. Anything sticks up, they will see it. Get down, get down in the mud. If you don't you're gonna die, you're gonna die." He stood right in back of me and kept repeating, "You're gonna die," over and over. I needed a new clip and turned around. The lieutenant was crying. Everybody on the line stopped shooting and turned to look at the lieutenant. A non-com walked over to him and led him off, then someone behind us called out, "Resume firing."

Whenever we returned to the barracks, there was a race to the one radio. Whoever reached it first turned the dial to his favorite station. In this part of mountainous eastern Pennsylvania, our radio drew in a lot of stations and, all of them played music that I knew as hillbilly, and detested. The one other station was WQXR from New York, the station that played the classical music that I was used to from home, the music that announced a life of reason, regularity, and culture. I knew that the radio could play QXR because in the first week of our training, I was a barrack guard. (Each day, one member of the platoon remained behind from the day's training to guard the barracks.)

I participated in the daily race for the radio dial, but I never won, and as the days went on the race became nasty. There were pushes from the side, or a group of boys would simply stand in front of me and not move. I was frequently tripped. Still, I persisted. It seemed as if all my anger and hostility at the regimentation, the constant drilling, the foul base plate, the repeated warnings about death, became focused upon changing that dial, just once.

Finally, after being pushed one more time, I grabbed the ridge-runner nearest me and we began wrestling on the ground. "Fight, fight!" was the scream from several dozen. We rolled on the ground, no one landed a punch. I was bitten on the shoulder, and my head butt on his brow drew blood. At the sight of it, Zach Marantis and several others pulled us apart.

Later, when we were both on KP scrubbing pots, John Harmon said to me, "You're going to get yourself killed."

"That's what everybody around here says all the time."

"Long before you get to Korea."

"How? Killed."

"You don't know that they've got guns and live ammo in this place?"

"You're serious?"

"Yes, I'm serious. You wouldn't be the first Jew these Yahoos got."

"There were others?"

"Don't be funny. I've been dealing with these people all my life. They're even angrier than you are. They're the same as blacks, except they don't know it. They're as angry as black folk. One thing, maybe the only thing that keeps them in place, is when they're told blacks are lower than them. They hear that so they can be screwed with the prices they get on their farms, screwed out of wages in mines and factories, shot or beat up if they want unions, same as black folk. If you explain things right, they are the salt of the earth."

"Salt?"

"Don't be funny. My folks were organizers with the Wobblies;

you know about them?"

I nodded. "Majored in American History. Black and white, unite and fight."

"No," John said with a laugh, "that came later — but you got to know when not to fight. You got to know when to relax, and you really have got to relax. Think what you want, but keep it to yourself. If it gets too much, and sometimes I know it gets too much, talk to me." Still smiling, he looked around. "But don't let them hear you say that thing."

"What?"

"You know. Black and white."

We were riding in a car, on our first weekend pass at the end of our first month of basic. Morty Zucker, somehow, had a car garaged in a town near the camp, and for a share of the gas money he took Zach, John and me back to New York City. Driving away from camp felt very liberating. "Ta, ta, ta, taaahhh." I slapped my belly to the rhythm of the opening notes of Beethoven's Fifth. "Liberation. V for Victory." I slapped victory on the seat, window, John's head. "I'm going to every concert I can afford, I'm going to stay home and run QXR loud. I'm going to wash that corn-pone music, that corn-pone twang out of my ears. Out of my brain."

"I once got beat up in college, in a bar, in Philadelphia," said John, "because I said, maybe a bit loud for somebody my size and considering where I was, that one of the sources of country music was in the black people's blues."

"Am I offending you?" I said.

"No, you're a snob. A white snob."

"Why white?"

"In distinction from a black snob, which is what I am and have got to get over."

"I don't understand that, but okay."

"What you have to understand is that Tex Ritter and Charley

Pride, all those Kentucky fiddlers, are great. Maybe not Shake-speare . . ."

"Beethoven."

"Maybe not Shakespeare, but their language and even those tunes, mostly, are from that time. Seventeenth, eighteenth-century people living in those hills. You know, 'Black, black, black, is the color of my true love's hair?' Mix that with what they heard from the colored churches, the shivarees, and you can get 'Your Cheating Heart,' or any one of a hundred others. Its poor people's music. It's great."

"Oh, come on."

"Zucker, turn on the radio."

For the rest of the two-hour trip John made us, me, listen to country music. I listened because I liked John. I still didn't care for it then, but John started something for me. And I began to relax. John was right. To have kept the contest up was stupid. There would have come some night on a bivouac when some Sterno can would be kicked over and I would really get hurt. I decided that John had kept me from a big injury.

In fact, I had already decided to like the "ridge runners." It took me a while, but I was impressed by the very long time they took to clean their rifles, sitting on their bunks for long hours, swabbing the barrel, cleaning it. I was impressed by the long time they took cleaning and spit-shining their boots until they were bright cordovan mirrors. The boy next to me was from somewhere beyond Beckley; he and John had struck up a friendship. I told him that he really had a great shine on the boot. He looked away and then at me. His lips didn't move but I knew that silently he was saying, "Asshole." Then he said, with contempt in his voice, "You don't get bored, do you?" I knew I deserved it, and from then on I began to spit-shine my boots for long hours. I liked doing it.

Every few weeks I would receive a package from home with the same contents: two cans of liver paté, a package of pumpernickel, a jar of strawberry preserves, and a can of chocolate-covered almonds. The package came from Oma. There was usually a brief note in the package, to the effect: *I always sent my brothers this when they were soldiers in the First World War. They liked it. I hope you like it too. Your Oma.*

Fowler dumped the package on my cot, and with it, always, came the same admonition: "Anybody gets a package in this platoon you share it with the guys." Morty Zucker said that on those occasions, "Sarge sounds like a goddamn camp counselor."

The radio was on, a group's loud nasal drone threaded through by a banshee violin and a constant beat from a banjo. I sat on my cot, undid my package, and called out, "Anybody want some goose liver paté?"

"Fuckin' what?"

John Harmon called out, "Fucking paté. It's French. They force-feed geese, stuff corn down their gullets. Enlarges their livers. It's great."

"No fuckin' way. French goose shit."

John had saved me again. I would have hated to part with any of my paté. So we partied, John, Zachary, Morty and I. Paté on pumpernickel, with the jam on pumpernickel for dessert, all washed down with cold 7-Up. It was a feast.

We began "field exercises." That meant lugging our mortar some five miles or so into a snow-white noplace, then pitching pup tents, with ponchos on the ground so we might sleep dry. Lighting up cans of Sterno in the tent to provide some warmth was no help, but we did it, anyway, then froze in our sleeping bags.

In the middle of the night, John, my tent mate, began moaning. In the morning, he was burning with fever. I found Fowler, who came to look. "Fuck, he's the fourth one. Ain't no doctor, but that's pneumonia." Fowler called for a truck that got John to a camp dispensary.

"Buddy's lucky," Fowler said. "Ain't crossin' the ocean with you fellas. Four weeks in a hospital gets him to the next cycle. Oh, well, be spring by then."

Soon after, I went to company HQ to ask for permission to visit John in the base hospital. Morty Zucker said that no one could see him yet, but I should get me to the next Friday evening service.

Friday evenings was the time for cleaning the barracks. It was a wet and sloppy business, a pain, especially if one was detailed to clean the latrine. Although Jewish boys were excused from work on Friday evenings so we could attend religious services, I had, early on, after hearing nasty remarks about Jews "cutting out" when there was work to be done, decided not to go to Friday evening services. Zucker knew of my practice, so I was surprised at his request. I went and I waited.

After the service, while I was munching on kosher cookies and drinking soda, Zucker came over. "There have been three guys from the F.B.I. or army intelligence or something, asking about John."

"About John? What about John?"

"He didn't sign the loyalty oath."

"What?"

"They asked me if I knew he was a communist. I said I never had any conversation with him about politics. Then they said who were his friends and I said everybody, he seemed to be a nice guy. Anybody come to see you?"

"No. When do you think we can visit him in the hospital?"

"I'll see if I can find out."

It was maybe a week before I received permission to see John. When I found him, he was walking around the hospital hall with pajamas on. I gave him one of my cans of goose liver paté and walked with him. "You seem a lot better than on bivouac," I said.

"I'll be here another week, but I won't be coming back to the company. Little gray John is very blue. They want to discharge me."

"Medical discharge? You will be the envy of everybody in the platoon."

"Uh, uh. Nothing medical. I think it's legal. I'm getting a lawyer."

"Morty said . . ."

"It's not only the loyalty oath. They want me to talk to them about my parents."

"What about them?"

"What have their activities been? Are they communists? Am I a communist? Are they anti-American? I told them I would have nothing to say about my parents, and they told me that if I didn't talk to them, I'd get a bad conduct discharge. So I called a lawyer."

"What did he say?"

"Haven't heard from him yet. I'm going to be a lawyer, but with a bad discharge, anything less than honorable, no law school will take me. Let's sit down."

We sat on a bench. John seemed resigned. I could do nothing. I was also afraid to try.

Fear pervaded our training. Our cadre had all been to Korea, and if they cried or screamed at us, it was out of fear. In the mess hall, our quartermaster sergeant sat at an empty table, hunched over, reading the *New York Times*. Suddenly he crumpled the paper, kicked the table and walked out. Sergeant Fowler said, "Lost another buddy. Back off him. Don't get near."

I began basic just as the bloody fighting over "Triangle Hill" ended. Then the winter's cold seemed to inhibit fighting, but from what our cadre kept telling us, "What the cold don't kill, snipers can." Toward the end of basic, fighting erupted at "Little Gibraltar" and "Old Baldy." Spring offensives had begun. We all heard and read, but made no sign that we had heard or read. No one wanted to go, but we all knew that we were slated to go into the Korean meat-grinder.

The snows turned to mud, and we marched through the mud. Earlier, snow on the hills both near and far away often presented a sweet Christmas-card vista. Lung-piercing as our marches were, the pain was made almost bearable by the sight of Hallmark country. Now, with the snow gone from the hills, the raw work of winter's rust stared us in the face. Nearly everything was brown, a wide screen of brown, with leafless trees on the hills, brown. The green of the occasional pine only emphasized the brown. And the marches got longer with each succeeding week. Fowler's "Close it up, close it up," chased me in my sleep.

A truck followed the marches and picked up any soldier who needed to fall out. An ambulance followed the truck. The word was that if you did fall out, it was KP for the rest of your basic training. Though I was now in much better shape tromping through Pennsylvania hills than I had been walking around Washington Heights, all too often the only way to get through the slog was to tell myself that if I get to that next tree, if I get to that next stand of pines, if I could make it to the next group of boulders, I'd be all right. "Close it up, close it up." There were others from the long line ahead of me who stood at the side of the road holding their sides, leaning against a tree or sitting on their backpack, but I was still marching. Every time we passed one of the out-fallen, the pain visible in their very posture, Fowler would point at them, not saying anything, just pointing his long accusing hand at their gasping, blanched faces. How often I wanted, even needed, to join them — but I never did.

The big one, the big field march that had been talked about for days, the very long march to a very distant bivouac area, our final test, had arrived. Fowler clapped his cold hands together and screamed, "This'll tell you if you're fit to fire an' fight in frozen Chosen. Joe Stalin died today. Shut up and close it up. Nobody drops out. You all are going west with the sun." Didn't "going west" mean death? And what did he mean by announcing Stalin's death and coupling it with going west? We knew that negotiations were going on to end the war and we also knew that some of the very worst fighting in all the years of the war was going on right now while we were preparing for this last ordeal. So why was he so upbeat?

The march began in a cold rain, and was to go twelve, maybe fifteen miles, maybe twenty miles. Fowler lined us up. I stood under the eave of our barrack while the early rain slid down from the roof and over me. I remember pulling boots out of ankle-high mud that made a sucking sound. The march began, and after half an hour our sucking breath met the sound of the sucking mud. The straps of the backpack cut into my shoulders; the base plate bouncing against my shins ground away at old scabs; it was all uphill. Now I knew why they called infantrymen "grunts." Fowler walked by, his voice low: "Gettin' a break soon. Thirty-degree hill. But then it goes up again. You're doin' good. Doin' good. Good enough to join the best we got on Pork Chop Hill."

Some two hundred men of Charlie Company walked uphill in single file. I was somewhere near the rear. Most of the uphill was on a narrow trail that ran through a forest of tall pines. When the pine branches arched over us, the rain slackened, but then the pines parted again. About every hour there was the cry, "Fall out." Then the column halted, and many of us, literally, fell out to rest inside the margin of the pine forest, where the rusty ground of old needles was soft. I fell down once, but no more, because it was so difficult to get up again. Lying down on the soft forest ground, I saw mush-rooms, stick-like and yellow chanterelles, gray-capped mushrooms, and light brown ones capped like those I picked with my Oma in Germany, in the woods beyond our meadow.

"Okay, boys, sing out, and step out. 'There was a girl lived up on a hill . . .'" For minutes we all marched to Fowler's call-and- our response, but then the muddy ground began to break the rhythm of our march and the singing broke off as well.

We emerged from the narrow confines of the pine forest, and as we did the rain ended, and our mountain climb began to straighten out. When we came to level ground, we saw that we were on a high and narrow ridge with a view into a deep valley. Now we could un-bend, look about. The ground fell away on both sides, and on the left, in the far distance below, we could see, as from an airplane's height, the checkered farmers' fields in many shades of brown and tan. On the other side were the Allegheny Mountains, whose repeated humpbacks rose and fell. Windswept, the clouds broke up quickly, and there was soon blue in the sky. On the pine-green flanks of the mountain nearest us, wispy threads of clouds, long thin tendrils, drifted downward into the valley between us.

Our ridge broadened out. Banks of puffy cumulus sailed in the blue sky. The sun was lowering, leaving yellow and orange scraps in a distant stand of pines.

Our trail bent around a nearer stand of pines, and when I could finally see around that bend, it seemed as if our ridge would suddenly end out there in a sheer drop. Near that drop hung large, intertwined balls of clouds that seemed, very slowly, to rise from below us. They scrolled upward, and as they did, pink chromatics, every hue of pink and red, modulated by the white of the clouds, appeared on the rising face of this cloud curtain.

As I marched toward this spectacular sunset, I began to be enveloped in a great joy. Never mind the weight on my back, the effort to move forward: Here was a show in front of me, as if put on for me and me only. Here was a blessing, not spoken, but demonstrated.

Two days later we received our orders. Everyone in our company was detailed to the east, to Korea, except for five Chinese kids and myself, who received orders for Germany.

I was given a ten-day leave before having to report to Fort Dix for transfer to Germany. I went home by bus, subway, then walking up 160th Street in my uniform. The sidewalks, houses, stoops, and manhole covers that I had known for over a decade suddenly felt strange, distant; I was home but not home. The gray fronts of the apartment buildings seemed to say, "You don't live here anymore, do you?" Still, Mom and Oma hugged me around the neck,

Karl and Peter punched my shoulder, Frankie wanted to try on my Eisenhower jacket. Pop stood back, red-faced, smiling, proud of his son in uniform. It was a Friday afternoon, and Mom said, "Go with Pappa to synagogue tonight," then quickly added, "You don't have to go in the morning. In the morning you can sleep late. He would like that very much."

We walked to synagogue. "My son defending his country," Pop said, still smiling. Very nice. You know, when you get to Germany, maybe you can go to Ruppichteroth."

"Sure," I said, "if I can, I will. And I'll wear the uniform, walk all the streets with my uniform when I get there."

When we got home from *shul*, there was the white tablecloth and the candles. First came the chicken soup, then potato shalet and roast chicken, wine cream for dessert. All through the meal, I felt like a guest. All that weekend, I slept.

There were photographs to be taken. "Out, out on the street," said my mother. "The light is better. One with each, one with each."

At the end of the leave, Pop insisted that he would drive me back to Fort Dix. Quietly, when she had me alone, Mom said, "Maybe you could take the bus. It's a long ride there and then back. Right now, Pappa is a little bit nervous."

"Nervous? About what?"

"I really shouldn't say. I don't know. But I think it's maybe about you going. Going back. The Russians. Oh, I don't know."

It had never been Mom's manner, in the past, to sound confused. But when I suggested to Pop that maybe Mom should drive to the base and he could drive them back, he barked, "No!" and I didn't argue.

The evening before leaving, there were calls from Uncle Theo and Aunt Irma, each brief and each ending with "Be careful." Oma loaded me up with several cans of paté, lots of hugs, and an embarrassed, "I know you like it." In the morning there were punches to the shoulder from the brothers, and we were off. About halfway to Fort Dix, Pappa pulled into a service station. In a peculiar voice he said, "Somebody else has to drive, I have something in my eyes." As he rounded the front of the car, I saw him wiping his eyes with a handkerchief. Mom took the wheel. When Pop sat down beside her, Mom stroked the back of his head. She looked back at me, her lips pressed together. We drove off. I was reminded of how dumb I had been, how for so many years my cosmos, as regarding my father, had been ruled by my ego.

On just about the last day at Indiantown Gap, John Harmon told me, "Scuttlebut. I heard that when you get on your ship, go to the chaplain, tell him you want to be on the ship's newspaper; you'll get the run of the boat. No sweating with the grunts down below."

"How do you know this?"

"Your friend, this un-American commie pinko, picked it up in the officer's mess, where I am now employed as cook."

Once on the ship, I did as John suggested. The chaplain said, "Yes, we used to have a paper but not this trip. But here, you seem like a nice guy." He handed me an armband that said something about journalism. Then he added, "But you'll have to help the chaplain's assistant set up for Passover the next few days." How he knew I was Jewish, I will never know.

I was hanging over the ship's railing. The spume from heavy, North Atlantic waves reached the high deck, the salt water cooling my face. I had just finished throwing up when somebody tapped me on the shoulder. He was very tall, blond, and blue-eyed. His armband read "Chaplain's Assistant." "You're Hess? I'm Steve Burns."

I was feeling a bit better after my exchange with the ocean, "Funny,"I said, "you don't look Jewish."

"Just camouflage for life in Sioux Falls, South Dakota, and it used to be Bernstein. Let's get you something for your stomach."

"Please, no gefilte fish right now."

"What makes you think . . . ?"

"All the chaplain at the Gap ever handed out was gefilte fish and Tam-Tam crackers."

We were now inside a huge club-like room. Small tables with wire-backed chairs were scattered about it, and a dark, wine-colored carpet covered the floor. On either side, port and starboard, a vast array of windows gave views onto the gray ocean as it churned up the waves, which made me feel like we were piggyback on a reeling drunk. Even in this hall, the ship's rush through the sea provided background noise.

Against one wall was a baby grand piano that someone was playing, quiet notes that wrapped themselves around the sea's noise and became part of the background. Against another wall was something that looked like a bar. That's where I was led.

"This is no bar," said Steve Burns. "You may never, ever, say that this is a bar. This is a place where officers may congregate and recreate, but never refer to it as a bar. As befits an ocean liner, this place is called a salon. Not a bar." I did not argue. Steve said to the guy behind the bar, "Give this guy some soda." He shook his head, but when Steve pointed to my armband, the guy reached underneath the bar and pulled out a bottle of soda and a glass. The soda settled my stomach.

Next to the piano, sitting on the floor, was a small, dark boy who from time to time looked up from the book he was reading to the player, whom I could not see until I went over and stood behind the boy. Playing the baby grand was a very beautiful African-American woman. I had actually seen her once before when, shortly after graduating CCNY, a bunch of us, celebrating our graduation, had splurged and gone down to Café Society, in the Village.

The tune she played was Gershwin's "Soon" — slow, drawn out, shaped and reshaped, modulating from a blues to pop song to a pathetic torch song, then returning to a different blues, a different pop, a different torch. Throughout there were interpolations of other Gershwin songs with such subtle and shimmering changes that only later, trying to replay them in my head, did I then even vaguely understand what she had been doing. I stood there a good while before she looked up from the keyboard.

"I don't take requests. And please be careful, that's my son."

I stepped back away from the boy. "Sorry. I saw you at Café Society last year."

She smiled, "You saw me? I am wonderfully flattered to have a fan on this ship. Then okay. I'll take a request."

"More blues."

"You want blues?"

I nodded. She turned back to the piano and began to play, but it wasn't blues, it was Chopin, it was the Barcarolle. I knew the piece; Pop played his Chopin record often. I had heard him say to Rabbi Lieber once, after synagogue, with great relish, "I have Rubinstein in my house." With the Barcarolle, Pop would say, "You see the dancer?" And if I paid attention I would see the dancer, but this time I heard it all new. I heard the waves, I heard memory, I heard loss. I heard blues. I heard a piano being played every bit as fine as Rubinstein ever played. I clapped when it ended, and she started in on Tico Tico. I shook my head.

"Don't care for my bread and butter?" she laughed. "Okay, I know. Some more blues." With her hands folded over the keys, she drew a long breath and began to play. Very low and slow, it was the Chopin Berceuse. I wanted to cry. The whole time I stood there I wanted to cry, but of course I couldn't. I saw Ruppichteroth. The cobblestones were shiny. A late sun turned the white walls of houses to orange. A knot began to form in my stomach. And I saw train tracks, and swooping electric lines, that led us from Germany to Holland.

She stopped, looked up at me, "See, Chopin knew the blues." I quickly said, "Yes. Thanks." Almost stumbling over her son, I ran out to the ship's railing again. I didn't want to hear any more blues.

A few days later, early in the day, a brief blare over the ship's public address system announced, "Anyone wishing to celebrate the Passover can show up on the top deck salon at 19 hours sharp."

The salon was empty except for the grand piano and about fifteen uniforms standing among a row of folding tables in the center of the room. It was *erev Pesakh,* the night for the seder, and the North Atlantic was not happy. Hard waves were slapping the sides the ship, and the spray reached our high deck and striped the glass walls of the salon. With each bounce, the strings of the piano sounded an eerie discordant whisper.

"Where's the rabbi?" someone called out.

"The ocean's got something against Jews?"

"Please, no brisket tonight. Who can hold it down?"

Burns stumbled through a door carrying a heavy carton. Haggadahs tumbled down from the top of it. "Please, everyone, pick them up. Take one and let's all sit." He put his burden down, and went over to the bar. We all sat, and he came back with a stack of little plastic thimbles and a bottle of wine. "Our wine glasses." The thimbles were distributed. Burns screwed off the top of the wine bottle. "Let's see if we can make it reach four glasses for everybody." I noticed that the Haggadahs were all blue-covered with a streamer, "Compliments of Maxwell House," printed along the bottom. I began to feel at home.

Someone began to read, "And it was evening and it was morning; the sixth day." I sat down next to an officer, surprised at the silver leaf and cavalry patch on his shoulder. He was a colonel.

Burns ripped open another carton, pulled out jars of gefilte fish, and distributed them around the table. "Please don't open them until we get to eating. These you can eat." He set out boxes of Tam Tam crackers. "They're going to have to do for matzohs."

The colonel smiled at me. "Just about eight years ago I was at Mauthausen," he said, then shook his head and clamped his lips together before saying, almost to himself, "Son of a bitch. Son of a bitch. Ironic, isn't it?

"What, Sir."

"Now I'm going back to save those bastards from Uncle Joe. Ironic, isn't it? Where are you from?"

I told him, New York City. I wanted to tell him that I'd been born in Germany, but I couldn't. Yet as the ship steamed on and as the story of the escape from Egypt was being retold, I felt myself more and ever more as having come from Ruppichteroth, the place I had escaped from, and the country to which I was returning. We were two days out of Bremerhaven.

"Yes, Sir," I said, "hell of an irony." The telling of the Jew's liberation from Egypt went on.

Nowhere in the Haggadah is there any reference to a place, any chunk of ground in Egypt, that some slave might have cared about, never mind loved. That's not what the Haggadah story was about. There wasn't much anger in the text, either, just the multiplication of plagues visited with gusto on the Egyptians — from ten to fifty to 250 in the retelling by the rabbis, the sages, centuries later. I always smiled when I heard this *midrash*, this story, told, imagining some small group in the Middle Ages, or later still, having only recently escaped murder, now praying in exile, in their pointed caps, or with yellow patches stitched onto their coats — how they must have relished the piling on of plagues.

I thought of how they might have told the Passover story in Mauthausen.

But this time, I couldn't smile. Instead, I wanted to cry when I heard all the Passover songs after the meal of Tam Tams and gefilte fish: songs of praise for His mercy that endures forever; songs of thanks for all the miracles, the miracles in the daytime and the miracles at midnight. The songs all sounded like blues to me, songs of loss and anger.

Chapter Twenty-Five

The *Buckner* was in the English Channel, and I was leaning over the railing. The sea was calmer now, and the sun was making sparkling splinters on the low wave tops.

I remembered making Peter walk the top of the rail on the *Caribia*.

"What the hell you doing up here?" Brown-faced and gray-headed, he was a master sergeant with more stripes on his sleeve than I had ever seen before. I quickly lifted up my arm to let him see that I was a member of the press. Master sergeants had a way of intimidating PFCs, but he answered very gently: "Oh, okay, didn't see that. Wanna write about me?"

I explained the dormant nature of the ship's paper. He shook his head and smiled. "That's okay. That's okay." He leaned out over the railing with me for a long while. "That's Cherbourg out there. You can't see it, but that's Cherbourg out there."

"That's the tip of Normandy," I observed.

"You know about Normandy?" He seemed surprised.

"June 6th, 1944. Everybody knows about that." I was about to tell him my *bar mitzvah* had been two days before, but I stopped myself.

"You be damned surprised how many don't know. Goddamn shame."

"I followed the war on a map. I followed the whole hedgerow campaign."

"You were just a kid."

"I was thirteen in '44."

"I was twenty-six in '44." He said it low, as if talking to himself. "Had a bazooka team in the hedgerows."

"You took out tanks with bazookas," I said with awe.

He didn't answer, just looked out towards where he had indicated Cherbourg.

The hedgerow campaign had been fierce. I had read of the bazookas standing up against German Tiger tanks. You had one shot, and if you missed with that shot, you were dead.

"Big cemetery out there," he said. "First leave I get, gonna look up some old buddies."

I was about to say, "Lots of cemeteries out there," when he turned and left me alone, leaning over the rail.

I was often at that rail, day and night, looking for lights, for cities, and hoping to hear some of those sounds I had loved so many years ago — in Le Havre or Dieppe or Boulogne or Calais, or Dunkirk or Ostende — trying to follow the route back that I had once taken out. The more I stood there the sadder I became, thinking of all those cemeteries out there beyond the water.

Still, in the morning I was at the rail again. The day was glorious, the sky washed to a light blue, the clouds small and very white, and happy, the breeze happy.

Burns appeared at my side. Couldn't they all leave me alone? "That's Heligoland Island over there," he said.

"I know. The Brits blew half their island to hell last year."

"Lots of bombers went down because of that place."

"One time, when I was a kid," I told him, after a sad beat, "my class was invited someplace in town where they showed movies. Just as we entered the hall each of us was handed a cup of soup. We were told that the soup was a gift from our 'Führer.' Somebody stopped me from going in. Somebody said, 'This Jew?' Then somebody nodded, and this Jew was handed a cup of soup. Inside the hall we saw a documentary on Heligoland. The island had been changed from whatever it had been into a resort for nice blond boys and girls to do all kinds of calisthenics on a beach. All their nice holidays were also a gift from their 'Führer.' The Brits should have blown the whole place up."

"You're German? One of those refugees?"

"One of those, yeah. As to German? Yes, no. What the hell do I know?" There must have been something peculiar in my voice, some kind of resentment, some kind of anger. Burns leaned over the railing next to me.

"You know, we Jews have a lot of rituals to help us get over our mourning, to get over our losses."

"So? I should say *kaddish* for . . . Oh, hell." I turned away, then almost ran to the other side of the ship. What the fuck did he know? He was just a chaplain's assistant.

The ship turned into the Weser estuary, and now there were coastlines on both sides of the ship. As we neared Bremerhaven, the two coasts narrowed, like pliers, and I could see, on one shore, great cranes waving their giant arms, dropping loads into the bottoms of anchored freighters. Dangling at the end of these great arms were huge wooden rectangles that looked from my distance, like the "lifts," the cargo boxes in which some of those leaving Germany, had packed everything that still belonged to them. Were there still any people who hadn't left?

On the other shore, I could see rows of houses, spanking white, their red roof tiles seeming to smile beneath the happy clouds, their windows reflecting the blue of the sky. There were roads on which cars moved, and green gardens around the houses, and green trees — all as if nothing had ever happened. How could this place still exist? How come there was still this firm earth surrounding the

Weser estuary? How come there was still a Weser estuary? They had blown up half of Heligoland — why not all of it, and all of the mainland too?

The busy cranes, the shining houses, the sky and clouds, were mocking me. Didn't they know what had happened? Didn't they know about the lost places, the loved places, the lost people, the loved people? Why did any of this damned place still exist?

Over the ship's loudspeakers came the order that the uniform of the day was fatigues, that we were to gather our duffle bags, that we were to be prepared, shortly, to debark and then board a train for Pirmasens, the trip to take about eight hours.

The *Buckner* docked. We stood somewhere in the bowels of the ship. A large black panel opened, two gangways were let down to the dock, and down we tumbled. Across from the *Buckner* were huge warehouses, and between the ship and the warehouses were railroad tracks. A long train rested there, its coaches fancy, like Pullman cars. Far ahead, smoke rose from an engine that I could not see. It whistled, and a sharp, knife-shaped plume rose.

Several NCO's waved us into the cars: "Let's go. Let's go. Move your ass." A man in a dark uniform, papers under one arm, waved us on as well. He was smiling, waving one arm to make us go faster: *"Schnell, schnell, Kinder. Schneller, Schneller. Müssen fort."* As I came up to the man, I yelled at him, *"Wo sind die verdammte Lastwagen?"* Where are the damned freight cars? His smile disappeared.

We boarded second-class cars, which looked better from the outside than inside. The seats were covered with a fuzzy green felt. Thousands rubbing against the felt had raised a nap that would never be combed down. The cars' interiors were old and neglected, the wooden trim around the ceiling and sides dull, and with gray and green splotches spreading outward onto the dingy white ceilings and walls. I thought, "They didn't clean these cars very well. How very un-German." Oh, well, they were just for the Americans to use, so who cared how they looked? Yet they felt familiar, the green felt especially. *Could we have ridden these same cars to Holland fifteen years ago? No, those cars had been bombed to hell during the war. Must have been, should have been.* But these cars were so very 1930s, so very old.

I had a window seat. The train took off. White smoke billowed past the window. I was making a return trip.

For the hundredth time, it seemed, somebody with stripes walked through car shouting variations on: "Y'all goin' to Pirmasens. Pirmasens. Germany. Dutchland!!! Dutchland!!! You are in Dutchland. Dutchland's now our ally. Don't want any you to make any illegal moves against these fine frauleins they got over here, Dutchland's now our allies. You all are replacements and you all are replaceable. Two, three months now y'all won't be wearin' no class A's outside your base, goin' drinkin' that fine Loewenbrau beer. Beer's the best thing they got over here. Except maybe Jaegermeister. Don't do no shots with it, except maybe if you get a letter your wife is leavin'. Yeah. Jaegermeister. Know that these Germans are sensitive and don't want nobody to remind them of what happened. Anybody here know what happened? Didn't think so. But you guys goin' to Pirmasens. From there you will be sent to some place else in Dutchland. Maybe Division, maybe someplace else. You all are replacements. From division you will be sent to some rifle company guarding the borders of freedom, unless you got some kind of MOS where you don't never have to clean no rifle. Don't think none of you guys got that. It might be a while that you are in Pirmasens; be a while before they decide what to do with you. You will be bored out of your skulls waiting and there will be no going outside the base for beer or frauleins or Jaegermeister. You will keep Pirmasens clean. You will be asked to pick up any cigarette butts on the ground. The will be no cigarette butts on the ground because all the previous replacements will have picked up whatever there was on the ground, but you will do a lot of walking stooped over. You will pick up anything that even looks like a butt even if it's bird turd. You are going to Pirmasens. It's an eight-hour trip. Get yourselves sleep. You will not get much sleep later on 'cause you'll be defending Dutchland, their beer and their frauleins."

I was actually grateful for these interruptions because they kept reminding me of where I was rather than being so preoccupied with where I had been, years before. Still, where I had been kept rushing through my head. There were all those railroad stations we had passed through in 1939, with familiar names, from Bremerhaven to Bremen. In my childhood, no one had ever mentioned Bremen without sarcasm. People from Bremen were snooty. They spoke *hoch Deutsch,* was "high German." Everybody else, anywhere else in Germany, spoke it wrong. Snooty people were bad people. I knew that. I was given that from the age of 3. The fact that my father, mother and grandmother could still summon a resentment toward Bremen and all of north Germany whenever Bremen was mentioned in the kitchen of 652 West 160th Street made me angry. I once yelled out, "You are not living in Germany any more. Forget Germany!" And I ran out of the house. That had been loud anger. My anger was silent most of the time.

After Bremen, the train pushed through the Teutoburger Wald. Passing through Osnabrück, I saw a sign, something about the Teutoburger Wald. The subject of the Teutoburger Wald had not come up often in the apartment on 160th Street, but when it did, silent anger roiled my gut. Sometime in Caesar Augustus' reign, Herman, or Arminius (my father called him Herman), thoroughly annihilated three Roman legions led by one Varus. My father could go on for quite a while proudly detailing the precise course of the Roman defeat by the Germans and lauding the fight for German independence from Roman subjugation. Then, at the end of the lecture, with a broad grin, he would intone a little jig about "Varus, Varus, Varus, where is your army?" How, how, how could he do that, carrying on with that grinning recitation of German victory? The Germans were barbarians then and barbarians still. Didn't he know that it was the Germans who should have been annihilated, subjugated to Rome until the end of time?

Münster, Hamm, Dortmund, Essen: The train pulled on, the cities were left behind. There was a story my grandmother read to me about Münster; Pop had relatives in Hamm; Dortmund, more relatives; Essen, now we were in the Ruhr and the Rhineland, my home. We had bombed the hell out of the Ruhr. There were the wires, telephone or electric, that rose and fell the whole route of the train, but their gentle bellying, which had been so calming to me on the way out, now only reminded me of that exodus. There were the small green gardens behind the little red-tiled houses, where women were puttering with rakes and hoes, or kneeling, planting, ripping up weeds. It was all just like it had been on our way out. How could these women do this? Didn't they know?

Düsseldorf: Somebody had an aunt there who ran a store. We had bombed the hell out of Düsseldorf. Now we were on the industrial Rhine, not the romantic part. From a distance I could see the spire of the great Cologne cathedral. Thirteenth or 14th century? I had to know, and there was nobody to ask. The train stopped at an isolated siding in the Cologne station. Here we were let out of our cars for a few moments and allowed to walk about. Through a fence and across a narrow street, I could see the stony grayness of the cathedral. There were cars on the street, taxis. People walked. Was anybody going to the place where I had seen my first movie? Somebody whistled for a taxi. Was anybody going to the offices where Mom, half- crazed, had tried to find out where Pop had been taken on *Kristallnacht?* The cathedral was up close, blocking the sky. I could see an entrance where women, mostly older women holding net shopping bags, crossed in and out. The up-close cathedral was a taunt: "I've been here all the time, all the time, not you, not you."

The train went on. It rushed through Bonn, where Oma and Pop went on Fridays to buy groceries for Oma's store. Bonn, where twice the little train had taken us to the big train, on the way out. And there, to the east, not very far away, was Siegburg, and the hospital where I was born — and just a bit further, a very short distance further, Ruppichteroth, the place where I had lived. Ruppichteroth, "Ruprecht's clearing in the road."

All along the way were the rising and falling wires, and cars on the roads, and people walking and, in this spring, planting their little plots and pulling out weeds.

Now came the romantic part of the Rhine, through the great gorges, past the hillsides where grapes grew, past pinnacles where sat the ruined castles of the robber barons. We stopped briefly in the Koblenz station. There had been a cattle market in Koblenz where Opa and Pop bought and sold cattle. Like Opa, the market was surely gone. I wanted to see the great fortifications that Pop had often talked about so admiringly, Ehrenbreitstein high on its pinnacle, guarding Koblenz from the French. *"Die Wacht am Rhine," the watch on the Rhine*, blared out by the hundred kids marching in their brown uniforms and the hooked cross flags; somebody had called it the "Whine on the Rhine," but I couldn't remember who, and I didn't get to see Ehrenbreitstein.

Boppard, Oberwesel, Bachrach; who wrote "The Rabbi of Bachrach?" Was it Heine? *Ich weiss nicht was, soll es bedeuten, Dass ich so traurig bin, Ein Märchen aus uralten Zeiten, Das kommt mir nich aus dem Sinn. Don't know what it means that I'm so terribly sad, an ancient tale keeps murmuring about in my head.* Yeah, it was Heine, and tales and other stuff were whirling about in my head.

Now Bingen, but I didn't see that peak sparkling in the evening sun, nor that most beautiful virgin combing her golden tresses and luring the sailors to their deaths. There was no luring, no luring at all. I didn't know why I was so sad, so angry. I didn't know that I lost something that I wanted and didn't want, didn't know why I wanted the whole place to sink into the ground, to relieve me from feeling that this was a place that I'd ever cared about. I didn't know that I still cared.

"You have come to Pirmasens, Germany," said the sergeant. We were lined up in front of army bunks in a huge dormitory. "You are lucky that it's not Korea, but if you'd had any real luck they'd have sent you to Hawaii. You've come to Pirmasens by the grace of your Uncle Sam and your MOS. You'll be here two, three days an' then off to some division headquarters where they'll send you somewhere else. An' if you stay lucky an' keep your noses clean, you draftees, after eighteen, twenty months, you'll go home with a good conduct medal an' a dose of the clap."

We slept for two days, and then some of us were told that we were going to Göppingen, Cooke Barracks, the headquarters of the 28th Infantry Division, the Pennsylvania Keystone Division. Okay, not bad, but where were their regiments stationed, their battalions, their heavy weapons platoons? "You'll go where they tell you," we were told.

On a train again. We stopped briefly in Stuttgart. *Can I get out? Can I get directions to the American consulate from someone, anyone here in Stuttgart, where Mom went half crazy in 1938, trying to get papers for America?* I couldn't get out. When the train stopped again, the signs said, "Göppingen." I had never heard of Göppingen. We were loaded onto trucks. I badly wanted see the town through which we were passing, but because of where I sat and the truck's canvas cover, I could see nothing.

When we jumped out of the trucks, there were maybe a hundred of us. A sergeant waved us into motion. No lining up, no marching, no "hup two, hup, two," just a wave. The sergeant pointed, and we saw a huge sign stuck in the ground and the huge red keystone. I'd seen a lot of that at the Gap, it was the emblem of the Pennsylvania national guard. Then I read, "Welcome to Cooke Barracks — Headquarters of the 28th Infantry Division." Walking to where the sergeant was leading us provided a few moments to look around at the solid houses, some with two stories, some with gabled roofs. These were nothing like the wooden structures I'd lived in at the Gap. I heard somebody say, "These guys really built stuff to last."

Curving roads were lined with barracks and high-reaching trees, and there were green lawns that stretched out from the houses to the road's edge. It might have been an expensive suburban subdivision.

We passed Rogers Road, and then walked up tree-lined Terry Allen Avenue.

Now we were in a theater, facing a white screen. A warrant officer, holding papers, stepped out from a group on one side of the room. "You guys are impressed at our little town here, aren't you? The Germans built good," he said. "Good for a thousand years, they did. And yeah, we show movies. Got a bowling alley too. We built that. Eight lanes. Library, if you read. Got a photo lab, that's because everybody gets here gets themselves a Leica. Got a very nice chapel. Got a very nice nine-hole golf course, too. Anybody here play golf? No? Nobody? Good, 'cause you got to be here a while before they let you play, and none of you will be staying here. These goodies are all for those assigned to Division Headquarters; that's where you all are now, but in three days you'll be going down the road to Gablingen, that's the Gablingen just outside Augsburg, that's the Augsburg in Bavaria, Germany. You'll be going to Headquarters, 109th Infantry Regiment. A good outfit; they got a band and all. And from there you'll be assigned further. Okay? Can't tell you where they'll assign you down there, so don't ask." Then, without any transition, he began to read from one of the papers he held, things we'd heard repeatedly in basic, but now tailored to where we were.

"You are now in the 28th Infantry Division. The primary mission of the 28th is to close with the enemy by fire and maneuver in order to capture or destroy him, or to repel his assault by fire and close combat. The specific mission of the Division is threefold. First, to engage in a training program designed to improve its capabilities to fulfill its primary mission. Second, as a part of the North Atlantic Treaty Army, it is to help safeguard the peace and freedom of the people of Western Europe and North America, and, if necessary, to defend that freedom against any aggressor. Third, by demonstrating to the people of Germany the high standard of American moral, cultural and material life, it is to inspire them with confidence in democratic ideals. That last means we don't want to find anybody passed out drunk in the streets of whatever town you're going to be in. The beer here is potent. Do it and the consequences will be potent, too. For two cartons of cigarettes you can get laid. We'll call out your names and these guys here will hand you your orders. Be here when the bus for Gablingen takes off."

Orders in hand, we were led to one of the houses, now called "kasernes," for our three-day stay. On entering the building, we were simply awed: there were tiles, tiles for a thousand years, white tiles, floor to ceiling. The hallway floors were tiled, the walls were tiled, the toilets were tiled, the shower rooms were tiled, all floor to ceiling. The ceiling in the hallway was high, and from somewhere the sun was allowed in, but I saw no windows. The ceilings in our new dorms were also high, and there was wainscoting half way up the walls. Eight to a dorm, the last one in was in charge. "Make your bunks and keep it spic. We see garbage and we got kitchen sumps need cleaning. Do what you're told. We know your names. Best thing next three days is you sleep. Not going to get much after. No going off base for the time you're here. Enjoy."

The first day I slept. The second day I got bored sleeping and wandered about the base. There were curving roads, and trees and bushes graced the small paths circling about the solid rectangular buildings. I was in suburbia. I saw the huge PX, which was comparable to any food emporium in the U.S., and where they sold cigarettes for eleven cents a pack. I walked past a theater. A very small wall sign advertised "The Bad and the Beautiful." From another building I heard the crash of bowling pins. I went in and found all eight lanes busy.

My wandering stopped at a fence. The suburbs stopped at the

fence. Guards patrolled that fence. I stopped and looked at buildings that were in long decline from their bright tiled origins. The shabby structures stretched into the distance. Sometimes someone, man or woman, in shabby clothes, on the other side of the fence, would shuffle by and look towards the fence.

"What are you looking at?"

I spun and saw a grey-haired master sergeant. "Get out of here. No buying or selling today."

"Please, sir, who are they?"

"Not sir, the king hasn't seen fit to knight me yet. DP's. Russians, Ukrainians, Jews. Nobody wants 'em and these haven't got the energy to go. You a replacement?"

"Yes."

"Don't get involved with 'em. Man or woman. If you sell 'em a carton of cigarettes, the going rate is twelve Deutch Marks. Don't let 'em cheat you. Now get out of here. You got no business here."

I went and found the base library. I was awed by its fan of brightly shining stacks that were ceiling-high and fat with books. I stood a while just to look at the wonderful faded colors of the books' spines. The only people in the library were myself, a young woman who sat behind a very library-like desk, and another GI whom I could only see from the back. He was bent over, leaning both elbows on the desk.

"Ya, please, can I help you?" said the young woman. The GI at the desk turned around. The GI and I both smiled broadly as we recognized each other.

"Hess tess kiss my ess," he said.

"Rubel, you bastard."

"Hess tess kiss my ess; how about a game of eightball?"

"What, they've got pool rooms here? All I saw was a bowling alley."

"No, no pool rooms." He smiled. "But we've all kinds of other entertainment here."

The girl at the desk turned toward a typewriter next to her and began typing.

Bert Rubel had been perhaps the best pool player in Washington Heights. He was a year ahead of me in school and had been the center half on the Maccabi soccer team for older teens. On the same floor as our Club Maccabi hangout was a pool hall. If you wanted to find Rubel, you'd find him there. While so many of us at Maccabi had after-school jobs to pay for our various enjoyments, Rubel made his money at the pool tables. He was a great fan of Woody Herman and was the first person that I knew who smoked pot.

The young woman at the typewriter turned to me and smiled. "You two know each other?"

"Bert and I live in the same neighborhood. I'm 160th, he's on 162nd, between the drive and Fort Washington. Goddamn, we're in the same neighborhood again! How long have you been here?"

The young woman had brown hair pulled back in a bun, big eyes, an oval face ending in sharp chin, skin with a pinkish sheen. She wore a dark sweater with a brooch over her heart. She looked like the librarian at the Jumel branch on St. Nicholas Avenue. She looked at Bert: "Does he . . . ?" Bert looked a bit puzzled and then replied, "Yeah. All right. You speak German, don't you, Hess?"

"Yes?"

"How good is your German?"

"I don't know. Three years of B's at City. And they were easy markers. Probably just like you. Like all us refugee kids."

"You just come here? What's your assignment? Your orders?"

"I'm being sent to some infantry regiment." I sighed. "I'll be hauling a damn base plate for another two years."

The young woman librarian quickly said, "Eighteen months. Draftees are being sent home after eighteen months."

"I've been here seventeen, supposed to go home next month," Bert said. He looked at the librarian, then at me. "I've got two weeks of leave coming that I want to take before I go. But they won't let me take my leave unless they get a replacement for me. You are my replacement."

"But my orders say . . ."

"Screw the orders. I'll get new orders cut for you."

"I'm ordered to Augsburg. Tomorrow."

"You're staying. I'll have the orders cut this afternoon."

"You'll cut the orders? Rubel cutting orders? What?"

"A bunch of us corporals run division HQ. Corporals do all the work here. We're all friends. I tell them, they'll do it."

"Hard to believe, but what will I be doing? What have you been doing?"

"I work for JAG."

"What's JAG?"

"Judge Advocate General. I translate for them. General Courts Martial's where German witnesses are involved. And there are always German witnesses involved."

"Hope it's better than hauling a base plate. "

"It's a good job. People are all nice, mostly lawyers. Just watch out for Colonel Rood — but you like classical music. You'll probably get along."

Some hundred of us sat on our duffle bags. We had been called out of the Kaserne at 7:00 and now it was about two hours later. We had been standing in ranks for a long time when a gray-haired sergeant called out, "Everybody relax." It was no order I'd ever heard before, and when somebody sat on his duffel bag there was no countermanding.

Trucks rolled up and names were called out. The names clambered into the trucks and disappeared behind the rear canvas. Name after name disappeared, and I was sure that Rubel had been pulling my leg. Corporals do not run U.S. Army divisions. But as more and more men disappeared while I remained sitting, it began to dawn on me that indeed corporals did run the army. What had Eisenhower ever been thinking? I was the last one sitting, and when the gray-haired sergeant approached, I snapped to attention.

"At ease. You Hess?"

"Yes, sergeant."

"Your MOS heavy weapons?"

"Yes, sergeant."

"Then why the hell are you assigned to division HQ?" He continued on, but it was a mumble, and then he shoved the papers in his hand at me, pointed to a building some distance away. "Up there. Personnel. There's a sign. Take your goddamn bag."

Obviously, if you are a private in the army, stripeless, not even a private first class, and are invited to see Personnel in person, an alteration of your destiny has surely been decreed. I trooped to Personnel, where a corporal changed my destination from Augsburg and the 109th Infantry Regiment in the Gablingen Kaserne to HQ Company 28th Infantry Division, Göppingen. Another corporal then changed my MOS from Heavy Weapons Specialist to Interpreter (German). Another corporal showed me to my quarters, a large room with four bunk-beds and a row of wooden closets. On the way to my new digs I learned that my corporal guide was a graduate of Harvard, and that he was acquainted with the Agha Khan.

A day later, though my collar was still tan, there was now a whitish tinge to my collar, with a desk all my own in the office of the Division Judge Advocate General.

Rubel showed me around, introduced me to the several enlisted men, clerks and administrators with whom I'd be working, and to the several officer-lawyers with whom I'd be spending a good deal of time. The most imposing of them was Lt. Colonel Rood. He was large, his face pale, a collection of folds under bushy eyebrows. He talked with a twang that I was to learn originated in Arizona. I also was to learn that he'd been in what he called "the war previous," and that he'd been recalled to duty at the start of the Korean War.

"You a lawyer?"

"No, sir."

"Good. How do you know German?"

"I was born here."

"I don't hear any accent."

"I was eight when we left, sir."

"And that must have been…?"

"Nineteen thirty-nine, sir."

His eyebrows rose and he nodded. I thought that he was going to ask me something, but he seemed to change his mind. His eyebrows lowered, and in the kindest way, he asked about my schooling.

"History major, sir."

"History major?"

"Yes, sir. American history."

"American history, very good. How do you feel about Abraham Lincoln? Never mind, we'll talk about him another time. How do you feel about the Germans?"

I was silent. I shrugged. I felt angry, but I didn't know that I felt angry. In any case I liked the question. He was very smart.

"Get yourself a good dictionary," he said. "Talk to people. The language has changed a bit since the last time you were here, since the last time I was here. Get Rubel to tell you how to get your corporal stripes."

Rubel told me that to get my stripes, I had to wait: first, a period of waiting for PFC, then another period for corporal, but as soon as the periods were up, I could write the orders for my promotion myself and Colonel Rood would sign them.

It seemed as if all the officers were lawyers and spoke with a twang. Captain Herbert came from North Carolina. The first time we were introduced, I saw Gunner Myrdal's book, *An American Dilemma: The Negro Problem and Modern Democracy*, on his desk. Lieutenant Bullock was from a Texas oil family who, I later learned, had flown his new Jaguar sedan from England to the Stuttgart airport on a private plane. Captain Barry was black, from New York City. He hardly ever spoke, except in court, and while I might have extended conversations with all the officers — we were all college men — my exchanges with Barry were always brief and merely business. I often wondered how John Harmon might have fared in the JAG environment.

Divisional JAG had supervision over all aspects of the Uniform Code of Military Justice. I was mostly needed as a translator in General Courts Martial, where major crimes were adjudicated, and while I was sometimes called on to work on cases involving minor offenses, which were dealt with at a battalion or company level, I really had very little to do. Sometimes they gave me documents to translate.

My barracks environment was not very different from the JAG office. My friends here, though few could boast of an acquaintance with the Agha Kahn, were also college graduates, some with very advanced degrees. Nicholas, the Ph.D. in history, had written his thesis on Motley and the origins of his *Rise of the Dutch Republic.* Nicholas would not pal around with the Jews in the company. Richard did pal around, however, as did Ken, who knew the Agha Kahn, and Ross and Scott. We became friends. They were all draftees who had been assigned to the base, some for weeks, others for months, and were all part of the corporalship. Richard did some writing for officers on the upper level; Ken was assigned to intelligence; Ross and Scott did some sort of administrative work. Scott, who was Jewish, had a motorcycle that he was allowed to keep on base. He and Ross introduced me to bars and beer, and what to order in which restaurants.

Maybe I was the only Jew in the group who thought in Jewish terms, that is, who was conscious as to who else was Jewish and who was not. That consciousness was lost very quickly, however, as it became obvious that whether we were Harvard or CCNY, UCLA or Washington University, our interests were pretty much the same:

beer and girls.

There were girls on the base — Rubel's friend who worked in the library, sales clerks in the PX, secretaries in the various offices of headquarters. They all seemed to be of an age that interested recent college grads, and they all looked, as my friend Richard pointed out, as though they, too, were recent college graduates of the Seven Sisters. The girls working in the PX, he insisted, had all gone to Smith. Whoever did the hiring for the PX must have known and liked something about Smith graduates. Richard went on to insist that that the Headquarters secretaries had all gone to Vassar, and that the several women translators on the base were definitely Radcliffe.

Sam Spitzer, however, objected to Richard's classifications. Sam was Cornell '50, and had been in Goeppingen the longest of us. Spitzer was going for a Ph.D. in philosophy. "No," he said. "they're not girls from the Seven Sisters. If they were, they would not want to be going to the States, they'd be taking a summer off to tour Europe: Rome, Florence, Madrid, maybe the Balearics. These ones are doing what they'd be doing in the States, where they all want to go. They all want to marry an American, marry one of the victors, one of the heroes, and get to the States, the land of *unbegrentzten möglichkeiten*, the land of unlimited possibilities. And of course bring their mother along."

"What about their father?" Richard said.

"Stalingrad; the Ardennes." The girls, Spitzer insisted, sometimes mentioned mothers but never their fathers. "But unless you promised to marry, you'd never get them to bed. Make out a bit, maybe, but unless you alerted the chaplain and received permission from the general, never a bed. They are pure examples of middle-class morality."

Still we all went out with the girls, usually in groups, to a restaurant, where they often received desirous stares from other patrons. We also went swimming at the marvelous, large pool on the base.

For me and my friends, there was a certain friendly ease with these girls from the base, an ease that came from the recognition of membership in a similar class.

I did go out on two dates, just two of us, dinner and a concert in Stuttgart. On each occasion, at some point in the evening, each date began to tell me a similar story of how terribly they had suffered during the war and its aftermath: the bombings, but especially the Russians. "You cannot imagine how terribly they treated us; rapes and theft; they lined us up and made us hold out our hands and if they saw a wristwatch, they ripped it from the wrist." They were quiet after their tales, but why were they telling me this? Who had told them I was Jewish? Was there some kind of equivalency being sought between whatever they suffered and what I had lost in place and people? Ruppichtheroth, Oma and Opa in Terezin, six million Jews?

I stopped going out with German women one on one.

As soon as I learned where my permanent home was to be, I sent my new address to 160th Street. It was the only letter that I wrote for a long time. Then I began getting letters from home, always written by Mom, and always containing the plea that I should please visit Ruppichtheroth.

I didn't want to go. I neglected her letters, but they kept coming. Her injunctions were of course mixed in with news from home, Frankie's *bar mitzvah* and so on, but always with, "Could you, and why don't you, you really should go and visit Rupp. Bendix would love to see you, and when you go could you please bring him one of those new 'wash and wear' shirts?"At first I had no idea who Bendix was, but soon I was given to understand that he lived in our old house in Ruppichtheroth, that he was Jewish, and that he and his wife, who was not Jewish, and their one son, had all been hidden by someone, somewhere near the town, during the terrible times.

The reason Bendix had assumed such importance was that my

grandparents' property, the house and surrounding pastures, all had been returned to their heirs: Pop and his brother Albert. In dividing the property, Albert got the house and Pop got the pastures. Bendix had somehow acquired the job of managing these properties and those of the others dispossessed from our town and nearby towns, property that had been returned after the war by the new government.

Mom and Pop wanted to see pictures, so I bought a Leica, but I sent no pictures. "And I really don't understand," wrote my mother, "why don't you go see our old town. You really have to see Bendix. See what he's doing. Does he have any customers for our property, and what are the going prices for property in the area? It would really help us if you found out all these things." I knew that it wouldn't help a bit, because I was certain that Mom and Pop were very well informed on all these issues from Bendix himself, and from their German friends in the area.

"Tante Mina," wrote my mother, "might be in Rupp sometime in June. Why don't you write back to us?"

Why was Mina visiting after all she had suffered at German hands? I had been forced to be here, while she had a choice. Why would she want anything to do, whatever, with Germany?

Chapter Twenty-Six

We were coming back from a trial in Augsburg, where Colonel Rood had been the presiding judge. He was in a rush to get back to our base in Göppingen, and as the local train seemed to be quicker than army transportation, the train it was. I went along because the colonel had asked me to carry some packages for him. Rood found an empty compartment, and as it was not seemly for a private to sit with a colonel, I started for another, but he stopped and waved me into his compartment. "Get in here."

"I don't understand," he said, "why you aren't writing to your parents?"

I reddened and covered my mouth. How did he know?

"Why aren't you writing home? I got a note from the AG's office that there had been an inquiry from the Red Cross about the fact that you haven't been answering any of your mother's letters. She was worried and got in touch with the Red Cross. What's this all about? Nice kids write their parents."

I didn't want to answer; didn't know what to answer.

"Don't you like your parents?" he said. "Are you mad at them?"

I turned away. In the window I saw the billowing electric wires.

"Here. Write." He handed me a sheet. "Write." Now I knew why the colonel had wanted me to carry his packages. He didn't want to do this in the office with others nearby.

I wrote.

Until recently, Mom had been writing about affairs at home; Oma was fine, Pappa was fine, Peter was fine, then more on Frankie and his preparations for *bar mitzvah*. Eisenhower she didn't like. She felt sad for Adlai Stevenson, who was getting a divorce, so the *Daily News* said, though she didn't like the *Daily News* or the *Mirror*. And please, to get some news from Ruppichteroth would be nice, just to know how things are. But then every letter had become urgent: I must, had to, it was absolutely necessary for me to go Ruppichteroth. If I didn't want to go for myself, I had to do it for the family, for Pappa.

I well understood that the invocation of Pappa was to really make me feel guilty.

"You have to go to Rupp. Go and see Bendix, and see if what he does is all right. He wants to sell one of the pastures by the highway, by the Bről brook. See what the property in the area is going for. Compare. See if what he does is all right. I don't think we should sell anything, but I am discussing it with Pappa. Mr. Bendix would very much like one of the new wash-and-wear shirts. You have to talk to Walter Schenk. He is a friend and knows about such things."

A friend? Why was Walter Schenk still a friend? Why was any German still their friend? Why did she want to hold onto even an inch of German soil? *Sell it! Sell it! Have you no memory?*

But I didn't write any of that.

Often, there was an addendum to her urgings: "Pappa thinks you should see August Willach. He was a friend of Pappa's from olden times. He would know about land prices and things." August Willach was one of the brothers who owned the factory that had made machinery for Hitler's war machine. They had used slave laborers and hid their dead bodies under the floors of their factory sheds. *Don't you remember what Leo Baer told us, that when he got to Ruppichteroth with the army in '45, Willach wanted to bribe him so that he wouldn't inform on him and his past?*

I didn't write any of that, either.

Late one afternoon, I was in the JAG office, lost in making translations of some documents. I thought that I was the only one left, but then I felt Colonel Rood standing in front of me.

"Get in my office." I got.

"Have you been writing home"?

"Yes, sir."

"Since the Red Cross inquired, how often?"

"Not too often."

"What's not too often?"

"Once."

"What the hell's the matter with you? No, don't tell me." I didn't tell him. I just stood there. "What the hell's the matter?" he repeated.

"I don't know. It feels peculiar being here."

"Where? On the base? Here?"

"No. I don't know. Germany."

"Germany. You'd rather be in Korea? When did you leave Germany, '39 — right?"

"Yes."

"And you were what?

"I was eight."

"And you remember everything?"

"Yes sir." I may have smiled slightly. He had me sit down in a chair across from his desk.

"You remember November, 1938 — the tenth?"

"How do . . . ?"

"In April, '45, I had to brief Ike on concentration camps," he said. "He was going to a place called Ohrdruf, with journalists, lots of cameras. It was part of a place called Buchenwald. You heard of Ohrdruf?"

I had to shake my head.

"Buchenwald?"

I nodded and felt the knot in my stomach.

He was silent for a long time, with a hand over his mouth. " I, we, all of us, received an education at Ohrdruf and then Buchenwald. That's how I know about November 10th. Did they take your father?"

I nodded.

"Where?"

"Dachau."

"Jeeesus." He was angry, appalled. "Dachau. Did you ever go there, where they sent your pappa? To see? Did he get out?"

I nodded. "After two months. He got out."

"You know, we go to Munich a lot, and coming and going we pass the damn Dachau station. And you've never gone there to see? Never even been interested?"

"When I see the Dachau station sign, I feel peculiar. I don't want to see it, but I see it. I get scared."

Colonel Rood's anger left him The folds on his face grew still. He was quiet. I was quiet.

"You get scared?" he said. "It's only a sign."

I didn't know the words with which to answer him. "I don't want to see it," I said. "It makes me feel helpless. And angry."

He was quiet for a while longer. "No," he agreed, "it's not only a sign." He put his elbows on the desk and his hands knotted under his chin. "Are you depressed?"

"What?'

"Depressed. I don't know if you remember, but in that assault case in Grafenwohr, one of the psychiatrists talked about that woman's depression as anger turned inward. I'm no shrink, but you mentioned anger."

"No. I don't think I'm depressed."

"You haven't accumulated any leave time," he observed. I shook my head. "Been out on passes? Seen anything of beautiful Deutschland?"

"Just Göppingen. A few times to Stuttgart, to concerts."

"We've been to trial…"

"Yes, sir, and Augsburg, Munich, the various Kasernes . . ."

"And Munich, we were just in Munich. That rape case. Munich interesting to you?

"Yes, sir. "

"Hitler's beer hall — you go there?

"No, sir. Haus Der Kunst. They had an exhibition of what the Nazis called degenerate art. Kandinsky, Picasso, Braque . . ."

"Yes, Bullok and I went there. Good to know there's at least one man on this base interested in culture rather than . . . What do you make of Klee? No, never mind."

"A couple of weeks ago," I added, "a bunch of us went to the Nürbergring for the car races.

"Nurbergring? Where is that?"

"Not far from Cologne, sir."

"Not far from Cologne. That's where you told me your hometown is. Not far from Cologne. Do you want to see the old place?"

"No, sir." Then I blurted, "But my parents want me to go there and see it."

"The parents you never write to?"

"I guess."

"You guess. Well, I'll tell you, from now on I want to see a letter to your folks once a week. You can just come here and wave the envelope at me, but I want to see the envelope. And I'll see to it that next week — are you due for a three-day pass?" I shook my head. "Well, I'll see you get one. You'll use it to see your hometown. You obviously have a mother that's concerned about you. I want to see that you meet that concern — otherwise, think about living in a tent in Grafenwohr for the rest of your duty here."

Grafenwohr is a muddy, mountainous, desert in Bavaria, southeast of Bayreuth and northeast of Nurnberg, not far from the Czech border, where Army units were regularly sent on maneuvers. Our HQ company had been sent there several weeks earlier, and our unit had lived, all of us in one tent, playing Hearts every day, all day, while all around us, tanks and artillery honed their skills.

On Armed Forces Day, the base was opened to German visitors. Everything had been scrubbed and cleaned. The half-tracks shone, the tanks were cleared of mud. The visitors inspected the dependents' school, the photo lab, the bowling alley. Wherever I went, I saw a German shaking his head and whispering to a neighbor, *"Das haben wir besser getan"* — *We did that better* — or some version thereof. A friend of mine, an off-duty MP who also spoke some German, nudged me, and shook his head. "You should have been here last year," he said. "On the night before Armed forces Day. We got a call that some young natives had some MP's surrounded in the town square. We busted in and relieved the situation. Busted some heads. The rest of the night was spent patrolling the officer's family quarters. There were some rumors that they were going to be burned down. Next day they'd scheduled a parade in town and our vehicles were showered with bricks and bottles." He snorted a kind of laugh. "Some celebration. But it's a lot nicer now. Somebody must have gotten on the phone to somebody, let 'em know who won the war."

That evening there was a concert in the auditorium where movies were usually shown. In attendance were mostly German visitors, and the program was for them: the division band played marches, and then an African-American sergeant stood up and announced that he was going to sing some traditional American folk songs. The one I remember is "Shall We Gather at the River" — "the beautiful, the beautiful river that flows by the throne of God." It ends with a line, "Soon our pilgrimage will cease." I think I first heard it in a John Ford film.

A few weeks later, Colonel Rood stopped by my desk and dropped a piece of paper on it. There was an evil smile on his face.

My three-day pass.

I was on a train and feeling as if I had just landed in Germany. Again I wondered why these towns, cities, railroads, were still part of the planet. There were no ruins; I wanted ruins. I wanted to see women in aprons stacking bricks in front of bombed-out apartment buildings. I wanted to see old men in jackets pushing wheelbarrows full of rubble. I wanted to see children with brooms pushing dust from the sidewalks in front of bombed-out buildings. I wanted to see everybody coughing hard as the sweepings swirled, covering them all in a granite-dust fog.

Most of all, I wanted to be in the uniform of the U.S. Army, Class A's sharply pressed and bronze buttons shining, with people looking at me and stepping quickly out of the way for me as I walked past the blocks of neatly stacked bricks in shattered, bomb-excavated hollows of bombed out houses. *The only good German is a dead German:* That's what I wanted to say to Colonel Rood, that I hated Germany and Germans — yet at the same time, I was not even allowed to acknowledge to myself that I hated. "Angry" was as far as I had gone, before needing to cover my mouth and not talk. Hatred was not allowed. Most of all, helplessness was not allowed. Why had I used that word, "helpless"? Why was it not allowed?

The ticket-taker with the anonymous face, on the train to Bonn, the one with the dark blue uniform and the braided cords about his cap, who knocked on the door of the second-class compartment, held out his hand, bowed slightly, smiling, then suddenly straightened, his smile gone as he recognized my uniform — it seemed to hurt him to say it in English, "Ticket, please."

I gave him my ticket, and answered, in German, *"Wie lang nach Köln?"* *How long to Cologne?* His eyes grew large, and his bland face reddened. I wanted to add, *Ich bin Jude, I'm a Jew,* but I didn't, and accounted myself a coward. He punched my ticket and shoved it back at me without answering.

The train went on. The phone and telegraph wires bellied rhythmically downward. The early summer sun shined, and women were still out in their backyards, in those many yards near train stations, tending their little vegetable gardens as though nothing had ever happened. I slept, and when I woke the train was running along the Rhine. It had been my Rhine, but wasn't any more. The castles of the robber barons, the curving blue river, the hillsides green with grapes, weren't mine anymore. I'd had them once, but then I'd lost them. I began to tear up, with Heine's and Oma's song threading through my brain. I'd once had a lovely fatherland. There the oaks grew tall, the violets beckoned gently.

I had to change in Bonn; no more the little narrow-gauge railroad to Ruppichteroth, but now a bus, yellow, that wove through green valleys along a narrow road. We had come and gone on that narrow-gauge railroad, and I'd been able to tell with only a coin in my teeth how distant its iron engine was. This bus route, instead, lied to me that I was back in Massachusetts, in the Berkshires: Great Barrington, Stockbridge, Lenox. This green was too beautiful, and I didn't want it to be beautiful.

The bus went on, through large Siegburg where I'd been born, and through little Henneff, where once we used to change steaming trains, and through Schönberg, where I had met those joyous teenagers going to make *aliyah* to Palestine.

The bus stopped in front of the hotel, and I stepped out onto the chosée, the macadamized highway over which my father and I had driven cattle. The bus drove off, and, astonished, I turned in a circle, seeing everything in black and white, just as in the postcard in which my great-grandfather, cane in hand, stood exactly in the middle of the street on which I had just placed my foot; black and white like all those pictures, those very small ones, from the album that Mom might draw from the bookshelf on 160th Street and open a page at which she looked so very intently with a hand to her mouth.

There, across the street, was my Opa Nathan's house; there, a little further off, was the road leading up to Wilhelm Strasse, my street. There was the post-office, there was the bank.

I turned around, but the gas station in the postcard was gone. The black and white now turned to color thanks to a blinking traffic light strung high over the middle of the choseé, where there had never been a traffic light before. I saw that the Nathans' house was gone, the largest Jewish-owned house in Ruppichteroth, gone, become a parking lot. Further on, long stretches of factory buildings with red canted roofs, and a sign that read, "Huwil Werke." The Willach factories. They must have expanded greatly during the war.

As I began to walk up Wilhelm Strasse, from somewhere someone began to whistle a tune from "Hansel and Gretel," and suddenly I recognized, to my great astonishment, that the street that I remembered as being so very wide was now a narrow, very narrow gray track. I stood again on cobblestones, but my spit-shined boots would raise no sparks from all these stones. I continued up the street, which I remembered as steep and tree-lined, but now there was hardly an incline and the trees were gone. I remembered green hedges flanking the street, also now gone, replaced by thin wires through which I could look down onto the highway.

The Füllenbach house was gone. The marvelous garden surrounding their house, always so full of red tulips, was gone; all that I saw was a dirt brown lot. No more sweaty hugs from Mrs. Füllenbach. And then our house: It didn't loom over me, and there were shutters on the windows where no shutters had ever been. The posts of brick still stood at the corners of garden, and the connected railings still captured the little garden plot fronting the house, but instead of grass and flowers and lilac bushes, there now was dirt. And across the street, the garden where Oma grew her asparagus, and which had been surrounded by wonderful gooseberry bushes, that, too, was dirt, and the gooseberry bushes were gone.

I walked the flagstones to the front door. The incised glass, with frosted wreaths and streaming strangeness that I had puzzled and dreamed over, was gone. The door was all wood. Before I could knock, it opened, and there stood Herr Bendix. I had to retreat a step, since his stomach spoke of a great deal of good feeding, but his head was bald, his eyes hooded, and his nose like an eagle's beak.

"I saw you coming, you were looking about," Bendix said. "Have you eaten? Come in." This was all in German. I didn't want to speak German, but I did, a melancholy, stumbling German. Where was Oma's grocery? And across the entrance hall from the grocery, the dining room where nobody ever ate? What I wanted was to look in and about *my* house, not someone else's'.

"Are you tired? How was the trip? Would you like to lie down for a while?"

I shook my head and said, "Thank you," and felt eight years old, and I knew that this would never be my house again. What I wanted right then was to pull it down, to create a ruin that no one could use. I was angry and felt helpless.

Bendix led me into the hallway, where stood his wife and son, in the hallway where Mom and Oma had screamed, where Opa had screamed, as Pop was taken away, and I'd had to embrace the milk separator because no one was there to embrace me and calm my fears.

Bendix introduced me to his wife and son. The wife was short, had very white hair, a pink, pale face, and a sharp chin. The son was probably 16, and wore a tie. "You'll talk later," said Bendix, and led me upstairs.

"This is our guest room." No, it was our living room, where we lived, ate, and saw friends. The stove was gone, the window had curtains, and the walls were covered with friendly white and flowery wallpaper. There was a large bed with plump pillows and a feather-bed, surrounded with area rugs.

The more steps I took into the room, the more I withdrew. I pulled a wash-and-wear shirt wrapped in crinkly plastic wap out of my bag on the bed and handed it to Bendix. I forced a smile as he shook his head in admiration and said, "You Americans."

We had instant coffee in a downstairs kitchen that looked vaguely like Oma's kitchen. I excused myself and told them I would like to just walk around. They understood.

I tried walking out of the back door, thinking that I would enter the barn, but there was no barn, only mud. I stepped out further, saw that the barn indeed was gone, leaving just a blank, half-timbered wall that showed no connection to the place where, in the loft, sunk in hay, I did the reading that introduced me to imagination and the world, and spared me the heavy sighs of those I loved best.

I walked out further to the meadow in back of our house, but where the meadow had been, where the apple trees had been, and the slopes for sledding, there was just more mud.

On my return to the house, Bendix said, "Yes, I should have told you what they told me: During the war, there were soldiers quartered here, all around here, in tents and other temporary shelters. They tramped everything down, cut down trees for fires. It's been like this ever since the war, ever since I first came here." I had no answer to offer, just more anger. I should come inside, he said, for more coffee. I begged off. I wanted to walk. He would walk with me. I declined and started off. He followed. I stopped and waited for him, and swallowed more anger.

"That's the Schumacher house, you remember?" I didn't answer. From where I stood I could see that the Schumacher meadow, where we searched for Easter eggs, had not been spared: mud.

We came to the space in front of the synagogue, where, fourteen years earlier, I had learned about hatred and humiliation. I was grateful for Bendix's silence.

We came to stand in front of the synagogue: blank wall. The

building had been sold. The handful of survivors who were the congregation-in-exile had agreed for it to be sold. Who now lived in that building, with the red carpeting, with the balcony from where sweets rained down on me, the building where my Opa presided? How did these people feel living in my synagogue? Did they have children?

The three great rectangular windows high over the synagogue door were gone, their spaces were filled in with stone. The two marvelous round windows, one on each side of the door, surrounded by white stone wreaths, were gone, filled in with stone. Something had been taken from me and turned to stone.

I wanted to go on and see the rest of the village, but it was getting dark, and it had been a long day.

A black car was standing in front of our house, and someone was trying to extract a heavy object from the rear seat. With a heave he pulled out a large trunk, then swung around and dropped it down next to another trunk-like object resting on the walk. Bendix ran forward, then looked back at me and waved. "Come, they are here."

Who was here?

Bendix and two other men were standing next to the car. The one who had done the heavy lifting was a man of about my age, the other quite old. The elder man came toward me with a sad smile, and when we were quite close, he raised his hand and ran it through my hair, *"Ya Wolfgang, wie lang?"* He paused. *"So traurig?"* *How long has it been?*

Unsmiling, I looked at Bendix. "Joseph Lauf. This is Joseph Lauf, a friend of your Opa," he said. "And this is his grandson, Stephan."

Opa's friend was taller than I. His eyes were bright, his face was long and smooth, and he had a white mustache, and wore suspenders over a blue shirt.

I had no memory of Mr. Joseph Lauf. What right had he to touch my hair? "I'm not Wolfgang any longer," I said. "My name is Walter." Lauf smiled his sad smile and pointed to the two trunks. "These things are from your Opa Moses. He left them with us when . . . all that." He waved a hand in front of him, as though trying to assemble some words. "When all that happened. Your Opa, was a very good man, a good friend." Again he pointed to the trunks. "We kept them in the barn, where nobody could find them. Your Opa thought that when it was all over we might get them to your family."

I kept my mouth shut. I hated them all, but here was somebody who ... who was this somebody?

Bendix wanted us to go inside, "maybe get something to drink; we can talk then." Opa's friend and his grandson took the heavy trunks and brought them inside. I wanted to examine them, but Mrs. Bendix gathered us in the kitchen where she had made more instant coffee for us. Mr. Lauf laughed and said that he liked instant better than regular, that's all he drank now, and that the first he ever had tasted had come from packages my parents had sent after the war. Did I know about the letter?

"What letter? "

"The letter from your Opa, the letter we smuggled out of the work camp in Much. We sent it to your family in New York."

I hated the packages that we sent to the people I hated, but here was somebody who . . . What the hell did I know?

"Yes, I know about the letter. It was very brave of you to have done that."

"Not so brave." His face became serious. "The letter went from hand to hand to hand, among three of us. It was easy to hide. I put it in my Bible. If I think I did anything brave, it was to always think, to believe, that in the end, after everything, we would lose." He got up and signaled to his grandson that it was time to go. He turned to me smiling, "You know, Wolfgang, Walter, I don't think you remember, but once, when you were very little, your Opa and Pappa came to our farm with you. You ran after the chickens, and you were surprised to see our turkey, and I remember you saying over and over again, 'What's that? What's that?'"

I watched them getting into their car and drive off. And I wondered: Why had they kept the trunks so very long? Why hadn't they shipped them to us? Why did he deprecate what he had done? Because it only made him seem more courageous, his modesty? I didn't want him to be courageous. If he was courageous, then . . . What the hell did I know?

I knew about trunks. These two were just like the ones Mom and Pop lugged around half of the world: dark brown leather, with two straps at the ends, scuffed all over. The locks were shiny bronze, and the keys were strung about Mom's neck. Those trunks contained everything we still owned; they were our kitchen and bedroom, and as a child I thought them miraculous. Mom pulled out dishes, flat-ware, wooden spoons, and spatulas; she pulled out towels, bedding, sheets, pillow cases and linen napkins. Those trunks held all our wealth, and the residue of generations from Germany.

We brought my Opa's trunks into the kitchen and hauled them onto the table. The first one held a large, leather-covered box that contained a silver table service for twelve. Remarkable, Mrs. Bendix said. There was also a beautifully decorated set of dishes — the very old set a Rosenthal, the other a Hutchenreuther, Mrs. Bendix said. The dishes were wrapped in linen and in some very beautiful shawls.

The other trunk was mainly linens, but there were also some women's dresses. I wanted to cry, but I couldn't. I skipped the offer of supper from Mrs. Bendix and went to sleep in their guest room — my living room, where we always had guests.

I didn't sleep well, but I slept long. I pulled on my khakis and headed downstairs where Mrs. Bendix had breakfast for me: a bowl of farina and strawberry syrup. The last time I'd had that, I was 8. Opa had prepared it for me and Karl on the morning that we were leaving Germany. When Mrs. Bendix put down the bowl of farina, she said, "You know, you can't hate a whole country."

Yes, I could — but then there was Mr. Lauf, and the hand to hand to hand. Now Mr. Bendix came in and sat across from me. "He put himself in some danger with those trunks," he said. "If somebody had found out . . . I will send those trunks to your family in New York. It's expensive, but some of your rentals from your property will cover the cost."

"Is that why . . . ?"

Bendix smiled. "I don't know. Farmers are a strange people."

I needed to know from Bendix where the Willach family lived. In the letters from home there had been the frequently repeated injunction to give Pop's old friend his greetings. I would do that this afternoon, but first I wanted to walk the streets of my old village wearing the uniform of the U.S. Army. I wanted an overcast day, but the sky was blue and the day was warm. I wanted to walk where once I had wanted everybody to see my new shoes, but now I wanted them to see my uniform.

What I hadn't seen yesterday now became visible: The chestnut trees were all gone. My tree was gone. Coal briquets had run out during the war, so they'd cut down my tree.

I followed the thread that once was my grand street. There did not seem to be many people, but whenever I did pass one, man or woman, there was a quick look and a quicker turning away: my uniform.

There, on the corner, was the Gaertner butcher shop. The large store window, through which one might see Gustav in his bloody apron, was gone, replaced by stone, just like the synagogue.

There was no ringing hammer from the blacksmith's shop. There was no blacksmith shop.

I was in front of the Hertzfeld Villa. The stone wall arced its way around the property, the lawn was green, the house still impressive. Was the Nazi Loewenich still its owner? Maybe, but the glass case on that wall was gone. That case, with its cartoons, had tried to tell me for much too long who I was, and that I was hated and should hate myself.

I continued on to Tante Lydia's house, but Tante Lydia didn't live there anymore; Tante Lydia had been dispersed in the smoke rising from the smokestacks of Auschwitz.

I went on to the Regensburger bakery, but the bakery had been transformed, like all the other places I once had loved.

I went on to Willy's house, but it was no longer there. The vacant space was all mud.

Later that afternoon, I walked to the Willach house. The sky was still blue, the afternoon still warm. The house was Old Victorian, pillared and balconied. It sat in the middle of much green grass, an intimidating house, the house of a family that profited from forced labor.

I reached the front door, and before I could ring a young woman in a white apron stood there, looking me up and down.

"Herr August Willach," I said, "*bitte. Ich bin . . .*" I stopped; I needed to decide who I was. "Wolfgang Hess. My father was a friend of Mr. Willach." My words ended with a question mark.

She stepped out from the door and pointed toward the back of the house. There stood an immense gazebo, and a number of men in suits stood on its high deck, with champagne glasses in their hands. I drew close to a flight of stairs reaching up to the deck, and stood and the bottom, trembling. "Herr Willach? Herr August Willach?"

A number of men turned and leaned on the railing that seemed so high above me.

"*Ya, Ich bins.*" He had a large round head with gray hair on its sides. I tried to smile, but he looked offended.

"I'm Wolfgang Hess. My father is Oscar Hess, your old friend. He wanted me to give you his greetings."

I had an expectation of being invited up on the deck, but Herr

August Willach just said, "*Ya*, okay," and turned around. All the others leaning on the railing turned with him. I stood at the bottom of the stairs, and I was eight years old again, trembling, with clods of mud flying at me.

I walked along the choseé, and came to a field that looked very much like the field where we cut hay. The brook, the Bről, was close by, and the woods on its other side were swept by wind, inviting me. I crossed the brook, stepping carefully on jutting stones, and walked into the woods. The floor was covered by chanterelles, but I heard none of Oma's hallooing. Instead I heard her telling me: "Let it go. It's not yours any more. Let it go. Let it go."

Walter Hess was born in Germany and emigrated with his family to the U.S. in 1940, via Ecuador. Educated in New York City schools, he earned a B.A. from CCNY in 1942 and a M.A. from CCNY in 2003. He is a retired documentary film editor. Films on which he collaborated have won numerous prizes, including three Peabody Awards and three Emmy Awards. His book of poetry, published in 2010, is *Jew's Harp*. In 2001 he received an award from The Academy of American Poets. In 2003 he received an award from the Nyman Foundation for a portion of this memoir.